SCBS

Please return/renew this item by the last date shown.

To renew this item, call **0845 0020777** (automated)
or visit **www.librarieswest.org.uk**

Borrower number and PIN required.

Libraries**West**

MERCY SHIPS

Mercy Ships

David Miller

continuum

Continuum UK, The Tower Building, 11 York Road, London SE1 7NX
Continuum US, 80 Maiden Lane, Suite 704, New York, NY 10038

www.continuumbooks.com

First published 2008

British Library Cataloguing-in-Publication Data
A catalogue record for this book is available from the British Library.

ISBN 978 1 85285 572 7

Typeset by Pindar NZ (Egan Reid), Auckland, New Zealand
Printed and bound by MPG Books Ltd, Cornwall, Great Britain

Contents

Illustrations

This book is dedicated to all those who, whatever their motives, kept talking to each other throughout the war and obtained the release of many tens of thousands who would otherwise have spent many more years in captivity.

Acknowledgements

I first learnt of the wartime voyages of the Swedish liner, *Gripsholm*, ten years ago when I ordered a file by mistake in the (then) Public Record Office in Kew. This led to six years of low-level research leading to a decision that the subject of wartime exchanges deserved a book, and this is it. On that long route I have encountered many kind and helpful people by post, telephone, increasingly by e-mail, and in some instances in face-to-face meetings.

Goeren C-O Claesson was an early contact whose deep knowledge of the Swedish-American Line and its ships has been invaluable, both in direct contact and through his excellent website www.salship.se/salpage.asp. Peter Levitt has been of great help on the complicated story of the *Zamzam*, and the eventual exchange of its passengers, all of which he lived through as a boy of ten. It was an extraordinary experience to sit in a quiet Wiltshire garden and hear how Peter abandoned ship in mid-Atlantic after being shelled by a raider, then traveled across France and Germany to an internment camp and finally reached Haifa by way of Vienna and Istanbul. Another survivor is Paul Atyeo, now of Oxford University, whose education started in an internment camp in southern Germany after deportation from the Channel Islands and eventual exchange through Gothenburg.

Bram Oppenheim, author of *The Chosen People*, proved of the greatest assistance, not only on the subject of the '222 Exchange' but also on Palestinian exchanges in general. He has been particularly generous in pointing me towards people and archives. Siri Lawson knowledge concerning Norwegian merchant seamen in World War Two has also been of great help; her website is at www.warsailors.com.

A man who deserves to be much better known is the late Captain David Nelson of the Strait's Settlements Volunteer Corps, who was a prisoner-of-war in Singapore throughout the Japanese occupation, whose deeds are recorded in Chapter 19. I came across his story in David Tett's monumental work on the postal history of prisoners-of-war and civilian internees in east Asia between 1941 and 1945. David Tett gave helpful advice and also introduced me to David Nelson's son, Mason, who presented me with a copy of his father's book, which, apart from being a fascinating and gripping account, also proved to be a mine of information.

Many others gave help along the way including: Philip Haythornthwaite, Miss Sarah de Graaff-Hunter, Dr Susan de Graaff-Hunter and the latter's daughter, Diana Gibson, Juliana Nel of the Universal Postal Union (UPU), Dr Alexandra-Eileen Wenck, author of *Zwischen Menschenhandel und 'Endlösung'*, and Beth Hatefutsoth of the Nahum Goldmann Museum of the Jewish Disapora. Jack Wort also generously sent a manuscript describing his personal experiences.

I am also grateful for advice from Sir Martin Gilbert, CBE, DLitt, Dr Alastair Noble of the Foreign and Commonwealth Office, and Lieutenant-Colonel Alasdair Morrison of the Adjutant-General's Corps (Army Legal Services). The Far East PoW Community at www.fepow-community.org.uk also advertised for survivors to come forward.

As ever, I am deeply grateful to Pauline Eismark whose research skills and deep knowledge of the British archives have saved me a great amount of travel and many fruitless journeys down archival dead-ends. My good friend, Josepha Altersitz also provided valuable insights into US archives and resources.

This country continues to be blessed with many wonderful museums and archives whose holdings are priceless to the researcher and whose value is greatly enhanced by their excellent staff. The National Archives at Kew remain in a class of their own, as do the Imperial War Museum and the Guildhall Library's shipping records. On this project I made contact with three less well-known specialist archives, but they too hold treasures and their staff were ever helpful. All located in London, these were: the British Airways Archive and Museum Collection at Heathrow Airport; the British Postal Museum & Archive in Phoenix Place and the British Red Cross Archives in Moorfields.

Robert M. Spaulding, the editor of *Japanese Philately*, (Haddonfield, NJ) very kindly provided a copy of an article that was crucial to my research.

Many others also helped and if I have failed to name them, I apologize. Finally, while I gratefully acknowledge all this help and advice, the opinions expressed in this book are mine alone, as is the responsibility for any errors or omissions.

The Historical Background

Since the earliest times prisoners taken in war have posed the captor with a series of dilemmas. They are of benefit because they have been removed from the enemy's order-of-battle, but they are a hindrance because they have to be prevented from escaping and if taken in large numbers can pose a potential threat, even though disarmed, simply through being present in the rear area. But, if they are to be held securely, they impose a significant administrative load, requiring a proper camp, manpower to guard them, medical facilities, food and general administration.

It may seem an antiquated example, but the events surrounding the end of the siege of Acre in 1191 in the Third Crusade illustrate many of the problems associated with prisoners-of-war. The siege started in August 1189 and dragged on for 23 months. The walled city was occupied by a Saracen garrison, which was encircled, apart from the western wall that lay along the Mediterranean shore, by a Crusader army which, in its final months, was under the joint command of Richard I of England and Philip II Augustus of France. This army was, in its turn, threatened by the Saracen field army, commanded by Saladin, which occupied the hills overlooking the city.

In early July 1191, the Saracen commander in the city proposed terms, but such a first offer was always rejected out of hand, so this was quickly followed by a more realistic second offer. The most significant feature of this was to offer to return many Christian prisoners, hand over a considerable sum of money, and, of great importance to the Crusaders, return the fragment of the Cross – the problem was most of these would have to come from outside the city, and, because there was no means of communication with Saladin and his army, the commander was unable to consult his general as to whether he would meet such terms. Nevertheless, agreement was reached and the city capitulated on 12 July 1191, with the surrendered garrison, some 3,000 strong, serving as hostages. Richard gave strict orders that there would be no molestation of the captives who were initially placed in a guarded camp outside the walls, but after several days were returned to the city where they were housed in accommodation set aside for them.

Saladin never sought to avoid the obligations placed upon him, excepting only in the matter of timing. It was in the terms that delivery of the fragment of the

Holy Cross, the prisoners and the money would take place one calendar month from the date of the capitulation (i.e., on 12 August 1191) and that, provided these conditions were met, the Saracen prisoners would then be released; if not, the prisoners would become slaves. There were repeated meetings between Crusader and Saracen representatives and it was clear that Saladin was doing his best to meet his obligations. Just before the deadline, however, he informed Richard's emissaries that he needed more time and it was mutually agreed to extend the deadline to 20 August.

Richard was desperate to move his army, which was the only Crusader army in the Holy Land, away from Acre. First, following the lengthy privations of the siege, most of his troops were living a life of debauchery in the city, and the efficiency of the army was decreasing rapidly. Secondly, the longer he delayed the more time Saladin had to make preparations to counter the Crusaders' next move. But the greatest obstacle to any move was the large mass of prisoners; if Richard took them with him they would form a huge, ill-disciplined and discontented mass, slowing the advance, requiring a large guard force to prevent them from either escaping or being freed by the Saracens, and having to be fed and watered. But, if Richard left them in Acre he would have to leave a large force behind to guard them, which he could not afford to do. Finally, simply to release them would not only run counter to every custom of the day but would also infuriate his own troops.

On 15 August Saladin sent a message that he was still having difficulties and requested a meeting with Richard on 16 August, but he did not turn up and Richard was still awaiting a response on 20 August, when the exchange deadline was midday. Once the sun had passed its zenith Richard called a council where it was decided that there was no point in waiting any longer and the only course remaining was to kill the hostages. Accordingly, the captives were bound with ropes and killed. The action was approved by the council but Richard was the undisputed commander-in-chief and on the spot throughout, and he never evaded personal responsibility.

The massacre must be judged in the light of the morals and customs of the twelfth and not of the twenty-first century. Similar massacres were by no means uncommon; indeed, Saladin had ordered the execution of some 300 Templars captured at the Battle of Hattin (4 July 1187). In the 1370s, the greatly admired French knight, Bertrand du Guesclin (1320–1380), twice captured large numbers of English prisoners; some 500 on the first occasion, considerably more on the second. When it could not be agreed to whom each prisoner belonged and thus who would gain the ransoms, he ended the quarrels by killing the lot.

Curiously, there was a much more recent parallel, which took place over 500 years later, but only 50 miles down the Palestinian coast. During his Egyptian campaign, Napoleon Bonaparte marched up the coast of the Levant, arriving eventually at Acre. His greatest problem, however, occurred at Jaffa, where, after a short siege, his troops captured some 4,000 Turkish soldiers. Like Richard the Lionheart, the problem was what to do with them, and after a series of conferences with his divisional commanders where they considered and rejected every alternative course, Napoleon decided that they would be shot – every last one of them – which was done on 9 March 1799.

The concept of ransom began to appear in the Middle Ages and meant that a knight captured in combat could be sold back to his relatives and friends. The sum involved was decided upon by the captor, but the general convention (although by no means universally applied) was a sum equal to the knight's annual income from his lands, while a common soldier (if allowed to survive at all) would be required to pay about three months' wages. Such a process involved the captor communicating with the captive's family in order to inform them of the sum and any attendant conditions, and to set up a procedure for the transfer of the funds. One significant development was that the question of surrender and the terms of the ransom became enshrined in law and in numerous cases one or other party went to court, an early example of the involvement of law and lawyers in the conduct of war.

To give just one example, following the Battle of Poitiers (1356), John de Hellenes, a French squire, wounded and captured the Lord Berkeley, an Englishman. John carefully nursed his prisoner back to health and then ransomed him for 6,000 nobles, a princely sum in those days that was duly paid and resulted in John becoming a wealthy knight.[1] *Parole d'honneur* (word of honour) is also of ancient origin and involved a captive in giving a solemn undertaking not to do something, such as escape, in return for some easing in the conditions of captivity. In the British experience in the Napoleonic Wars (1793–1815) the majority of French soldier and sailor prisoners were held in the notorious prison hulks, long-redundant naval and mercantile ships moored in rivers and creeks around the coast. The great majority of officers, down to sous-lieutenant in the army and its equivalent in the navy, were allowed to reside in 'parole towns' provided they were prepared to sign a legal undertaking to live within a closely defined boundary, to 'behave decently', to remain within their lodgings from 5 p.m. in winter and 8 p.m. in summer until dawn, and not to communicate with France except through authorized channels. Breaking any of these rules incurred a return to a proper prison and a reward of ten shillings to any Briton who apprehended them. The British paid such officers half-a-guinea per week subsistence allowance and the captives were allowed to obtain local work to add to this. A relatively large number broke their parole, 310 in 1812 alone, but the British maintained the system until the end of the wars in 1815.

Parole was very much a discretionary option: governments were not obliged to offer it, nor prisoners to accept it, but it proved attractive to both parties. For the captors it greatly reduced the administrative costs and logistic support needed for prisons, while for the captives it meant a life with some degree of freedom.

Parole was sometimes given in World War Two, but almost invariably for very short-term activities, such as walks outside the perimeter fence. This usually took the form of every individual signing a slip of paper, which held good only for the duration of activity. The giving of any form of parole was banned by the British authorities, but those in the camps considered it acceptable by British prisoners for the benefits in fitness and morale. It was also practised in at least some civilian internment camps.

Quite when exchange became an accepted part of military conflicts is not clear, but it would appear to have been practised at least as early as the sixteenth century. The general procedure was to exchange like for like; i.e., a colonel for a colonel, a lieutenant for a lieutenant, a private for a private and so on. This could, however, be modified by exchanging a man in a higher rank for a greater number of men of inferior rank, one example of such a codification being the cartel agreed between the United States and the United Kingdom in 1813. The tariff meant that the rules were clearly understood and allowed for any person to be exchanged one-for-one with another of equal rank, or for a number of men as laid down in Table 1 below:

Table 1: Exchange Criteria in the War of 1812[2,3]

Naval rank	Army rank	Tariff
Admiral	General	60
Vice-admiral	Lieutenant-general	40
Rear-admiral	Major-general	30
Commodore	Brigadier-general	20
Captain (line-of-battle ship)	Colonel	15
Captain (frigate)	Lieutenant-colonel	10
Commander	Major	8
Lieutenant/master	Captain	6
Master's-mate	Lieutenant	4
Midshipman, warrant officer, master of merchant vessel	Sub-lieutenants/ensigns	3
Lieutenants/mates of privateers, all petty officers	All NCOs	2
Seamen	Privates	1

In almost every exchange, the man concerned was required to give his parole not to take up arms again in the current conflict.

The United States Civil War (1861–1865) brought new problems, with the administration on both sides eventually being overwhelmed by the sheer scale of the problem. Conditions became dire and approximately 26,000 Confederate and 30,000 Union officers and soldiers died in the camps. Prisoner affairs were initially hampered by Lincoln's refusal to admit that a state of war existed and thus captured Confederates were not soldiers but traitors taking part in an insurrection, to which the Confederate government threatened to respond in kind. After some months Lincoln relented and an agreement was reached between the two sides for exchanges, to be based on the tariff system agreed with the British in 1813 (see above). Thus, up to about mid 1863, the prisons on each side were relatively small and coped reasonably well with the problem. In 1863, however, much larger numbers of prisoners were captured and the Emancipation of Slavery, coupled with the Union decision to raise black regiments, led to a hardening of attitudes on both sides and the virtual disappearance of exchanges. Serious overcrowding became common and in the most notorious example Andersons Ville eventually housed 33,000 men on a 26-acre site.

There was an exchange of severely sick and wounded prisoners in April 1864, but the emaciated state of the Union soldiers returning home resulted in a public outcry and led to the retaliatory reduction of rations in Union-run PoW camps. Shortage of troops in their own army, coupled with the increasing burden of the camps, led the Confederacy to agree to exchanges in early 1865, but by then the war was virtually over.

In 1864 the representatives of 16 European nations assembled in Geneva to sign the Convention for the Amelioration of the Condition of the Wounded in Armies in the Field, 1864, usually known as the 'First Geneva Convention'. Originating from the experiences of a Swiss businessman, Henri Dunant at the Battle of Solferino, the Convention sought in future battles to save lives, alleviate the suffering of the sick and wounded, and to protect those offering aid and assistance to the wounded. It also adopted the red cross on a white background as a protecting symbol, the design being, quite simply, the reverse of the Swiss national flag. Finally, the convention endorsed the establishment of the International Committee of the Red Cross (ICRC).

In 1899 all the great powers and most of the independent minor nations sent delegates to a conference held in The Hague in the Netherlands at the instigation of Imperial Russia. This established a number of rules and procedures, of which the establishment of a permanent court was, perhaps, the most important. It also established fairly precise rules for the treatment of prisoners-of-war, required belligerents to set up bureaux of information, and laid down that independent monitors should be allowed to inspect PoW camps.

The second Hague Convention was the outcome of a conference held between June and October 1907. This extended the rules regarding PoWs including the exemption of officers from labour (unless they specifically requested to do so), altered some of the rules regarding merchant seamen, and increased the duties of bureaux of information. This was the Convention in use during the 1914–1918 war.

It is a common feature of most modern wars that neither side has made any serious preparation for dealing with captured prisoners, and even when they have, they have always underestimated the scale. During World War One, on the Western Front alone, by November 1918, the Germans held approximately 182,000 British and Dominions; 350,000 French and 43,000 US prisoners. On the Allied side the British held about 328,000 Germans and Austrians, the French some 400,000.

On the Eastern Front the scale was even greater, largely because the more mobile form of warfare led to large concentrations of troops being encircled and captured. Thus, between August 1914 and the Treaty of Brest-Litovsk on 3 March 1918 the Russians had captured 2.1 million Austro-Hungarians and 167,000 Germans, while the Central Powers between them had captured 2.7 million Russians. These huge numbers simply overwhelmed all three administrations and they struggled to cope.

One of the earliest attempts at cooperation over PoW affairs came with the visit to Germany in 1916 by a Church of England bishop, Herbert Bury, whose diocese covered the whole of north-eastern Europe. Appointed in 1912, he travelled widely in the area, visiting churches, meeting Anglican priests, attending conferences and making many friends, until his travels were curtailed by the outbreak of war.[4] In 1915 the British War Office appointed him in charge of social and religious aspects of life in PoW and internment camps in the UK and he visited many, including Alexandra Palace, which held 2,500 civilian internees, and the Isle of Man, which held 30,000.

In 1916 one of Bury's friends, the *Oberbürgermeister* (lord mayor) of Munich arranged for the bishop to visit Ruhleben, the main internment camp for British civilians in Germany, which was on a racecourse just outside Berlin. Bury entered Germany via Switzerland and travelled by train to Berlin and then on to Ruhleben, where he spent several days, talking to the men, conducting services and learning of their problems and complaints. He then went to the German War Ministry for a meeting with General Friedrich, the man in charge of all PoW camps, who treated him with great courtesy and they discussed the problems of looking after two million prisoners. Friedrich then invited Bury to visit any camp he wished that held British prisoners, although, in the event Bury visited only one other camp (Blankenberg, 26 November 1916) and then returned to the UK. This remains an extraordinary visit by a leading churchman to PoW and internment camps in the enemy's country during a time of war.[5]

In early 1917 a meeting between French and German representatives was held at The Hague to discuss matters of mutual concern affecting prisoners-of-war. As these talks proved useful, further talks, this time between the British and the Germans, were held, also in The Hague, in June 1917. The British delegation was headed by Lord Newton, head of the Prisoner-of-War Department at the Foreign Office, accompanied by Lieutenant-General Sir Herbert Belfield, the Director of the Prisoner-of-War Division in the War Office and Lord Justice Younger, as legal adviser. The German delegation was headed by General Friedrich, head of the Prisoner-of-War Section in the War Ministry in Berlin. The meetings were chaired by the Dutch Minister of Foreign Affairs.

The meetings were surprisingly successful and agreement was reached on a host of issues.[6] These included repatriation of wounded, particularly disabled, PoWs and civilian internees, repatriation of medical personnel, and the amelioration of certain punishments. Particular attention was paid to the need for early notification by the captor state of individual captures and allowing such prisoners to make early communication with their families. There was also agreement to transfer many long-serving PoWs to neutral countries, where they would be interned for the duration of hostilities. The Netherlands promised to accommodate a maximum of 16,000 (both British and German), although all expenses incurred would have to be met by the respective governments, who would also provide the materials for the buildings, medical personnel and cooking facilities. Although not a party to these meetings, Switzerland gave a similar undertaking. Judging by the tone of the reports both sides set out to be reasonable and each gave sensible and, wherever possible, helpful responses to points raised by the other.

These meetings and the subsequent implementation of the agreements led to a further Anglo-German meeting also held in The Hague, which lasted from 8 June to 14 July 1918. This was also a success and resulted in agreement on many further areas, although other factors in the military situation leading to the Armistice in November meant that they were never ratified nor were many of the measures implemented.

Another unusual innovation during World War One was the large-scale internment of combat troops in neutral countries, a prime example being the brigade of the Royal Navy (RN) Division that spent virtually the entire war in The Netherlands. The RN Division had been formed hastily in August 1914, with the strong support of the then First Lord of the Admiralty, Winston Churchill, who sent it to help defend the Belgian port of Antwerp. The division comprised only two brigades with a total strength of some 5,000 men and when the Belgian Army was forced to withdraw on 8 October, the British had no choice but to split. One brigade withdrew first in good order, reached the coast and was evacuated to the UK. The second brigade withdrew later and because of bad information headed to the Dutch border, harried by Uhlans (German cavalry). After some 20 hours of marching the brigade reached the border and decided to go into neutral Netherlands and face internment rather than surrender to the Germans.

The main detention centre was a hutted camp outside the Dutch town of Groningen that was known to the sailors as 'HMS Timbertown', which was home to some 1,800 sailors from October 1914 to November 1918. They were allowed to go into the town and to obtain work, but nothing that could be construed as 'military', and many became friends with local families – some also married Dutch girls. They also organized education classes and various means of entertainment.

In what now seems a bizarre development, however, they were allowed 'home' leave to the UK. This started as a few cases of compassionate leave for individuals, but as a result of agreements between the British and Dutch governments, this became formalized in 1916 and regular parties crossed the North Sea for four weeks' leave, subject to a firm undertaking that they would return; indeed, one party was not allowed to leave until all members of the previous party had returned. This leave was not without its hazards. One ferry was intercepted by the Germans and ten British Royal Navy seamen on leave from Groningen were arrested and taken to Germany where they were held as PoWs until November 1918. In another incident, the ferry SS *Copenhagen* was sunk on 5 March 1917 and six people died, including three sailors.

The Turks had a very poor record for looking after PoWs. Captured officers were treated reasonably, and while food was poor, it was probably no worse than that issued to Turkish troops. For the soldiers, however, it was quite different. When the garrison at Kut-el-Amara surrendered in April 1915, some 3,700 British and 9,300 Indian troops passed into Turkish hands, of whom some 2,600 British and 2,500 Indians died while in captivity. They had to undergo several terrible marches and when static the conditions were bad, sanitation totally inadequate and food lacking in both quality and quantity. The guards were brutal at all times. Following the success of the meeting at The Hague a meeting between the British and Turks was held in Berne, Switzerland, in December 1917. This was chaired by a Swiss Foreign Ministry official and attended by representatives of the Ottoman Empire and the United Kingdom. It resulted in some useful agreements but it is doubtful if many were implemented by the Turks before they capitulated on 30 October 1918.

There had been some major developments in the treatment and rights of PoWs during World War One and the two Anglo-German meetings at The Hague in 1917 and 1918 had been of particular importance in achieving this. In the early 1920s a number of countries and organizations such as the ICRC decided, despite the prevailing 'peace in our time' attitude following the slaughter of World War One, to develop these ideas, eventually reaching the stage where an international conference would be worthwhile. This was held in Geneva from 1–27 July 1929, with delegates splitting into two main groups to consider, respectively, the treatment of the wounded, and the treatment of PoWs.

The agreement on PoWs had no fewer than 97 articles and an appendix and set out to define the minimum standards acceptable to the international community in the hope that most countries would seek to achieve more. Some of its provisions were of great value, such as the formal establishment of Mixed Medical Commissions and the appendix setting out the medical conditions for repatriation, although others, such as moves of PoWs to neutral state, were never used. The Soviet Union chose not to be involved at all, which meant that in World War Two its nationals held by the Germans and Japanese did not enjoy the protection of the Convention. Imperial Japan signed the Convention in 1929, then decided not to ratify it, but in 1942 announced that while still declining to ratify it, they would nevertheless observe its spirit – although, in many cases, they signally failed to achieve even that.

The Geneva Convention Relative to the Treatment of Prisoners-of-War, 1929, was signed by over 40 countries and was of great importance as it was the document that laid down the rules for the treatment of prisoners-of-war that were applicable in World War Two – although not all nations adhered to it, e.g., the Soviet Union and Japan. It was signed at Geneva on 27 July 1929 and ratified by over 40 countries shortly thereafter; for example, by the president of the United States on 16 January 1932.

Over the centuries belligerents have always been forced to speak to each other about the means of bringing a particular conflict to an end, but what changed prior to the 1939–1945 war was the steady increase in talking to each other about the conduct of those wars, and topics such as the treatment of wounded and of prisoners-of-war. From the mid-nineteenth century onwards there were a number of major international conferences, which, while they did not actually prevent wars taking place – and certainly failed to avoid the huge death toll of 1914–1918 – did, nevertheless, provide a framework. One significant development, however, was the increasing preparedness of many of the participants to talk about the treatment of the wounded and of PoWs actually during the conflict.

British–German Exchanges

The British and Germans had managed to establish reasonably civilized contacts during World War One concerning PoWs and even managed to hold face-to-face meetings. Thus, after the first phase in hostilities in 1939–1940 they both made tentative approaches through the Protecting Power, which at that time was the United States. The first attempt at an exchange was aborted at the last minute but once the lessons of that failure had been absorbed the subsequent exchanges took place relatively smoothly, although, like all exchanges, they required an immense amount of planning and involved agreements with every government and agency involved.

Despite the overall success, there were various difficulties relating to repatriation that were never properly resolved. The first concerned the division of captives into three categories: prisoners-of-war, protected personnel and civilian internees. The simplest of these was the prisoners-of-war, where the rule was quite simple – they either passed the examination of the Mixed Medical Commission (MMC), or they did not. As discussed elsewhere it was possible to mislead the MMCs, but the recorded instances were very few in number. In World War One long-serving PoWs were sent to a neutral country to be interned until the end of hostilities, but although this was considered by both the British and Germans later in World War Two, it was never implemented.

Protected personnel were entitled, as of right, to be repatriated, but the detaining power was quite specifically entitled to ensure that sufficient doctors and other medical support staff would remain to run the hospitals and medical treatment centres for the PoWs. It was the detaining power's prerogative to decide which medics should be retained or repatriated, which sometimes led to unfairness, with more recent arrivals in the PoW camps being released well before those who had been there much longer.

COMPLICATING FACTORS

One factor that affected all planning was that these exchanges did not – indeed, could not – take place in isolation from more warlike activities. Thus, operational commitments involving large-scale sea movement had to be taken into consideration, such as Operations Torch (invasion of North Africa), Overlord (invasion of Normandy) and Anvil (invasion of southern France). Such operations required huge amounts of shipping and operational chiefs were reluctant to give up even two or three troopships or passenger liners, no matter how worthy the cause.

A further problem was that from the fall of France to late in the war Switzerland was physically inaccessible to the Allies, meaning that Sweden, Spain, Portugal and Turkey were the only neutral European countries where exchanges could take place.

Another factor was publicity. This was inevitable at the time of exchange and afterwards, but public knowledge of what was intended could be very unhelpful, especially if an exchange had to be postponed, or, as in the Newhaven–Dieppe case, cancelled altogether. It was usually left to the Protecting Power to try to coordinate a news embargo, which aimed at ensuring that there was no premature leak in the country of either party, or, if one was also involved, the neutral where the exchange was actually to take place. A further problem, particularly with the Japanese exchanges, but also with some of those from Germany, arose when repatriates or newsmen broadcast horror stories that might then discourage further exchanges.

Getting people to the right place at the right time for an exchange was relatively easy for Germany and Italy. But almost from the start of the war, the UK pursued a policy of dispersing as many PoWs and internees as possible to camps run by Dominion and colonial governments and, as a result, once the exchanges started such people often had to be brought all the way back in order to be exchanged. The status of merchant seamen was always a problem, since the British treated them as PoWs and repatriated them when passed by an MMC, whereas the Germans treated them as civilians and tried to arrange exchanges for them on a head-for-head basis.

The factors involved in such sea voyages included the following:
- Safe passages had to be obtained, which could be very complicated, especially in confined areas such as the Baltic, Mediterranean and Irish Seas.
- Minefields were being constantly laid and cleared.
- By night any ship on safe passage had to be brightly illuminated and by day had to have prominent markings visible both from the surface and from the air.
- Advantage was taken for these ships to carry Red Cross supplies, which meant that dock and cross-loading facilities were necessary at each port.

THE ROLE OF THE RED CROSS

The Red Cross offered its good services in the negotiating and planning stages of these exchanges. If invited to do so, it also played an increasingly important role in the implementation of the exchanges, principally by checking that the agreed terms were being complied with, ensuring that there was no friction between the authorities of the two sides concerned, and also in dealing with any complaints by the repatriates themselves. In detail these representatives were required to:

- Obtain two copies of the nominal rolls of those to be exchanged.
- Travel to the place of departure, assist generally and verify that those boarding the ship/train matched the names on the rolls.
- During the journey, liaise between authorities and those to be exchanged.
- On arrival at the place of exchange, liaise with the neutral authorities, meet their Red Cross opposite number arriving with the other party, and exchange nominal rolls.
- Generally assist with the actual exchange, ensure names/rolls tally and deal with any unexpected problems.
- Send an interim report to Geneva.
- Accompany the returning party back to their homeland.
- Send a final report to Geneva.

THE PLANNED BRITISH–GERMAN DIEPPE–NEWHAVEN EXCHANGE: OCTOBER 1941

Within weeks of the outbreak of war in 1939 the United Kingdom and Germany had established contact through the Protecting Power, at that time the United States, and agreed to establish Mixed Medical Commissions (MMCs). It took some time for these to get to work, but by the end of 1940 the MMCs in both countries had completed their first tours. Negotiations on the next step, an actual exchange of those passed by the MMCs, started in February 1941. It was quickly agreed that it would be a cross-Channel operation, but the initial difficulties centred on the relatively simple matter of the choice of which ports would be used.

The two governments sparred for position for several months, with each side putting forward one name after another, only for it to be rejected, without reason given, by the other. This went on until September when the Germans proposed that they would use Fécamp, a small port on the French coast approximately halfway between Dieppe and Le Havre, and said that they would accept any port the British wished to suggest on their own side of the Channel. The British chose Newhaven, upon which the Germans changed their choice to Dieppe, which made for an even shorter route. This agreed, the naval staff on both sides insisted that, due to the tides, the exchange had to take place between 4 and 7 October and in daylight.

In 1941 there were far more British prisoners-of-war held in Germany than Germans held by Britain, so the British hesitated because they thought that the Germans might insist on a one-for-one exchange. At first it appeared that this would not be the case and both parties agreed to exchange all those sick and wounded who had passed the MMCs, together with any surplus Protected Personnel; in round figures, this meant that some 150 Germans would be exchanged for 1,600 British.

All seemed to be proceeding smoothly, when on 20 September, and just three weeks before the exchange was due to take place, the British were informed by the United States that the German government was now unhappy with the imbalance in numbers and proposed that the vacant slots on the UK–France leg of the voyage be filled by sick and elderly German women internees. A few days later (26 September) the Germans wanted to change the criteria yet again, this time proposing that the British should also include fit, younger women and children, as well as men beyond military age. The British were so keen to get their people back that, despite the short notice and apparent German high-handedness, they agreed and as a gesture of good faith offered to release 60 civilians at once.

On 2 October the Germans alleged that the British government's attitude had created a new situation which meant that they, the Germans, could no longer guarantee to meet the agreed date. This was despite the fact that the British sick and wounded, accompanied by a number of protected personnel, had already been moved from Germany to a holding centre in Rouen. For their part, the British continued with their arrangements for an exchange on 7 October, as planned, with the Germans to be exchanged being concentrated on the south coast and the two ships standing by at the quayside in Newhaven.

But on 6 October, as so often throughout their history, the Germans over-played their hand, in this case with the public announcement that they would only agree to a limited exchange on a strictly head-for-head basis. This flew in the face of Article 68 of the 1929 Convention which stated that exchange of those passed by an MMC was to be 'without regard to rank or numbers' and the British, considering that the very short notice made this tantamount to blackmail, cancelled the entire operation.

Both sides immediately blamed the other and the British government was given a hard ride in both Parliament and the Press. The British laid the blame squarely on Joachim von Ribbentrop, the Third Reich's Foreign Minister, who had been a much-disliked ambassador in London from 1936 to 1938. The Germans, on the other hand, blamed British arrogance and deviousness. The British did, however, examine the episode carefully and thought that prior knowledge of and newspaper articles concerning the exchange by the press were partly to blame.

They also saw that whatever the 1929 Convention and their own inclinations might say, future exchanges would have to be on an approximately 50:50 basis.

What should not be overlooked in this game of diplomatic chess is the effect this had on the people who were to have been exchanged. In the case of the British prisoners-of-war in German hands, their hopes had first been raised when they were told by the MMC that they had been selected for exchange. Then, when they set out for Rouen everything appeared certain and the first few days in the transit camp were full of high expectation. But all those involved report how crushed they all felt when they were told that it was all off, not least because they were told that it was the British who had cancelled it. Although no records have been found, the effect must have been just the same on the Germans in England. The effect was made worse because, apart from some Protected Personnel acting as escorts and carers, these were all wounded and sick men, many of them on stretchers.

The abortive operation also led the British to set up a more formal consultative structure of their own, with Repatriation Committee Number 1 handling policy and Number 2 operations and administration. As usual, the committees grew in size, eventually including representatives from the Foreign Office, War Office, India Office, Colonial Office, Commander-in-Chief Home Forces, Dominion High Commissioners, and so on, with both committees being chaired by the Director of Prisoners-of-War (DPW), an army major-general. The Foreign Office was responsible for dealing with the Protecting Power, as well as with the Vatican and the International Committee of the Red Cross, both of which tended to interfere at times when the Swiss Government was coping perfectly satisfactorily. The Foreign Office also had to deal with foreign governments, especially neutral countries, when exchanges were due to take place in their countries or on their ships.

BARCELONA, GOTHENBURG AND ORAN:
20–27 OCTOBER 1943

Despite the failure of the Dieppe–Newhaven exchange and the subsequent recriminations, it was only a month (24 November 1941) before Germany proposed a comprehensive exchange of British and German civilian nationals. The initial British reaction was that this approach was intended primarily for propaganda purposes, but it was also clear that it must be followed up, even though there was a new complication only two weeks later, when the United States entered the war. This meant that the US could no longer serve as the Protecting Power, although this role was quickly assumed by Switzerland. Having considered the German note, the British responded that the implementation of Article 68 of the Prisoner-of-War Convention and of Article 12 of the Sick and

Wounded Convention was separate from the repatriation of civilians, but that the British were ready to carry out an exchange of civilians, although not including men of military age.

The Swiss did not immediately pass this to the Germans, but, with British agreement, delayed while their Foreign Minister tried to establish personal contact with Ribbentrop, who was still thought to be responsible for the events in October. Such direct contact, the Swiss thought, might ease the process, but nothing happened and in April 1942 it was learnt that the only decisions that mattered were being taken by Hitler, although all was not lost as the Swiss were told unofficially that even he might be keen on some sort of an exchange. As a result, the Swiss prepared a proposal that would include both sick and wounded PoWs, as well as protected personnel and civilians, the latter whether they were interned or not, but only if they were willing and there were no security objections. The British agreed, but repeated their basic line, that any exchange of PoWs must be on the basis of Article 68. No mention was made of merchant seamen.

At this point the row over shackling prisoners-of-war and internees erupted and nothing was heard from the German government until the British ordered shackling to cease in March 1943. This long-running incident had its origins in the discovery by the Germans that during the Dieppe Raid in August 1942, Canadian troops had been under orders to handcuff prisoners to prevent them destroying documents and maps. The Germans protested and when a similar order was discovered following the raid on Sark (7 October 1942) the Germans ordered that 1,376 Canadian prisoners be shackled during daylight hours. The British then asked the Canadian government to shackle a similar number of German PoWs in its charge, which was implemented on 10 October, whereupon the Germans shackled a further 2,752, making a total of 4,128 Allied prisoners in seven separate camps. Public opinion in Allied countries eventually compelled the British and Canadian governments to rescind the order in their camps, but the German government, which was inherently much less susceptible to public opinion, continued until October 1943 when, under Swiss supervision but with minimal publicity to prevent a loss of face, the Germans did so, too.[1]

By this stage in the war the British were beginning to take increasingly large numbers of German PoWs, including wounded, particularly in the Middle East. This presented problems of guarding and dispersing, but, on the other hand, it also prompted the Germans to restart proceedings, but with a repetition of the condition that there must be an overall equivalence in numbers.

The British had reservations, primarily because they did not want any deviation from the 1929 PoW Convention which, they thought, if allowed would weaken the overall treaty. However, as reports were being received that the condition of some British sick and wounded was deplorable, they decided to accommodate the German wish for a general exchange of civilians including, for the first time, those of military age, provided they signed an undertaking not to serve in the war. But, as always, they wished to exclude those who did not wish to leave, as well as those serving sentences or awaiting trial for offences against British Law. Also, the British still refused to accept that merchant seamen were civilians, although they were quite willing to exchange them if certified as sick or wounded by an MMC.

The Germans might have haggled over merchant seamen but in mid May their forces in North Africa collapsed and virtually all their forces there were captured. As a result, new proposals, agreed with the Italians, were soon sent from Berlin to Berne and from there to London, which were much more accommodating than previously and included a proposal to send German and Italian hospital ships to any North African port designated by the Allies. Further as there was no MMC in the area, the Germans suggested that they would be willing to accept Allied doctors' views.

At this point it was learnt that, despite the large number of Axis prisoners taken in North Africa, the number of German sick and wounded was still rather fewer than the British: some 1,400 compared to 4,000. As a result, the British decided to reduce the numerical disparity by including as many German protected personnel as possible and there was then a further delay while the British consulted their ally, the United States. All this took time and as a result it was not until 9 August 1943 that a comprehensive reply was dispatched to Berne, for onward transmission to Berlin, proposing exchanges at three separate places. This duly took place in what can only be termed a masterpiece of logistical planning and implementation. Details of dates and numbers are shown in Table 2 below:

Table 2: October 1943 – British–German Exchanges

Place	Category	British/Empire	German
Gothenburg, Sweden (20 October 1943)	Sick/wounded PoWs	2658	403
	Protected personnel	1244	199
	Merchant seamen	152	176
	Civilian internees	105	54
	Totals	**4159**	**832**
Barcelona, Spain (27 October 1943)	Sick/wounded PoWs	454	401
	Protected personnel	582	608
	Merchant seamen	0	0
	Civilian internees	0	48
	Totals	**1036**	**1057**

(continued)

Place	Category	British/Empire	German
Oran, French North Africa (20 October 1943)	Sick/wounded PoWs	0	342
	Protected personnel	0	3534
	Merchant seamen	0	0
	Civilian internees	0	0
	Totals	**0**	**3876**
GRAND TOTALS		**5195**	**5765**

The first element took place at Gothenburg, Sweden, on 20 October 1943. The Germans assembled the British and Canadian prisoners-of-war from their camps and hospitals by train and took them to two Baltic ports. One assembly point was Sassnitz, from where the repatriates were taken by ferry to Trelleborg. Others were taken by train to Swinemunde from where they were taken by the ships *Metrero* and *Rügen*, also to Trelleborg. All were then taken by train to Gothenburg. The British brought their prisoners to Gothenburg in the liner *Empress of Russia*, hospital ship *Atlantis*, and chartered Swedish liner, *Drottningholm*.

German sick and wounded held in Tunisia were collected by the Germans from Oran, also on 20 October. They used the hospital ship *Gradisca*[2] which had to reposition from Patras, Greece to Marseilles, France, plus two former French ships *Sinaia* and *Djenné*, which had been requisitioned by the Germans. The use of these two ex-French ships caused great resentment among French officials in Oran, but the British officials in the port calmed them down.

The third part of this complicated plan took place on 27 October at Barcelona, Spain, where Germans held in the Middle East were exchanged with British and Commonwealth prisoners-of-war intended for return to homes in India, Australia and New Zealand. The Germans for exchange were taken from Alexandria, Egypt to Barcelona, Spain aboard two ships: hospital ship *Tairea* carried the wounded and the liner *Cuba* the protected personnel.[3] The Germans transported the British and Commonwealth prisoners[4] aboard hospital trains to Marseilles from where they sailed to Barcelona in the ships *Aquileia* and *Djenné*.

The exchanges at Oran and Gothenburg on 20 October involved 4,000 British and 5,000 German repatriates, with a further 1,000 British and Germans at Barcelona on 27 October. Gothenburg and Barcelona were both neutral, so the Swedes and Spanish were able to serve as guarantors. Oran, however, was not neutral, being by now under Free French control, so the Swiss government provided the guarantors.

The only problem of any significance in this very complicated three-way plan concerned a party of 150 British prisoners-of-war in Germany who had been passed by the MMC and who, it had been agreed, were to be routed by train and then trans-Baltic ferry to Gothenburg. For operational and transport reasons this proved impossible to achieve so the Germans then tried to send them to Barcelona, but this, too, failed to happen. This was due to administrative difficulties that were immediately and honestly admitted by the Germans. The Red Cross and the British accepted that there was no bad faith involved, the men concerned were included in the next exchange, and with that the incident was closed. The unfortunate men involved had to spend a further eight months in prisoner-of-war camps, but commonsense and openness on both sides prevented this from turning into a major incident, which might well have prejudiced future exchanges.

BARCELONA: 18 MAY 1944

Following this success, the next repatriation was through Barcelona, with the Allied prisoners being taken the whole way to Spain by train. Unlike ships, these trains were not under any 'safe passage' protection and had no special markings, but despite the heavy attacks by Allied air forces on many other parts of the Continental railway systems in the lead up to D-Day, none of the trains was attacked.

The Swedish *Gripsholm* was chartered for the Barcelona voyage. On her return from Barcelona she dropped off a number of Allied returnees (Australians, Indians, New Zealanders and South Africans) at Algiers and then, as there was a blanket ban on neutral ships entering ports on the British mainland due to the forthcoming invasion of France, she dropped off her British passengers at Belfast, in Northern Ireland. She then continued to Canada to deliver the Canadian returnees, while the British were taken by Irish Sea ferries from Belfast to Liverpool.

In this exchange the Allies passed over 900 German sick and wounded PoWs and protected personnel, including some who had been brought across the Atlantic from Canada aboard *Gripsholm*, and a small number who had been held by the French. In return, they received 979 sick and wounded and merchant seamen, plus 64 civilian internees.

GOTHENBURG: 8–9 SEPTEMBER 1944

The Allies invaded the north of France on 6 June 1944 and the south of France on 15 August, so that by the late summer of 1944 exchanges were only possible through Sweden. But then, and despite all the fighting on Continental Europe, an exchange of sick and wounded prisoners-of-war, protected personnel and civilians took place at Gothenburg, Sweden, on 8–9 September.

Drottningholm was again chartered and started by picking up a number of Germans from North Africa. She then proceeded to Liverpool where she embarked some German civilians who had been brought across from the Isle of Man, and then sailed in company with *Arundel Castle*, which was carrying more German returnees, to Gothenburg. *Gripsholm*, which had also been chartered, sailed direct from the United States to Sweden. The Allied returnees were again brought from Germany aboard Baltic ferries. On completion of the exchange the German repatriates crossed the Baltic on the ferries, while the other three ships returned to the UK, from where *Gripsholm* alone proceeded to New York.

In this exchange the Allies received a total of 2,654, comprising sick and wounded PoWs: 1,988; merchant seamen: 83; and civilian internees: 583. In return, the Germans received the slightly lesser number of 2,233 made up of sick and wounded PoWs: 1,533; merchant seamen: 83; civilian internees: 583; and 34 sisters of the German Red Cross. The exact parity of civilian internees exchanged was no accident.

One incident showed how closely the Allies stuck to the rules. Two British PoWs had escaped from a camp in Germany and made their own way to Sweden where they succeeded in infiltrating the returning group of British repatriates and boarded *Arundel Castle*. Once the ship had sailed, they announced their presence and to their dismay, the Master, who was not only under very clear safe passage rules but also determined to abide by them, immediately handed them over to the Swedish authorities, who interned them for the rest of the war.

KREUZLINGEN, SWITZERLAND: JANUARY 1945

A Franco-German exchange took place through Switzerland in November 1944 (see Chapter 9) followed by the simultaneous release of USAAF and *Luftwaffe* internees (see below) in late 1944, so it was decided to hold the next major exchange at Kreuzlingen, Switzerland. The Germans to be repatriated were brought to Marseilles aboard the liners *Arundel Castle* and *Letitia*, and then taken by train, under Red Cross supervision, first to Geneva and thence, now under Swiss government supervision, to Kreuzlingen, a small town on the Swiss side of the border with Germany. At the same time, Allied PoWs to be repatriated were brought by German trains to the town of Konstanz on the German side of the border. This exchange involved some 5,000 Germans, all sick and wounded PoWs, who were exchanged for approximately 2,500 Allied PoWs, including 497 from the US, and a small number of civilian internees. Among the British repatriates were a small number of paratroopers who had been seriously wounded and captured during the Battle of Arnhem.

The exchange was organized and run by the Swiss government. British repatriates were taken by British liners back to the UK while US repatriates were taken aboard the Swedish *Gripsholm*.

GOTHENBURG, 15 MARCH 1945

The final exchange of the war took place at Gothenburg, Sweden, on 15 March 1945. This was primarily a German–Turkish exchange, but it did include some British nationals; it is described more fully in Chapter 4.

INDIVIDUAL EXCHANGES

There were occasional individual exchanges, one of which took place in January 1944. German General Hans von Cramer was the last commander of the *Afrika Korps*, and was captured in Tunisia by the British in May 1943. Taken to the UK, he was held prisoner for a year, but was found to be suffering from increasingly severe asthma and it was decided that he should be repatriated on health grounds. At this, the British chiefs-of-staff concocted Plan Gilmerton in which several very senior British officers would have casual conversations with the German prior to his departure, in the course of which they would plant seemingly disingenuous remarks about Allied strengths. He would also be driven to his departure airfield through parts of south-western England and 'accidentally' allowed to see major troop concentrations, but told that he was actually in south-eastern England, which would lead him, it was hoped, to believe that the planned invasion would be directed against the Pas de Calais.

This plan required endorsement by the Deputy Prime Minister, Clement Atlee, who was well known for his forthright and pithily expressed views. In this case he fully lived up to that reputation with a devastating judgement. 'I do not like this proposal,' he wrote, 'I doubt it will be effective. I do not think the game worth the candle. It will tend to discredit all our Service chiefs (of staff) with their German opposite numbers which might be necessary some time.'[5] In other words, Atlee thought that the chiefs-of-staff had far better things to occupy their time than playing silly games of this nature.

Cramer was duly repatriated via the Swedish Red Cross, and on reaching home was debriefed, as was to be expected. Following the Allied invasion on 6 June 1944, however, he was appointed, first, as adviser to *Panzergruppe West* and then adviser to OKW. In the event, his return to service was very short as he was compulsorily retired in August in the aftermath of the 20 July bomb plot, although since he was not murdered the SS presumably had no evidence against him.[6]

The curious feature of this obscure affair is that, having been repatriated on health grounds and under the aegis of the Swedish Red Cross, he should not have been given any military employment at all. Article 74 states that: 'No repatriated person shall be employed on active military service.' This clearly prevents a junior rank being employed as, say, a combat infantryman, but a general is unlikely to carry a rifle. However, the British clearly did not think that he had breached the rules as they did not charge him with any offence when he fell into their hands for a second time in 1945.

REPATRIATION OF LONG-TERM PRISONERS-OF-WAR

Article 72 of the Geneva Convention, 1929, stated that:

> Throughout the duration of hostilities and for humane considerations, belligerents may conclude agreements with a view to the direct repatriation or hospitalization in a neutral country of able-bodied prisoners of war who have undergone a long period of captivity.

In mid 1942 discussions started in the British War Office about its application, since the longest-serving men had by then been behind the wire for three years. The matter was raised in the British House of Commons in October and the initial government reaction was that Axis prisoners were now spread around the world and the logistic requirement of bringing all such long-serving men back to Europe was almost too huge to contemplate, not least because of the shipping requirements for current and known future operations.

But, following the success of the October 1943 exchange, the British decided to have a new look and one of their first conclusions was that, if done, it would have to be on a head-for-head basis. The first suggested criterion was that it would cover those prisoners-of-war who would be over 48 years old on 31 October 1943 and who had been held prisoner for more than 18 months. On assessing the application of these criteria, however, it was discovered that the number of Germans in British hands was small, and most of those were U-boat crews while many of the remainder were merchant seamen, neither of whom the Royal Navy was keen to lose. As a result, the proposal was vehemently opposed by both the Admiralty and the Ministry of War Transport, and never left British government circles.

However the objections would not apply if the men were to be transferred to a neutral country, as had happened in World War One. So, in March 1944, and following agreement with the Dominions' governments, it was proposed, through Switzerland, that both sides should transfer to neutral countries willing to accept them all men who were over 42 years old on 31 March 1944 and had been held for 18 months or longer. It was further proposed that the criteria be applied regardless of numbers (i.e., not head-for-head), that merchant seamen would be included and that no individuals would be excluded on security grounds. The British estimated that this would involve 3,551 (including 559 merchant seamen) in German hands and 8,080 in British and Commonwealth hands (including 86 merchant seamen). The British intention was that all of these should be sent to Sweden, partly because Switzerland was already holding large numbers of internees, but also because there were numbers of Allied escapees already in Switzerland who were awaiting a legal opportunity to leave but whose position might be compromised if large internment camps were set up. It was also stipulated that the belligerent countries would be responsible for meeting all the costs of holding, administering and feeding such internees.

The Swiss agreed with these proposals and put them to the Germans, but met with a cool response and the Swiss indicated to the British that there were two main reasons. First, the Germans were reluctant to expose such released prisoners to anti-Nazi feelings in neutral countries. Of greater immediate concern, however, was the fact that the German Treasury was desperately short of foreign currency, and simply could not meet the expense involved.

By early 1945 there were over 40,000 British and Commonwealth prisoners-of-war who were more than halfway through their fifth year of captivity and although German defeat was by now inevitable it was by no means certain how long it would take and it was known that conditions in the country were becoming increasingly desperate. So, on 15 February 1945 the British proposed an initial small-scale exchange direct to their home countries rather than internment. This would take place, the British suggested, through Switzerland, whose western land border was now accessible through France. This British proposal was to exchange 3,000 Germans being held in the Middle East (mostly Afrika Korps veterans) who had been captured prior to 1 July 1943 for British and Commonwealth prisoners captured prior to July 1940. A somewhat bizarre additional proviso was that the proportion of officers to other ranks would be 1:19.

This was passed by the Swiss to Germany, but at the same time the Swiss received a German proposal for a much larger exchange involving 25,000 on each side. The Swiss supported the latter proposal as both they and the ICRC were already aware of large columns of Allied prisoners being marched around the ever-decreasing Third Reich, who were not only exhausted and hungry, but were also facing increasing hostility from the German civil population, particularly over the bombing.

When this proposal was notified to the US government its first reaction was to object strongly on the grounds that the Germans were simply trying to get their hands on men who could be sent to fighting units.[7] After further consideration, the US government modified its position somewhat and stated that it was simply opposed to the full figure of 25,000 but was prepared to agree to 5,000 or even 7,000.

The British quickly agreed to exchange 5,000 men, a figure later increased to 7,000, in an operation that would take place at Gothenburg, Sweden on 27 March. The Germans did not reply until 4 April, when they stated that the proposals were unacceptable due to a variety of factors, but by then Germany was in a state of complete collapse, the Allied armies were squeezing the Germans into an ever-smaller area and the ability of the Germans to transport such a large number of prisoners overland to the Baltic ports was questionable, to say the least. As a result the process simply ran out of time.

A SWEDISH EXCHANGE

The majority of exchanges fit into the general categories, but there were a few that did not. One such took place in late 1944, when 57 German soldiers escaped in a small boat from Estonia in order to return to Germany. Either by accident or design, it was never clear which, they put into a Swedish port where they were interned, but quickly released for onward travel to Germany. To maintain fairness, the Swedish government released 33 Allied internees in what was termed 'on account'.

3

US–German Exchanges

Following the Japanese attack on Pearl Harbor, Germany and Italy declared war against the United States on 11 December 1941. US diplomats in all countries allied to or controlled by these two European members of the 'Axis pact' were promptly interned and on 14 December many of them, including all 155 of the staff from the Berlin embassy, were taken to Bad Nauheim, a small spa town in the state of Hesse, some 22 miles north of Frankfurt-am-Main. There, they were confined to the Grand Hotel, which had been deserted since 1939 and, to the indignation of its involuntary guests, was in a somewhat rundown state. Other groups arrived from Budapest, Copenhagen and Rome, and with little else to keep them occupied there was plenty of time for gossip and rumour, with the most important topic being 'going home'. In late January 1942 there was a report that a Portuguese ship would conduct an exchange, which proved false, but a further report in April that they would return to the United States aboard the Swedish liner, *Drottningholm*, proved much more accurate. The American diplomatic party left Bad Nauheim on 12 May 1942 and travelled by train across France and Spain until they arrived in Lisbon two days later.

Meanwhile, German, Italian and other Axis nationals had been similarly rounded up in the United States (and in some Latin American countries, as well), and were concentrated in three locations pending exchange. The United States had chartered the *Drottningholm*, which had been lying idle in its home port of Gothenburg. It left Sweden on 1 May and was in New York on 6 May, taking its passengers aboard the next day and sailing that evening. She carried 948 passengers, mostly German, but with a few Bulgarians, Italians and Hungarians; there were also 267 crew and five US government officials in charge of the arrangements. *Drottningholm* was painted white, with her name in large letters along the side and cruised at a somewhat leisurely speed, sailing alone and brightly lit.

On arrival in Lisbon on 16 May the ship disembarked its passengers and was then cleaned and victualled for the return voyage carrying the Americans. She sailed on 22 May and arrived in New York City on 30 May. *Drottningholm* sailed again on 3 June with more German repatriates, exchanged them for the second group of Americans and was back in New York on 30 June 1942.

With that second voyage completed, there were few, if any, US citizens left in Continental Europe and there were no further civilian exchanges, all future efforts being concentrated on the return of prisoners-of-war. There were a few German nationals in camps who had been declared a danger to national security by the FBI, but after President Roosevelt formally forbade any further civilian exchanges in August 1942 they were there for the duration.

Most of the remaining US exchanges were conducted in conjunction with its British allies, which have been described in Chapter 2. There was, however, one rather unusual exchange.

USAAF AIRCREW EXCHANGE IN SWITZERLAND

Quite apart from all its other activities as a neutral arbiter and home of the International Committee of the Red Cross, Switzerland was also an involuntary host to a large number of members of belligerent armed forces.

By far the largest group were some 15,000 members of the 2nd Polish Infantry Division, which had been raised in France in 1939 and fought as part of the French Army until it was cut off by the German advance. Having disarmed themselves at the border, they crossed into Switzerland where they were interned for the duration of the war. They lived a life of relative freedom, being allowed to study at schools and universities, or to work in mines and forests.

A second group were airmen of several nationalities, who, for a variety of reasons, landed or crashed on Swiss territory. Some 12 British and German aircraft are known to have landed there, but by far the greatest number belonged to the United States Army Air Force (USAAF) – see Table 3 below.

Table 3: USAAF Aircrew/Aircraft Interned in Switzerland 1943–1945[1]

Year	Month	Aircraft Landed/ Crashed	Surviving aircrew Interned
1943	August	4	40
	September	5	49
	October	3	15
	November	0	0
	December	0	0
	Totals	**12**	**104**
1944	January	1	10
	February	2	19
	March	23	195
	April	33	293

Year	Month	Aircraft Landed/ Crashed	Surviving aircrew Interned
	May	8	59
	June	4	38
	July	49	393
	August	4	39
	September	9	89
	October	3	13
	November	2	21
	December	2	13
	Totals	**140**	**1182**
1945	January	0	0
	February	15	94
	March	1	9
	April	4	34
	Totals	**20**	**137**
GRAND TOTALS		**172**	**1423**

Most of these were bomber aircrew whose aircraft were damaged by hostile fighters or anti-aircraft fire while conducting daylight raids on targets in Germany, Austria or Italy, while others were affected by technical problems or bad weather. Not every airman survived the air combat or the crash, and a small number of survivors were wounded, but the great majority were fit and healthy.

Even in the early part of the war the Swiss were prepared to release balanced numbers – for example, in early 1943 the crew of an RAF Mosquito that had crash-landed in their country were repatriated at the same time as two Luftwaffe Bf-109 pilots were returned to Germany. In late 1944, however, there was a massive repatriation in which 793 fit USAAF aircrew were released, the sole proviso being that they must not fly again in Europe, although that, of course, did not stop them replacing a man in the United States who could then be sent to Europe. The counter-balance was the release of 1,500 Germans, including some aircrew, to Germany.[2]

The United States did not tell their allies about this until after it had happened, which upset their British allies somewhat.[3] In a similar manner to the British exchange with Italians who had been held in Saudi Arabia (see Chapter 8), this was a government-to-government exchange, involving neither the ICRC nor the Geneva Convention, and the rules imposed on the repatriates were unique to the exchange.

4

German Exchanges

Germany conducted exchanges with France, the United Kingdom and the United States, as described elsewhere in this book. But it was also involved in two other exchanges, neither of which was totally successful.

A FAILED EXCHANGE: GERMANY AND ARGENTINA

Argentina and Germany severed diplomatic relations in March 1944, whereupon Germany immediately proposed an exchange of diplomatic and consular staff in accordance with established procedures. Unfortunately, for both these parties this could only be achieved with the concurrence of the Allies who controlled the Atlantic, and the Swiss, as was by now usual, set about brokering an arrangement. It was eventually agreed that two ships would be involved, both heading for Lisbon, but by way of Trinidad. It was, however, an absolute condition of the British agreement that they would inspect every item of baggage (i.e., hand, cabin and hold) of those returning to Europe, and they sent teams to both Rio de Janeiro and Buenos Aires to do this.

The inspections, which were described as 'very vigorous', took place, much to the indignation of those being inspected, and the ships duly sailed. The Argentine-registered *Rio Jachal* sailed from Buenos Aires carrying 128 passengers and the Spanish *Cabo de Buena Esperanza* from Rio de Janeiro carrying 291. When they arrived at Trinidad all the inspection seals were carefully checked by a fresh set of officials following which the two ships sailed from Trinidad on 27 July 1944. By the time they arrived in Lisbon, however, all rail communications between Portugal and Germany had been cut, with the result that the Germans were stuck in Portugal, while in Germany the Argentines were unceremoniously dispatched to Sweden where most of them sat out the rest of the war. The two ships then returned to South America via Trinidad, but without their intended passengers. *Cabo de Buena Esperanza* sailed empty, but *Rio Jachal* carried some 270 distressed Argentine nationals who had been trapped in Portugal for several years.[1]

GERMANY–TURKEY

The final successful exchange of the war took place at Gothenburg on 15 March 1945 and was unique in several respects, the first being that on this occasion, the Swedish liner *Drottningholm* was chartered by the German government, the only time in the war this was done. The primary aim of the voyage was to sail to Istanbul to recover German diplomats and other citizens from Turkey, which had broken off diplomatic relations in August 1944, followed by a declaration of war on 23 February 1945. Turkey had traditionally enjoyed close relations with Germany and there were many German civilians in banks, insurance companies and other commercial undertakings.

Planning and negotiations were well under way by January 1945. Because the ship would sail through British-controlled waters, they had to be consulted to obtain safe passage, and the government seized the opportunity to insist that the ship should carry some British repatriates, particularly Channel Islanders. The exchange began at Gothenburg on 8 March 1945, when *Drottningholm* sailed with 246 Britons from internment camps in Germany, of whom 212 were from the Channel Islands; this British group was accompanied by a doctor, a nurse and six paramedics provided by the Swedish Red Cross. The largest single group was 480 Turks, of whom approximately 80 were from the Turkish embassy in Berlin, the remainder being mainly businessmen and students. There were also 113 Argentinean diplomats who had been stranded in Sweden since the aborted exchange of July 1944. A number of others took advantage of the opportunity to leave Sweden, including 130 Swedes, mostly diplomats, businessmen and missionaries proceeding to posts abroad, some 50 British who took the opportunity to go home, 26 Portuguese and a number of Peruvians.

Drottningholm sailed from Gothenburg on 8 March and called at Liverpool to disembark the British group, Portugal to disembark the Argentines and Portuguese, and then on to Port Said and Istanbul. She spent three weeks at Istanbul and then returned via Lisbon and Holyhead (Liverpool) to Gothenburg arriving on 5 June. The German group were on this return voyage but their numbers cannot be discovered.

A signal sent by the Foreign Office in London to the Embassy in Stockholm on 10 March 1945 gave a valuable summary of the British position:

1. This present exchange is primarily exchange of Turkish and German, and Argentine and German officials for which *Drottningholm* was chartered by German Government. British Government have given safe conduct to this vessel on condition that 250 British civilians from Germany are repatriated in this ship to United Kingdom. Number of British from Germany to be repatriated is governed by number of German civilians immediately available for a head-for-head exchange.

2. Channel Islanders deported to camps at Wurzach and Biberach. We pressed German Government a long time ago to include Channel Islanders but none were included in first exchange which took place at Lisbon. Some were repatriated to Gothenburg in September, but many husbands were quite unnecessarily sent without wives or vice versa. We pressed Swiss Government to ensure that more Channel Islanders would be included in future exchanges and that families should never be divided. We have pressed in particular that families, one member of whom has already been repatriated, should be given priority.

3. Since agreement was reached last April between British Empire and Germany to exchange civilians approximately 1,800 (repeat 1,800) British Commonwealth civilians have been repatriated from Germany and German-occupied territory in three head-for-head exchanges. In 1943, before this agreement was reached, 400 British civilians were repatriated in small exchanges.

4. In addition some 630 British merchant seamen have been exchanged.

5. It is hoped to arrange a further exchange of British civilians.[2]

There were, of course, no further exchanges as the war was coming to an end and the situation in what was left of German-controlled territory was deteriorating day by day. Nevertheless, the British note shows that the efforts to repatriate people from Germany continued right up to the last.

Jewish–German Exchanges

Among the exchanges that took place in Europe, there was one type that was highly focused, very emotive and beyond anything envisaged by those who framed the 1929 Geneva Convention – the exchange of Jews from German-occupied territory for German citizens interned in various Allied countries. As a proportion of those murdered by the Nazis, the numbers involved in the exchanges were very small, but for each Jew concerned it meant an escape from almost certain death, while for those involved in the negotiations the potential for exchanges on a much greater scale always seemed to be just around the corner, so they kept on persevering, right up to May 1945.

As with other exchanges, numerous organizations and groups were involved, but in this case there were strong and unique political pressures, and, as a result, it required months, sometimes years, of negotiations and only took place when each side had not only something to gain, but, of equal importance, something to offer in return. In essence, the people actually exchanged were mere pawns in a much larger game, although, as will be shown in the case of Mary Berg, those people were real, too.

In the initial exchanges, the situation revolved around two groups of people: those Jews in Europe who had a demonstrable connection with the then British-Mandated Territory of Palestine, and a group of German settlers in Palestine, known as the Templers. Palestine, at this stage, was essentially a geographic area rather than a political entity and had been part of the Ottoman Empire for many centuries until the Turkish defeat in 1917, when it passed under British control, whose policy was laid down in the Balfour Declaration.[1] Then, in 1922, the newly established League of Nations granted a mandate to the British to rule the country on behalf of the League of Nations.[2] This led to the establishment of a British High Commission, supported by the usual apparatus of colonial rule – judiciary, police, civil service, and so on – in Jerusalem, which reported to the Colonial Office in London. The British created Palestinian citizenship, holders of which were entitled to a British Palestinian passport. Within Palestine there were several different ethnic and religious communities, with the ever-increasing number of Jews causing distinct unease among the majority Arabs.

Article 4 of the Mandate required the setting up of a 'Jewish Agency' and this was established in 1923, with the leaders being elected by the Jewish community in Palestine as a whole. The agency's headquarters were in Jerusalem but it also established several offices overseas, including London, Geneva and Istanbul. The Jewish Agency was given official recognition by the High Commission in 1929, but its authority was confined to its own community.

Under strong pressure from the Arabs, the British High Commission imposed a limit on Jewish immigration, essentially restricting it to those with relatives already domiciled in Palestine. The number allowed was 7,500 per year and responsibility for assessing eligibility and then issuing the 'Immigration Certificates' was delegated by the High Commission to the Jewish Agency.

In the UK, the Colonial Office was responsible for the affairs of the Mandated Territory of Palestine, but the Foreign Office became involved whenever contacts with other governments were involved. One particular issue was wartime contact with Germany, which was only possible through the Protecting Power – the United States until 7 December 1941 and Switzerland thereafter. The Foreign Office also dealt with any other embassies or legations and established a special office, the Refugees Department, to handle such matters. The Cabinet Office became involved in matters of higher policy, particularly where relations with the United States were involved. There were also Jewish pressure groups within the British Parliament.

In the late 1930s, the British, as the Mandatory Power, found themselves in a major predicament. On the one hand were the Jews, who were demanding increased immigration, which in the short term was intended to accommodate the Jews of central Europe who were threatened by the Nazi's policies. In the longer term, however, the intention was to establish the 'Jewish national home' (i.e., a Jewish-ruled state) promised in the Balfour Declaration. On the other hand, the Palestinian Arabs, who had lived in the country for many centuries, were becoming increasingly alarmed by the escalating numbers of Jews. Both sides were taking military action, not only against each other, but also against the British. As a result, the British convened a conference in London in 1939, which was attended by Arab and Jewish delegates, but when they refused to talk to each other the British issued a Government White Paper.[3] This was rejected by almost everyone, and even repudiated by the next British government, but despite this, and in the absence of anything else, this document remained the basis of British policy during the war years.

The White Paper laid down that for the following six years (i.e., 1940–1945) there would be an annual quota of Jewish immigrants of 10,000 per year, with the proviso that a shortfall in one year could be added to the next, provided economic circumstances allowed it. In addition, there was to be a 'one-off' contribution to alleviating the current refugee problem in Europe by allowing 25,000 to be admitted at the discretion of the High Commissioner, with priority being given to children and dependants. This allowed for 75,000 immigrants over five years, following which there would be no further entry for a further five years, until, in 1949, a Palestinian state, composed of and governed by all inhabitants, would be established.

The main German interest in Palestine centred on a group known as *Tempelgesellschaft* (Temple Society), a religious community which had split from the Lutheran Church in the southern German state of Württemberg in 1861. These Templers (with an 'e') had no relationship whatsoever with the Knights Templar (with an 'a'), a movement that dated back to Crusader times. Instead, this new movement derived its title from the belief that individuals and communities were God's temple and that redemption came through hard work and a pious lifestyle. The aim was to 'bring God's people together ... in the temple of God in the Holy Land (i.e., Palestine)' and the first community of Templers arrived in the then Ottoman-ruled Palestine in 1868. They slowly overcame disease and tough conditions to establish a number of self-contained and thriving agricultural settlements. There was a second wave of immigration at the turn of the century and by 1910 the total number was about 2,200; total numbers never exceeded 3,000.

When the League of Nations Mandate was established in 1922, the British left these quiet, law-abiding and self-sufficient settlers to their own devices. By the early 1930s, few Templers had been born in Germany, but they spoke German within their community, retained German citizenship and maintained official ties with their home country through the German consulate. When the Nazis came to power, the Templers, along with many similar bodies around the world, were classified as '*Auslanddeutsch*' (overseas Germans), which, among other things, meant that their young men were obliged to return to Germany for their military service.

When war broke out in August 1939 those Templer men already in Germany were retained by the *Wehrmacht*, while men of military age in Palestine were ordered to go to Germany at once – which a number did. Realizing what was happening, the British then rounded up any remaining physically fit men aged between 16 and 60, declared them to be prisoners-of-war and placed them in a specially built camp near Acre. This left 174 elderly men, 463 women and 365 children in the four rural settlements, with a further number, again women, children and old men, scattered among the major towns, giving a grand total of just under 2,000. All Templers were then ordered to move into one of the four main settlements, Bethlehem, Sarona, Waldheim and Wilhelma, which were then surrounded by barbed wire fences to become large-scale internment camps, although within the wire the inhabitants had complete freedom of movement, administered themselves and carried on farming, assisted by their Arab field hands. In July 1941, the British, alarmed by the advance of the Axis armies in North Africa, sent 661 of what appeared to be hard-core Nazis, including women and children, to Australia, leaving the remaining women, children and elderly to maintain the settlements in Palestine.

The United States was not directly involved in the situation and people of Palestine, but its role as Britain's protecting power in Germany meant that it was involved in negotiations between the two governments until 7 December 1941, when this role was taken on by Switzerland. The United States was, however, subsequently involved in the Bermuda Agreement, where they and the British agreed that there should be no negotiations with Germany and, in particular, that there could be no exchange of Jewish civilians for German civilians or prisoners-of-war. By 1944, however, various lobby groups were becoming more vociferous and influential.

From its inception, the Nazi Party always intended to rid the German *Reich* itself of its indigenous Jewish population, but as the German-conquered territories grew in size, so, too, did its ambition to 'cleanse' them of their Jewish populations, as well. Despite the enormity of this evil project, the Nazi mind was also capable of making some very pedantic and nit-picking bureaucratic distinctions; thus, in many cases, they were prepared to differentiate between Jews born in Germany or its conquered territories and Jews with foreign, particularly Allied, nationality. They were also prepared to give special status to Jews of any nationality who happened to have a valid immigration certificate to Palestine. This was countered by the German desire to obtain the return of German citizens who were either domiciled abroad, as were the Templers, or had been caught abroad by chance on the outbreak of hostilities. It would also appear that, in parallel with their contacts with the Allies over other exchanges (e.g., wounded prisoners-of-war and civilian internees) some Nazis also saw contacts over these Jewish exchanges as a means of keeping open even a limited form of communication with the Allies.

Although many departments in both the government and the Nazi hierarchies were involved, the lead was taken by the *Auswärtige Amt* (Ministry of Foreign Affairs) within which the Legal Department had primary responsibility for international treaties and international law. Then, once war had been declared it also became involved in communicating with Protecting Powers and bodies such as the International Committee of the Red Cross over legal aspects of prisoner-of-war matters, as well as the actual exchanges of wounded prisoners-of-war. Another key department was the *Reichsicherheitshauptamt* (State Security Head Office), with *Department IV B4*, headed by the notorious *SS-Obersturmbannführer* Adolf Eichmann, constantly involved in Jewish affairs from 1936 onwards.

On the outbreak of war, a number of Palestine-based Jews, holders of Palestine passports, happened to be visiting relatives in Poland and were almost all rounded up by the Germans and interned. Their relatives in Palestine immediately pressed for their return and the Jewish Agency raised the matter with the

British authorities. Quite by chance, and as described above, the Germans were interested in their nationals in Palestine, particularly the Templers, although there were others. As a result, but only after lengthy and very painstaking negotiations, the first exchange took place. This was agreed in principle in May 1941, but it took until December to resolve the minutiae of the deal. The process involved the Germans, the United States (as Protecting Power), the British Government, the High Commission in Palestine, the Jewish Agency, and the Turkish Government, since the exchange was to take place on their territory. However, in this particular case, the International Committee of the Red Cross (ICRC) was not involved.

Thus, on 12 December 1941, 65 people of German nationality from Palestine were exchanged in Istanbul for 46 people with Palestinian papers, who had been held in Germany. Apart from crossing the Bosporus, all transportation was by railroad, with the Germans delivering their group to the Bulgarian/Turkish border and the British to the Syrian/Turkish border, and the Turks supervising both the travel across their territory and the actual exchange itself. This process obviously benefited the very small number of people involved, but this exchange was significant in establishing the feasibility of civilian exchanges through government–protecting power–government negotiations, as opposed to those concerning prisoners-of-war under the Geneva Convention and involving the International Committee of the Red Cross.

The first part of the second exchange took place on 12 November 1942. The negotiations started as soon as the first had been successfully completed (i.e., January 1942) and involved the same people as before, except that, since the United States was now an active participant in the war, its place as the Protecting Power for both the UK and Germany was taken by Switzerland. By this time the news of the Nazi extermination camps was beginning to spread outside German-occupied territories and there was an even greater feeling of urgency. Each side produced lists of their citizens they wanted the other to include in the exchange and both proposed a widening of the categories and an increase in numbers. The original date was to have been 1 October 1942, but this had to be postponed, first to 1 November and then to 12 November, when it actually took place. The numbers involved were 301 Germans plus four Italians who were exchanged for 69 Jews, 11 non-Jewish Palestinians, plus 71 British subjects, many of them survivors from the Zamzam – see Chapter 6. Again, transportation was by train, with the actual exchange taking place in Turkey.

The Germans were conscious that they had not met their quota and sent an official to Poland to look for more people on the British list, but in the event they dispatched a small group of three women and 12 children, all Dutch Jews. These arrived in Palestine by the same overland railroad route on 9 February 1943. Despite this, the imbalance – now 305 versus 166 – remained heavily weighted in the German favour. To confuse matters, some of the few sent by the Germans were not on any of the lists submitted to them, but the British accepted them in order to avoid compromising possible future exchanges.

Preliminary negotiations for the third exchange started well before the second had taken place and on the British/Jewish side there was a much-heightened sense of urgency as the scale of the German attempts to murder all European Jews became apparent. Once again it was a question of lists and categories, and in February 1943 the Jewish Agency in Jerusalem passed to the Passport Control Officer in the British Consulate in Istanbul a document that became known as the 'First Istanbul List'. This included the wives and children of Palestine passport holders, the great majority of whom were believed to be in Poland.

By now individuals, groups and agencies were flooding the British and Swiss authorities with lists of names and the British High Commission decided to clarify precisely who was eligible. This comprised: Palestine passport holders; wives and children of Palestine passport holders; wives and children of male Immigration Certificate holders.

This resulted in the 'Second Istanbul List' that included the names of some 800 families, complete with addresses and details of Immigration Certificates. This was passed to the Swiss by the British in the third week of December 1943. Somewhat confusingly, despite being known as the 'Istanbul Lists' these documents were actually prepared by the Jewish Agency and passed by them to the British High Commission in Jerusalem. The onward passage of the list was convoluted as the High Commission, if they approved the list, sent it to the Colonial Office in London, who passed it to the Foreign Office for transmission to the British Embassy in Switzerland, who handed it to the Swiss Foreign Ministry who cabled it to their embassy in Berlin who handed it to the German Foreign Affairs Ministry.

Two new factors now began to appear. The first was that, despite the documentation, many of the Jews on the Istanbul Lists could no longer be located by the Germans, probably because they had already been sent to the extermination camps. On the other side, the British were finding it increasingly difficult to find German civilians who were not only available to be repatriated but were also willing to be so. One possible answer might have been to exchange German prisoners-of-war for Jews, but this was specifically excluded by the Bermuda Agreement.

At this point the German internment camp for foreign civilians at Vittel in France entered the picture. In addition to the wives and children of British, Dominions and US citizens, it also held a number of Palestinians, as well as other Jews, such as 250 of Polish origin who had obtained, by one means or another, Latin American passports. A train carrying some 90 with Latin American passports was sent to Vittel on 9 March 1944, but then, despite the apparent safety of the camp, the Germans started to transport some of these same Jews to extermination camps in Poland, the first train departing on 17 April 1944, followed by another in May.

At the end of the war, the camp at Bergen-Belsen, located near Celle in Lower Saxony, achieved dreadful notoriety for its cruelty, the skeletal condition of those found alive by the arriving British, and the huge mounds of dead, but it was not always like that. It was originally established as a prisoner-of-war camp – *Stalag XI-C* – in 1940 for Soviet prisoners-of-war run by the *Wehrmacht*, but its role was expanded in April 1942 when it passed to SS control and was redesignated *Aufenthaltslager* Bergen-Belsen (transit camp) – where, among others, Jewish civilians who were potentially suitable for exchange were assembled and then held pending finalization of the arrangements.[4]

Another source of potential exchangees was the camp for Dutch Jews at Westerbork, where inmates were rigorously assessed for eligibility by a Fraulein Slottke, who based her judgements on a list provided by the RHSA, which was essentially that provided by the British. Many people from Westerbork were also being sent to camps in Poland, the Germans observing a distinction in the mode of transport in that those going to possible exchange from Bergen-Belsen travelled in passenger coaches, while those going to their death in the East went in cattle trucks. Five trains left Westerbork between January and April 1944 taking some 1,300 to Bergen-Belsen.

The Germans ran the affair in a way which, either deliberately or accidentally, resulted in the inmates being constantly off-balance and unsure as to what fate had in store for them. Thus, in late April all those with 'Palestine papers' were ordered to assemble, which resulted in some 1,300 moving to one side. A total of 300 were named from a list, which was reduced to 272 the following day and these were then marched to a separate compound, where they were held until 28 May. Another parade and roll call reduced the number to 222 being named and 50 rejected. The Commandant insisted that he was not permitted to deviate from a list he had received from the RSHA in Berlin, although there was a list of reserves who could be selected if any of the 222 fell out for any reason. The selected 222 were then warned on 1 June that they would depart the next day, but this was postponed without explanation.

As described earlier, the first two exchanges had resulted in an imbalance of exchanged numbers: 305 to the Germans, 166 to the British. As a result, the British asked the Swiss to inform the Germans that they must rectify this in the third exchange by producing an excess of 139 people. They further insisted that the people to be exchanged must be those on the named lists and this the Germans found difficult to meet – some had moved, some had disappeared in the chaos of war and some had already gone to the death camps. The Germans scoured their territories for more with 'Palestine papers' and, helped by the

French police, found some 300 in France, but, somewhat surprisingly, very few of them wanted to go – or, in some cases return – to Palestine.

It was not only the Germans who were having difficulty in finding people. The British had some 7,000 German civilians scattered around the Empire – Australia: 665; Canada: 253; India: 1,800; Palestine: 90; Rhodesia: 74; South Africa: 3,500; and the UK: 1,310. Although there were still some Templers left in Palestine, very few of these had any wish to go to Germany. The Germans suggested that the 665 Templers sent to Australia in 1941 could be brought back to Europe for exchange. The British looked into this but calculated that once the men of military age had been excluded together with their wives and children (who presumably would not travel without their husband/father) that left about 90 women, children and old men. The British turned this down and finally managed to find 74 in Rhodesia and another 40 individuals, all of whom were moved to Palestine pending the exchange.

This rather macabre bureaucratic dance lasted through 1943 and into 1944 but the problem appeared to be solved when it was agreed to include some of the Dutch Jews in Bergen-Belsen, who were not on the British/Jewish lists. The resulting (but still not final) list comprised 11 people from Laufen (*Internierungslager VII*), 30–50 from Vittel (*Frontstalag 120*) and the balance from Bergen-Belsen, plus some individuals, only 38 of this total being named on the original British lists. However, the Germans were adamant that, given the circumstances, this was the best they could do.

The exchange was repeatedly delayed, sometimes by the Germans, sometimes the British, and once by the Turks. There were changes of individual names, but eventually on 29 June the Bergen-Belsen contingent was told to prepare to move. Even on this final day there were changes due to sickness, but on 30 June they marched to Celle station where they found a train with passenger coaches, a luggage van, a dining car and even coaches for the sick. The train took them to Vienna where they were put into a hostel where they were joined by 55 from Vittel and five from Laufen. Also in the hostel were some 100 Egyptians, who were scheduled to go on the same train to Istanbul, but who were delayed 'due to paperwork'.[5] On Sunday the party got into a new, modern train with 11 carriages (including sleeping cars and a dining car) and set out for Istanbul. They passed through Belgrade and Sofia, finally reaching Istanbul at 5.30 a.m. on 6 July where one woman from Bergen-Belsen had a stroke and died. The Turks placed all the passengers aboard a ferry that cruised in the Bosporus throughout the day, as did a second boat carrying the 114 Germans, while officials ashore sorted out the paperwork. When this was finalized, both ships docked, people went ashore and into trains and set off, the Jews reaching Haifa on 10 July.

Meanwhile, a completely different group of people had been brought into play, with the '*Benghasi Juden*' (Benghazi Jews) being involved in another exchange in

June 1944 in an episode that, to this day, remains something of a mystery. Prior to World War Two, there were a number of Jewish communities along the North African littoral who had lived there for many centuries, one of them being a Sephardic community in Benghazi, in the Ottoman province of Cyrenaica. These Benghazi Jews had been there since at least the mid-sixteenth century and lived in relative tranquility until the Italians took over three Ottoman provinces of Cyrenaica, Fezzan and Tripolitania in 1911. The Italians subsequently combined the three into a single entity named Libya in 1934.The Libyan Jews numbered between 25,000 and 30,000, and of these 1,600 were under French protection, while 870 had British nationality.[6]

At some point in 1942 someone in Germany appears to have realized that these British passport holders could be used as a negotiating tool in a future exchange and some 300 of them were taken to Italy. They passed through a number of camps, including Passoli, near Modena, but were then moved in smaller groups by train to Germany, arriving at Bergen-Belsen between January and May 1944 (January 31: 83; February 24: 70; 20–23 May: 147).[7] Once in Bergen-Belsen they were held in a special compound known as the 'Sternlager' (star camp, so called from the Stars of David worn by the inmates) until being moved on, again in small groups, according to some complicated German plan. Thus, on 18 February 1944, 89 left Bergen-Belsen, of whom 66 were taken to Liebenau and 23 to Laufen, and 49 of these 89 were subsequently moved to Vittel, where they were joined on 1 July 1944 by a further 70 direct from Bergen-Belsen.

The British–German exchange duly took place at Lisbon on 12 July 1944, some four months after that involving Mary Berg. On this occasion 919 German citizens who had been held in South Africa were exchanged for 920 British passport holders, including 119 Benghazi Jews. All those to be exchanged were taken in a variety of special trains, some of which, ironically, were attacked by Allied aircraft, which by then – it was three months after the D-Day landings – were roaming freely over France and attacking anything that moved. The Benghazi Jews were taken in a special train through Hendaye to Lisbon, where the actual exchange took place, and from there the British facilitated their return to their home city of Benghazi.

This incident is surprising for a number of reasons. The first is that the German government never released anybody on any of these exchanges except after protracted negotiations, which always involved some quid pro quo in the form of the return of an equivalent number of German citizens. Where Jews were concerned, the names of those to be included in such an exchange were usually the result of intensive lobbying, typically by the Jewish Agency in British-Mandated Palestine or the Jewish community in the United States. But there does not seem to have been anybody lobbying on behalf of the Benghazi Jews, who were a small and obscure group with limited financial resources and little or no 'political' influence. Thus, why they should have been singled out for exchange is difficult to understand.

Secondly, in the majority of Jewish exchanges the group concerned travelled eastwards by train to Turkey where the physical handover took place at Istanbul and the Jewish group then moved, again by train, to Haifa for processing and release. But, the Benghazi Jews were, for no obvious reason, sent in the opposite direction and added to a British–German exchange in Lisbon.

Thirdly, it is not known how and when these people came to have British passports. The only significant contact between the inhabitants of this stretch of coast with 'Europeans' was during the war with the United States at the start of the nineteenth century. A few may have had British passports because they were born in a British colony and then emigrated to Libya, but this could only have applied to a small number (see Table 4, below). This is not to say that they should not have had them, but only to comment that it is by no means clear how it came about.

Table 4: Extract from the List of Benghazi Jews Exchanged at Lisbon (first 20 names only shown).[8] *BSS (=British subjects) repatriated via Lisbon, Aug 1944*

Surname	First Names	Date of Birth	Place of Birth
Benjamin	Chaim	1937	Benghazi
Benjamin	Elise	1935	Tripoli
Benjamin	Lydia	[Blank]	Benghazi
Benjamin	Labi Messauda	1886	Benghazi
Benjamin	Labi Rachele	1906	Benghazi
Benjamin	Rachele	1926	Benghazi
Benjamin	Rahmin Clemente	1936	Benghazi
Benjamin	Samuel	25.8.1939	Benghazi
Benjamin	Smeralda	1921	Tripoli
Benjamin	Labi Tita Nantina	1906	Benghazi
Benjamin	Giulia	1911	Derna
Benjamin	Ester	1928	Benghazi
Benjamin	Esacco	1930	Benghazi
Burbea	Abramo	1927	Tripoli
Burbea	Gabriel	1925	Tripoli
Burbea	Rachele	1932	Tripoli
Burbea	Vittorio	1923	Tripoli
Burbea	Arbib Wassi	1903	Tripoli

Surname	First Names	Date of Birth	Place of Birth
Buaron	Ester	1925	Benghazi
Buaron	Dadusse Mezzala	1889	Benghazi

Note: Heading *BSS* … etc. is in manuscript in the original.

A fifth exchange took place at Gothenburg, Sweden in March 1945. This was a deal between the German and Turkish governments and was primarily intended to return diplomats and students following the cutting of relations between the two countries. The Germans also simply added 137 Jews of Turkish origin, of whom 99 came from Bergen-Belsen.

The 'Kasztner transport' resulted in 1,685 Hungarian Jews reaching Switzerland, although it was not, strictly speaking, an exchange, since the escapees purchased their places by money, gold or precious stones. It was engineered by Rudolf Kasztner (1906–1957), a Hungarian Jew, who was a lawyer and journalist by profession, but also a highly motivated Zionist, and a committee member of the *Vaada, Vaadat Ezra ve'Hatzalah*, a Jewish rescue and relief society, based in Budapest.

The Germans did not occupy Hungary until 9 March 1944, when the 800,000-strong Hungarian Jewish community quickly became the last national group to be targeted by Himmler and the SS. Adolf Eichmann was sent to Budapest to take personal charge, and he issued orders for the wearing of the yellow star, and with his usual chilling efficiency, the first deportations took place on 15 May. At the same time, Kasztner started negotiating with the SS, including face-to-face meetings with Eichmann, and various plans were discussed, including the 'sale' of one million Jews in exchange for 10,000 trucks, 200 tons of tea, 800 tons of coffee, two million bars of soap and an unspecified amount of tungsten (required for armour-piercing anti-tank ammunition). The Americans refused such a deal, but another and very much less ambitious deal *was* agreed, whereby a number of Jews would be enabled to travel to Switzerland by train at US$1,000 per seat, thus saving them from certain death in a gas chamber. The negotiations were both protracted and convoluted. Some of the seats were sold by Kasztner to wealthy Jews for well over the asking price in order to raise the money for those who were on the list but did not have the funds, while the SS sold some seats direct, also for sums well in excess of the asking price, but this time with the SS pocketing the difference. It was also alleged later that Kasztner unfairly allocated seats to his own family and friends, although he did not personally travel on the train.

The train, with its 1,685 passengers, left Budapest on 30 June 1944 and took its passengers to Bergen-Belsen, arriving on 8 July where they were housed in a special annex, separated from the others. On 21 August, Kasztner, accompanied by SS-Colonel Kurt Becher, met Saly Meyer, a Swiss Jew and a member of the

American-Jewish Joint Distribution Committee, on the Swiss border. As a result, the first 318 Jews were released from Bergen-Belsen and transported to Switzerland, arriving two days later, and on 7 December, after what must have been an unnerving wait in Bergen-Belsen, the second group of 1,367 Jews, also reached Switzerland.[9]

As usual with groups on the move over several months, there were a number of events that changed the overall total. According to a researcher, at least three members of the group died during the stay at Bergen-Belsen, while at least eight children were born. Also, for unknown reasons, a further seventeen were not allowed to leave Bergen-Belsen and proceed to Switzerland.[10]

PERSONAL EXPERIENCES: MARY BERG

There is a danger when dealing with the Jewish experience in World War Two to become overwhelmed by statistics; millions of Jews were murdered during the Holocaust and only a very small number were exchanged. But, every one of those millions had his or her own story of hardship and suffering, and just one is taken here as being representative of those few who managed to leave under one of the pitifully few exchanges.

Mary Wattenberg was living in Poland when the Germans invaded in 1939.[11] Her grandparents, Polish Jews, had moved to the United States in the 1890s where Mary's mother, Lena, was born in 1902. The family returned to Poland in 1914 and then back again to the States after World War One, but Lena stayed behind and married a Polish citizen, giving birth to Mary in 1924. The key to what happened to them during the war was that Lena was a US citizen and held a US passport, which under the rules followed by the Germans meant that the whole family was 'American' even though the father and two daughters were both born in Poland; indeed, had never actually visited the United States.

Mary was confined, with her family, in the Warsaw Ghetto in November 1940 and during that period the conditions became increasingly oppressive; life became a daily struggle for survival and the sight of corpses in the street was commonplace. For most of them there was virtually no hope of survival, but for the 'foreigners' there was just a glimmer and the first rumour of a possible exchange came in late February 1942. Then, on 17 July 1942 Mary and her family, together with some 700 other holders of 'foreign' passports, were moved into the Pawiak Prison, which was situated inside the ghetto and that now combined the functions of a prison for criminals and an internment camp.

From their prison these internees were helpless spectators of the decimation of their fellow Jews outside the prison, who were either taken away in the seemingly endless succession of trains 'to the East', or died inside the ghetto, either mown down in arbitrary shootings or from sickness or starvation. Those inside the Pawiak were by no means safe and there were many arbitrary shootings. Nevertheless, the hope of release remained, despite repeated setting and then cancellation of dates. They were held there until 18 January 1943 when Mary, her mother and her sister were among those finally taken to the railroad station and then by train to an internment camp at Vittel in France – they even received meals served by women of the German Red Cross.

The Vittel camp consisted of three large hotels, adjacent to each other and surrounded by wire, supplemented in March by a fourth. These were occupied by a mixture of internees including British who had been unable to escape when the Germans invaded France, some Americans, and Jews with foreign passports ranging from US to Haitian and Costa Rican. The food was insufficient but was supplemented by occasional Red Cross parcels. One curious feature of their stay was that they received occasional letters from their friends in Warsaw and were allowed to send cards in return, but they also received occasional letters from elsewhere in France and even from England.

The first group to leave Vittel for exchange departed on 21 November 1943, consisting of about 100 people, most of them over 60, but the turn of Mary and her family did not come until 1 March 1944 when, at long last, they were sent by train to Lisbon. There they boarded the *Gripsholm*, which sailed for the United States on 5 March arriving in New York ten days later.

Mary Berg arrived in New York, aged 19, having experienced more in the previous four years than most humans do in a lifetime. She had seen death, both through shooting and illness, at first hand, had experienced an almost daily uncertainty of seeing the following dawn, and had lost relatives and friends in large numbers. Memories of this dreadful period must have remained with her for the rest of her life.

6

The Zamzam *Affair*

On 7 April 1941, the liner *Zamzam*, a neutral vessel sailing under the Egyptian flag, was sunk in mid Atlantic by the German raider, *Atlantis*. One person died in the attack, but the adventures that befell the survivors illustrate how widely the treatment of civilians could vary, even though they were captured as a group and held by just one power.

Zamzam was completed in 1909 as the Bibby Line's *Leicestershire* and employed for some 20 years on the UK–Egypt–India–Burma route, apart from service as a troopship during the First World War. Afterwards, she was modernized, converted to oil fuel and then returned to commercial service, but sold in 1930 to be used as an exhibition ship. This project collapsed and the ship was sold again, this time to the Alexandria Steam Navigation Company, generally known as Misr, and, having been renamed *Zamzam*, she was used as a pilgrim ship between Alexandria and Jeddah until the war caused the *Haj* to be suspended in 1940.

Because Egypt was neutral, *Zamzam* could sail under the protection of the Egyptian flag, so on 28 December 1940 she departed Alexandria carrying 99 passengers, of whom 18 were US citizens, plus some 5,000 tons of Egyptian cotton. Her route took her through the Suez Canal, down the east coast of Africa, around the Cape of Good Hope and across the Atlantic to Brazil, arriving safely in New York on 24 February 1941. By this time, *Zamzam* was 30 years old and while her theoretical speed was 14 knots (16 mph) she was unable to proceed at more than about 10 knots (11.5 mph) although at least one passenger described the actual speed as 8 knots (9 mph).

In New York, *Zamzam*'s owners employed the travel agent, Thomas Cook, to drum up business for the return voyage and the prospect of a safe passage aboard a neutral ship attracted some 200 passengers. The largest single group consisted of 142 missionaries and their families, mostly Americans, but with a small number of Canadians, British and one Norwegian. These belonged to a wide variety of denominations, including Baptists, Catholics, Lutherans, and Seventh-Day Adventists, most of whom were going to Central Africa to replace German missionaries who had been interned by the British.

Next was the unique British-American Ambulance Corps, consisting of 24 young, mostly wealthy, American volunteers looking for adventure. Despite the word 'British' in their title, they were actually intending to support the Free

French forces in the North African campaign. Their ambulances and equipment were aboard *Zamzam* as cargo. There were also six American tobacco traders from North Carolina, en route to Southern Rhodesia at British request to help set up a tobacco market.[1] Finally came a mixed group of passengers, including several British and Canadian families en route to join their husbands, a Belgian family on their way to the Congo, two Greek nurses and an Italian, Prince Alfonse de Liguori.

The crew was 127 strong. The captain and chief engineer were British, the remaining officers Egyptian, and the others a mix of Egyptians, Sudanese, and Somalis, with one Greek stewardess. The cargo consisted of cars, tools, chemicals (including 1,000 tons of nitrate), paper, lubricating oil, and steel, and, as far as is known, all were intended for use by the Egyptian government or commercial companies.

Zamzam sailed from New York on 20 March 1941 and, following brief stops in Baltimore and Trinidad, arrived in Recife, Brazil, on 7 April, where she refuelled. Two American journalists, who had flown down from the States, also joined the ship; one was from *Fortune* magazine, the other a photographer for *Life* magazine, and both were en route to report on the British campaign in North Africa. Leaving Recife on 9 April, *Zamzam* headed for Cape Town, and all went well until 5.40 a.m., 17 April, when, without warning, the ship came under fire from the German raider, *Atlantis*, then disguised as the Norwegian ship, *Tamesis*. The fourth round hit the radio room, preventing the transmission of a distress call, and the bombardment of the unarmed vessel continued until the master managed to signal by torchlight that they were neutral.[2] The passengers and crew of the *Zamzam* were then rescued and taken aboard *Atlantis*, where they were correctly treated until transferred next day to the supply ship, *Dresden*. Loaded with some 300 survivors *Dresden* headed north and on 23 May, 35 days after leaving the *Atlantis*, she anchored off the French resort town of St Jean-de-Luz, just north of the border with Spain. Despite some close shaves, she had never once been spotted or challenged, probably because the entire British navy was in the North Atlantic looking for the German battleship, *Bismarck*.[3]

At that time the German high command was eager to keep the United States out of the war. Thus, from the moment they were told of the US passengers aboard the *Zamzam*, it was clear that the situation was potentially hugely embarrassing. So, as soon as *Dresden* reached St Jean-de-Luz, the United States citizens were given special treatment and the majority, with the exception of the members of the British-American Ambulance Corps, were released on 30 May 1941. They were then dispatched by train to Portugal, arriving in Lisbon on 2 June, where they were accommodated in Sintra while their passages home were arranged.

The first three to reach home were the two journalists, Charles Murphy and David Scherman, accompanied by one of the members of the British-American

Ambulance Corps, all of whom found seats aboard a Pan Am flyingboat, arriving in New York on 9 June. Next to arrive were most of the single women aboard the Portuguese passenger liner, *Mouzinho* (21 June), followed by eight families aboard another Portuguese vessel, *Serpa Pinto* (23 June*)*, and 53 aboard *Exeter*, an American Export Lines ship (24 June). More arrived on 30 June and 28 July.

Of the remaining members of the British-American Ambulance Corps, two escaped in France and made their own way to Portugal arriving on 28 July, and the remainder arrived on 2 August, less one man, the leader, Franco Vicovari, whose adventures are described below. One of the tobacco traders from North Carolina, Ned Laughinghouse, had been wounded in the shelling of *Zamzam* and was retained aboard *Atlantis*, where, despite excellent medical care, he died.

The sinking of the *Zamzam* had already caused a furore in the United States and this was exacerbated when the survivors began to reach home. The *Life* photographer succeeded in taking photographs of the entire affair, including the rescue, and although most were seized by the Germans he managed to smuggle a few and these appeared in a dramatic *Life* article on 23 June.[4] A number of other survivors produced books, at least four being published in 1941 alone, while many others gave lectures or wrote magazine articles.

The US citizens having disembarked at St Jean-de-Luz, *Dresden* sailed northwards, escorted by German warships, and then up the River Gironde to Bordeaux, where the remaining survivors disembarked and divided into three groups. The women and children were taken in buses to an old school building where they were looked after by the German Red Cross. The two other groups – the Egyptian crew, and all remaining men (i.e., those passengers with British or Dominion passports, plus the two British officers from the *Zamzam*) – were marched through the city streets to the village of St Médard, where they were held in a makeshift camp of wooden huts surrounded by barbed wire for nine days. On the tenth day they were taken, still in their three groups but all on the same train, from Bordeaux to Wesermünde, a small town west of Hamburg, a journey that in peacetime would have taken a day but which, in wartime conditions, took five.

The women's group comprised 21 adults and seven children, most of them holders of British, Canadian or South African passports, but with two Greek nurses who had been travelling as passengers, one Greek stewardess from the ship's crew, a Liberian mother and daughter, and one Norwegian female missionary.

On arrival at Wesermünde, these women and children were given just two minutes to bid farewell to the men, with no idea of when they would meet again, and were then moved from one prison to another. The first was in Bremervörde, where they spent ten days in very inhospitable conditions, before setting out for the south by train under heavy escort. The trains were slow, dirty and overcrowded, as were the city jails where they spent the nights: one in Bremen, two in Hanover, and a final one in Stuttgart.[5] Their odyssey came to an end on

16 June, when they left the train at Meckenbeuren, a small town in the state of Württemberg, some 20 miles north of Lake Constance. From there the adults and older children walked two miles through idyllic countryside, while one older woman and three infants were driven, to their new home, *Internierunslager V* (*Ilag-V* = Internment Camp 5), at Liebenau.

The women and children from the *Zamzam* settled down to make the best they could of the camp, a former lunatic asylum.[6] It consisted of four large buildings, which were surrounded by barbed wire and patrolled by a few armed guards, while the Franciscan sisters who had looked after the lunatics remained to serve as wardresses for the internees. In June the three Greeks (two nurses and a stewardess), the Belgian mother and daughter, and the Norwegian missionary were sent home to their respective countries, which were under German occupation, where they were released.

There then followed an extraordinary experience for some of the women, which started on 13 September 1941 when a number were summoned to the camp administration office and offered the opportunity to travel to Berlin at their own expense and then remain there, paid for by the United States embassy, while their eventual fate was decided.[7] They were given two hours in which to make up their minds and, in some cases, to borrow the rail fare. The offer was accepted by two South Africans, eight Canadians and four others, and the very next day they were taken to the railroad station. They were escorted only as far as Ravensburg, after which they were left to travel on their own.[8] Contrary to what they had been told in Liebenau, they were not expected in Berlin, but once they had made contact with the US Embassy they were provided with money and given help in finding accommodation. Thereafter, the US Embassy gave them a monthly living allowance until December, when, America having joined the war, the responsibility was taken over by the Swiss, but for almost all facets of their daily lives, the women were left to fend for themselves in the capital city of the country with which their own countries were at war. Shortly afterwards, Mrs Wright, at 70 the oldest female in Liebenau, was also sent to Berlin, where she was joined by her husband, aged 75, who had been the oldest man in Tost.

In mid June 1942 some members of the Berlin group were given very short notice that they were to be exchanged and ten of them (eight from *Zamzam*, consisting of the Canadians, Dr and Mrs Wright and two others) left Berlin on 13 June in a train that also carried diplomats from South and Central America and a number of United States citizens. The train travelled via Paris and Bordeaux to Hendaye on the Franco-Spanish border, where, after observing the arrival of the Germans with whom they were being exchanged, the party from Berlin boarded the recently vacated train for the journey to Lisbon. After a short stay there they boarded the Swedish liner *Drottningholm* for the voyage to New York and then home.

The departure of the Canadians left the two remaining ex-Liebenau South Africans in Berlin feeling rather lonely. One of them, Mrs Hankin, who had found a cottage in a wood outside Berlin, was on her own until the YWCA found another Canadian woman who had not been included in the exchange and the two lived together for four months.[9] Then, on Saturday 24 October 1942 these two were told that they were on the exchange list and would leave Berlin by train the following morning. Their group comprised twelve women: five South Africans (including Mrs Hankin, the sole ex-*Zamzamer*), the Canadian, who had been sharing the cottage with Mrs Hankin, two Australians, and four Jewish women of unknown nationality.

They left Berlin at 6 p.m. and arrived in Vienna at 7.30 a.m. on the morning of Monday 26 October 1942, to be met by a Swiss official who took them to a large house where they joined others on the same exchange. As near as can be calculated, once they had assembled in Vienna this party comprised 69 Jews from Bergen-Belsen on their way to Palestine, 11 non-Jewish Palestinians and 71 British and Dominion subjects, the latter made up of the 12 from Berlin, 40-odd from Liebenau, and the group from Paris.

The group spent ten days in Vienna sightseeing and left on Saturday 7 November, being forced to walk to the station in a straggling column led by a rabbi with a long beard. All were vaccinated and deloused before leaving, and then they were off, escorted by three Red Cross nurses, three policemen, one Gestapo man, one German Foreign Office official, and a Swiss representative. They were on the train for four days, and the journey was reasonably comfortable, even though part of the trip was through Yugoslavia where there was a serious danger of attack by Tito's guerrillas.

On arrival on the north shore of the Bosporus the exchangees were put aboard a Turkish ferry that then anchored near a second ferry carrying the Germans until all formalities of the exchange had been completed, when the two ferries proceeded to the opposite shores. The exchangees from Germany then boarded a train that took them through Turkey, Syria and Lebanon and finally to Palestine. They arrived in Haifa on 17 November and were put in Athlit camp for questioning and processing, before being released.

PERSONAL STORIES

A British woman, Mrs Kathleen Levitt, aged 28, with her children, Peter (six) and Wendy (two), was one of those aboard *Zamzam*, on her way to join her husband, an RAF officer serving at a flying training school in South Africa. She was struck in the feet by pieces of shrapnel during the shelling of *Zamzam* but recovered and, with the other women, went through France and Germany, ending in Liebenau. She was given the chance to go to Berlin with the Canadians and South Africans, but turned it down as she felt that with two small children she was safer where she was. Then, in January 1942 she was offered places on the first Palestine exchange, which she again turned down, this time because of the dangers she perceived to her children while passing through the Balkans and Turkey. But on 23 September 1942, she was able to write to her husband that she had been given places on the second Palestine exchange and in October they were duly dispatched to Vienna, as usual at very short notice.[10] They travelled unguarded by train from Meckenbeuren, via Munich to Vienna, where they joined the Berlin group, which included Mrs Hankin, where they awaited the onward journey to freedom. The regime in Vienna was more relaxed and Mrs Levitt managed to persuade the guard that she would not abandon the opportunity to be on the exchange so that she was allowed to go for walks in Vienna to exercise her children.

Dr James de Graaff-Hunter, aged 61, was a British citizen and a geodesist, well known in international circles who, with his wife and daughter, was caught in the US on the outbreak of war. Although over age, he offered to return to his previous post in the Survey of India, in order to release a younger man for military service, but his offer was turned down, so, eager to be useful, he went to Bermuda where he was employed in the British censorship service. His offer to return to India was eventually accepted in February 1941 and his first opportunity to get there was to sail, with his family, aboard *Zamzam* to Cape Town and thence to India in a different ship.

The de Graaff-Hunters survived the sinking of the *Zamzam* and, like the other British passport holders, were taken to Bordeaux and thence by train to Wesermünde, where they were forced to part. Mrs de Graaff-Hunter and her daughter went to Liebenau while James went with the other British men to *Stalag Xb* at Sandbostel for two months and thence to *Ilag VIII* at Tost-bei-Gleiwitz in Upper Silesia. But in November 1942 de Graaff-Hunter was suddenly told to go to Vienna, where he joined his wife and daughter, and became one of the two male passengers in this group to be singled out for exchange (the other was the septuagenarian Dr Wright). This was probably due to de Graaff-Hunter's age, an impression reinforced by the long, flowing white beard he cultivated in captivity. It also appears possible that a well-known Danish geographer, Dr N. E. Nørlund, may have brought pressure to bear on his behalf, perhaps through German fellow geographers in Berlin.[11] Whatever the reason, the de Graaff-Hunters travelled by train to Haifa and then went to Jerusalem and Baghdad, reaching India by air in January 1943.

The master of the *Zamzam* and his chief engineer were treated the same as all other British merchant seamen and taken to *Milag* (*Marine Internierten Lager* = Merchant Seamen's Internment Camp) at Westertimke, near Bremen, where they spent the rest of the war.[12]

Although neutrals, the Egyptian members of the crew were not released with the Americans, but were sent to Germany – 120 men in three cattle trucks on a five-day journey. Delivered, like the other two groups, to Wesermünde, the crew were then detained in *Milag*, together with many other merchant navy crews. The camp was regularly visited by representatives of the International Committee of the Red Cross and through them the crew received the invaluable food parcels and other supplies from Egypt. All members of the crew were given the option of working either inside or outside the camp, the latter as foresters; they were paid for this work, their working day lasting from 6 a.m. to 6 p.m., with two hours for lunch.

There was a flurry of German interest in the crew when Rommel's forces in North Africa appeared to be about to invade Egypt and German intelligence sought information from them on port facilities and conditions in Alexandria. The first attempt was by infiltrating spies into the camp, but when that failed the entire crew was taken to Berlin and accommodated in good hotels, with the officers separated from the others. They were asked about British deployments in Egypt and possible reactions of the indigenous population to a German invasion, but after 20 days they were sent back to *Milag*.

On 22 July 1944 the camp commandant suddenly held a roll call where he read out 84 names of men who were to be exchanged as a result of a deal between the German and Egyptian governments. The fortunate 84, plus 20 Egyptian students who had been arrested in Germany, were taken by train to the Bulgarian-Turkish border where, in early August 1944, they were exchanged for an equal number of Germans who had been arrested by the British in Egypt.[13]

The release of these 84 left approximately 35 still in German hands and there were two further, albeit conflicting, reports concerning Egyptian seamen. The first was in a statement issued by the Soviet news agency, TASS, on 23 October 1944 that stated that 104 Egyptian sailors from the *Zamzam* had been found in a camp in Bulgaria by the advancing Soviet Army, freed and repatriated. Finally, there was a report by Percy Knauth, a *New York Times* war correspondent, that he had found some of the *Zamzam* crew in a Yugoslavian village in 1945. Neither of these two can be verified, but it would appear that, one way or another, all members of the crew of the *Zamzam* eventually found their way home to Egypt.

Following their split from the wives and children at Wesermünde, the male survivors from the *Zamzam* were put into the nearby *Milag* on 5 June 1941, which was appropriate for the two British Merchant Navy officers and the Egyptian crew, but not for the rest of the party. As a result, the non-merchant navy internees immediately protested, but it took six weeks for the bureaucracy to decide what to do, and then, as was typical of the Nazi machine, immediate action was demanded. So, on 23 July all except the two ship's officers and crew were given a few hours to pack up and move, travelling next day to a civilian internment camp (*Ilag VIII*) at Tost, near Lamsdorf in Upper Silesia, where they remained until November 1943. Curiously, while at Tost one of the party, Reverend Guilding (and possibly others) was visited on two occasions by his wife, who 'came from Berlin'.

In November 1943 many of the inmates of Tost, including the *Zamzam* survivors, were moved to *Ilag VIIIH* at Giromagny in eastern France not far from the Swiss border. In late 1944 US forces neared the camp and all the internees were moved out. About half were exchanged in Sweden, but those from the *Zamzam* were not, and returned once again to *Marlag und Milag Nord* at Westertimke, where they were freed by the British on 27 April 1945.

Francis (Frank) Vicovari, the commander of the British-American Ambulance Corps aboard *Zamzam*, was badly wounded during the attack by *Atlantis*, suffering two broken arms, as well as fractures of the right ankle and left thigh. Once aboard *Atlantis* he was given excellent treatment, although he was judged not fit enough to be transferred to *Dresden*. Three *Zamzamers* remained aboard *Atlantis*, of whom one died (Ned Laughinghouse) and the second (Robert Starling) recovered and was sent back to Germany aboard one of *Atlantis'* later victims, the Norwegian ship, *Silvaplana*. Thus, Vicovari was still aboard *Atlantis* when she was found and sunk by the British cruiser, HMS *Devonshire*, on 23 November 1941 and was rescued by the German submarine, *U-126*, which on 25 November met the German supply ship, *Python*, and *Atlantis'* survivors, including Vicovari, were placed aboard. But on 1 December, while refuelling two other U-boats, *Python*, too, was found by the enemy, this time cruiser, HMS *Dorsetshire*, when some 1,000 miles south of the island of St Helena, and was immediately scuttled by her crew. Vicovari was rescued for the third time, on this occasion by *U-68* and during her voyage back to France, he was informed that following the outbreak of war between Germany and the United States he was now no longer a civilian internee but a prisoner-of-war. On reaching Lorient, France, on 24 December Vicovari, still suffering from his wounds, was taken to *Stalag VIII* at Tost, where he was held until exchanged on 25 February 1944.

Dr Robert Starling was a British chiropractor on his way to establish a clinic in Cape Town, accompanied by his wife, Florence. He was injured during the attack on *Zamzam* and detained aboard *Atlantis* with Vicovari and Laughinghouse when the majority were transferred to *Dresden*. When *Atlantis* encountered a Norwegian ship, *Silvaplana*, it was made a prize and Starling was sent aboard and they all reached Bordeaux in late November 1941. The *Silvaplana's* crew of 26 Norwegians, one Dane, four Swedes and one Pole were sent to *Marlag und Milag Nord*, but were subsequently repatriated to their respective countries in April 1942. It is presumed that Dr Starling was retained until the end of the war, possibly with those at *Ilag VIII* at Tost, while his wife went to Liebenau with the other British women.

A FRIGHTENING EXPERIENCE

The treatment meted out to the survivors of the *Zamzam* illustrates many of the points about exchanges, but also introduces a few of its own. First, a great deal depended on the passport, with Americans, British, Canadians, Egyptians, and South Africans being treated differently. Secondly, while the principle of an exchange could be agreed fairly quickly, the detailed processes – numbers, names, place and travel arrangements – always took a long time. Thirdly, the internees were usually pawns in a much larger game and, at least on the German side, were seldom told what was going on, but once a decision had been made it had to be implemented immediately, and every contemporary report tells of the way in which Nazi officials shouted at everyone, almost as their normal mode of conversation.

Whenever there appeared to be a *system* there were always examples of it being breached. Thus, while most of the women were confined to the internment camp at Liebenau, some were allowed to live in relative liberty in Berlin. On some occasions the internees were under armed guard, but at others they were simply put on a train and left to make their own way to the destination. All the British and Canadian men were, so far as is known, retained until the end of the war, except for Drs Wright and de Graaff-Hunter, almost certainly because of their ages, Wright being 75 and de Graaff-Hunter 61 years old.

While in France and Germany, none of the *Zamzam* survivors was in immediate and overt threat of death, as were the Jews in the concentration camps. Nevertheless, they found themselves in situations that were totally beyond their experience and for a young woman such as Kathleen Levitt with two young children to feed and protect it was a very frightening experience. As she wrote to her husband: '… we are prisoners a year … there seems to be very little justice in the world.'[14]

7

The Channel Islanders

The Channel Islands lie some 20 miles off the French coast, but have been dependencies of the British Crown since 1204. Once the Germans had overrun the whole of the French coast in 1940 the islands became indefensible, enabling the Germans to arrive unopposed between 30 June and 4 July 1940. The Germans then occupied the islands in some strength, although their only real value was as the sole British possession to be taken by the Third Reich. Foreign slave labourers of the Organization Todt were brought in to construct some massive coastal defences.

Hitler took a personal interest in the Channel Islands when he learnt that, following the British invasion of Iraq in 1941, some 500 German nationals resident there had been interned. He ordered that, in reprisal, 2,000 Channel Islanders were to be interned (i.e., four for each German) and that they would be housed in camps to be constructed in the Pripet Marshes, an area lying between modern Belarus and Ukraine, which was known to be unhealthy. Somewhat surprisingly, the German government, usually only too anxious to comply with Hitler's orders, managed to 'lose' these documents, apparently deliberately, although administrative incompetence may have also been to blame.

Whatever the reason, the order was not complied with and it was not until August 1942 that Hitler discovered that the deportation had not taken place. He immediately issued an order that 2,200 men, women and children were to be deported at once, albeit their destination was changed to southern Germany. The deportees comprised 800 from Guernsey, deported on 26–27 September and 1,186 from Jersey taken on 16, 18 and 29 September; this was still 214 short of Hitler's total, but a substantial number, nevertheless. The great majority of these were people who had been born on the British mainland, or who had served as officers in the British armed forces during World War One. A further group of 201 was deported in February 1943, but this was in retaliation for a raid by British commandos on Sark on 3–4 October 1942.

The main camps housing Channel Islanders were all in southern Germany. *Ilag VB* at Biberach-an-der-Riss in Württemberg was a hutted camp, which accommodated some 1,000 internees in total, including men, women and children. *Ilag VC* at Wurzach, also in Württemberg, was an eighteenth-century castle and housed 618, all from Jersey. The third major camp was *Ilag VII* at Laufen in

Bavaria, which housed 417 Channel Islanders, as well as 48 other British people and 120 Americans. As with all other prisoners-of-war and civilian internees their rations were very short and they depended for survival on the regular supply of Red Cross food parcels.

The deported Channel Islanders were in an unusual situation. The normal concept of repatriation was that individuals had been captured when abroad from their home country and were seeking to return there. In the case of the Channel Islanders, however, their homes had actually been overrun and were being occupied by the Germans, so the only two options open to the British government were that the Germans would eventually relent and allow them to return home, or that they could be brought to England. Since there appeared to be little prospect of the former, the British government made frequent requests that at least some Channel Islanders should be included in the Gothenburg exchange on 18 May 1944. They were firmly convinced that this would happen and were dismayed when they discovered that it had not. They also came under strong pressure in both the press and Parliament where there were active 'lobbies' working on the islanders' behalf. The government therefore brought even stronger pressure to bear, as always through the Swiss government, and this was more successful when a group of 125 sick and elderly Channel Islanders were included in the exchange at Gothenburg on 10 September 1944, reaching England aboard SS *Drottningholm* on 16 September 1944. The choice of who was to be in this party lay with the Germans and it included at least two septuagenarians, but in a number of cases, and for no discernible reason except, perhaps, administrative incompetence, some husbands were repatriated without wives and in other cases wives without husbands.

The British brought yet further pressure to bear on the Germans and eventually succeeded because they were able to make it a condition of agreeing to the safe passage of the *Drottningholm* on the German–Turkish exchange of 8 March 1945 that it had to include significant numbers of Channel Islanders. As a result, 212 Channel Islanders travelled northwards across Germany by train, which took some seven days, eventually reaching Denmark where they sailed across the Kattegat from Vyborg to Korsov, whence they were taken by Swedish railroad to Gothenburg. There they boarded the *Drottningholm*, which did not sail for seven days, but they were allowed ashore each day and were very well treated by the local Swedish Red Cross and the general population. Carrying the Turks being exchanged, and the British civilian repatriates, of whom 212 were the Channel Islanders, *Drottningholm* arrived in Liverpool on 23 March 1945.

There was a very limited mail service and numbers of Red Cross cards were sent to and from England. The postal service in the Channel Islands was closely supervised by the German authorities and all external mail was taken from the post offices to the local German headquarters which sent it to Paris. The mail then went to Germany and from there to the International Committee of the Red Cross at Geneva. From there it went, by way of France and Spain, to Portugal and then by ship. These messages could take between two and five months to reach their destination, meaning that a family query could take up to nine months to receive a reply. Mail to and from addresses outside the United Kingdom was handled by the German Red Cross. At least one who took part has commented that it was far easier and quicker to send letters to and from the United Kingdom from the internment camps than from the islands themselves.

When the Allies invaded France in June 1944 it was a deliberate act of British government policy not to invade the Channel Islands, leaving them increasingly cut off, and resulting in extreme shortages of food, medicine and other supplies – which affected the garrison and the islanders in equal measure. The British government and the British Red Cross pressed hard for relief supplies to be allowed through and eventually a small ship operated by the ICRC, SS *Vega*, was allowed to make six voyages between December 1944 and 8 May 1945, when the first British forces arrived.

PERSONAL EXPERIENCES – PAUL ATYEO[1]

Paul Atyeo, aged 14 in 1940, was the son of a Church of England vicar, who was not a Channel Islander but had been transferred to a parish on the island of Jersey in 1935 in the normal course of his ecclesiastical career. The family comprised the father, mother, Paul and an older sister, who was a nurse in a local hospital. In May 1940 the Reverend Atyeo was warned of the imminent German invasion and offered the opportunity to return to England, but considered it his duty to stay with his flock. Following the German arrival, Paul's father continued with his parochial duties until September 1942 when he was suddenly informed that, as he had not been born in the Channel Islands, he, his wife and Paul would be in the second group to be deported, although his daughter would be permitted to remain at her hospital post. Like all the others, the three Atyeos were given no idea of where they were going, or why. Their journey started on 18 September, when they sailed by ship to St Malo, where they were put on a train. They then travelled in normal French second-class carriages and were not too uncomfortable, which was just as well as it took two-and-a-half days to reach Biberach-an-der-Riß, a small town located some 25 miles north of Friedrichshafen on Lake Constance. There, they were put into a vacant German Army barracks, now designated *Intiernungslager VB (Ilag VB)*.[2]

After only six weeks in Biberach, Paul was among 618 Channel Islanders, all in family groups, who were moved some 12 miles south to Bad Wurzach, a small *Kurstadt* (spa town) in the Oberschwaben region of Baden-Württemberg, leaving the singles and childless couples behind. The new camp was a *Schloss* (castle), which had been built originally as a ducal residence, but more recently had been a Roman Catholic seminary. In its new role it was surrounded by barbed wire with armed guards on patrol, and was designated *Ilag VC*. The regime was irksome but not excessively severe, with the internees confined for most of the time, but allowed up to three walks per week, although sometimes Paul was also able to leave the camp on fatigue duties, such as unloading Red Cross parcels at the railroad station. All such expeditions were always accompanied by an armed guard.

There were numerous children in the group, so a school was clearly necessary and qualified teachers were quickly pressed into service, while other adults dug back deep into their past in order to cover other areas, the Reverend Atyeo, for example, teaching Classics, based on 40-year-old memories. This school was properly organized and all the smaller children attended, but older children less so. Progress could be remarkable; Paul Atyeo, for example, then aged 15, was reading Sophocles in the original Greek. The school was in contact with the UK for the supply of books and Paul even wrote to the redoubtable Miss Herdman at the Oxford Library asking for a specific book and although she replied that it was not immediately available, it did arrive later.

The internees were allowed to listen to German radio, with the bulletins being taken down by German-speaking Channel Islanders, translated into English and then passed around. But, there were no films that Paul can recall. One particular memory of Paul's is that in late 1944 (or, possibly, early 1945) a party of some 40–50 Dutch Jews arrived, who, to the best of his knowledge, then stayed with another 500-odd until the end of the war.[3]

Another memory concerns the mail. While they had been in Jersey it was possible to send Red Cross letter cards from and to the UK, but only 20 words were allowed and it took a very long time. Somewhat bizarrely, it was much easier and quicker to send and receive mail to and from the UK when they were in Wurzach.

The first mention that Paul can recall of the possibility of repatriation came during late November or early December 1942 when a visiting Swedish princess mentioned the subject. But, rumours apart, nothing happened until September 1944 when a group of sick and elderly Islanders were suddenly told that they were to be repatriated. Great concern was caused by the fact that other family members were not allowed to accompany them, even if it was the head-of-family who had been selected. Others staying behind rallied round and everyone looked after everyone else, so it was not too severe a problem.

The second group went in February 1945 and this time sick people were accompanied by the rest of the family. Unfortunately for the Atyeo family, Paul's father was selected but died five days before he was due to leave. Clearly Paul and his newly widowed mother were very upset, but in a rare example of magnanimity, the commandant allowed them both to go, anyway.

To the best of Paul's recollection, he and his mother were in a group of about 50–60 Channel Islanders who were put on a local train that took them a short distance to a minor station, where they got off and spent the night sleeping on the waiting room floor. The next morning a Red Cross train arrived from the south, with many other repatriates from other camps already aboard. They all then spent five days and nights on the train, as it meandered slowly through war-torn Germany, taking a roundabout route that took it through Magdeburg before eventually crossing into Denmark and thence to Elsinor, where they left the train. They then carried on until they reached Sweden, where Paul can remember the arrival of a large party of Turks a little later. They boarded SS *Drottningholm* on Thursday 15 March 1945, which Paul remembers well as it was his seventeenth birthday. *Drottningholm* sailed through Kattegat to a point off the southern tip of Norway where the ship anchored for two days and nights (Friday night to Sunday morning), with a small German warship guarding them. They then sailed on the Sunday morning, without the escort, and passed through some severe storms until arriving at the Faroe Islands where they spent 24 hours (Tuesday–Wednesday) at anchor off Thorshavn but were not allowed ashore. They then sailed around the north of Scotland and then down the west coast arriving in Liverpool on Friday, where they were put on a train to London where the party dispersed.

8

The British–Italian Exchanges

In their campaigns in Africa in 1940–1942 the British Imperial forces quickly captured vast numbers of Italian prisoners, and, in many cases, their advance was so rapid and the penetration so deep that they also captured large numbers of 'protected personnel', such as doctors, nurses, chaplains and stretcher-bearers. During Operation Compass, the first attack across Cyrenaica (December 1940–February 1941), British forces captured some 130,000 Italian soldiers, while in the East African campaign (January–April 1941) they captured another 100,000. These were vast numbers that had to be dispersed quickly, not only to spread the administrative burden, but also because such a huge number of potentially hostile men in the rear areas posed a major danger, at a time when it looked possible that Rommel might break through to the Suez Canal.

The first suggestion came in September 1941 and was a British proposal for 500 sick and wounded Italians to be exchanged for a lesser number of British servicemen. This was agreed by the Italians on 12 January 1942 and took place at the Turkish port of Smyrna on 8 April. This process seems rather slow, particularly as neither side raised any strong reservations, but was, in fact, surprisingly fast when compared with setting up other exchanges. British hospital ships brought rather more than had been planned – 344 sick and wounded, plus 575 protected personnel – all of whom came from camps located in the Middle East. The ships sailed from Alexandria and in return they received 59 sick and wounded, and 69 protected men of the British, Australian, New Zealand and South African forces.

The first exchange was very successful, but it was not until August 1942 that the British suggested a second and much larger exchange, which was agreed without any major difficulty and took place between 19 April and 3 June 1943. There were two elements, the first taking place, as before, at Smyrna, using British hospital ships from Alexandria to bring Italian personnel from Middle East camps and hospitals. Again, as before, Italian ships sailed from Italy to Smyrna. This time, however, there was a second element, with Italians being taken from the UK to Lisbon by ship, whence they were taken home by train, through Portugal, Spain and southern France. No British personnel were returned by this route.

The totals involved in this exchange were 9,114 Italians and 1,916 British and Imperial personnel, making it by far the largest exchange of World War Two.

The imbalance in numbers reflected the disproportionate numbers of Italians held by the British, but the British felt that the Italians had reneged to a certain extent by failing to return all who had been certified by the Mixed Medical Commissions.

The third British–Italian exchange took place on 20 March 1943 and is described separately below.

Building on their successes, the British and Italians agreed to yet another exchange, which was to have taken place at Lisbon, Portugal, on 13 September 1943, the agreed numbers being 500 Italians and 170 British. Unfortunately, outside events intervened. The Allies had invaded Sicily on 9 July and completed their conquest on 17 August. During this operation, Mussolini was overthrown on 24 July, leading to the Italian surrender to the Allies, which was signed on 3 September and announced on 8 September. At this point the Italian prisoners-of-war due to be exchanged were already at sea from the UK, while the British had been assembled in Italy but had not yet started their rail journey to Lisbon. In a very quick revision of the plan, the ship carrying the Italians was diverted to Algiers, where they were held until they were quietly shipped to southern (i.e., Allied-held) Italy and released. The British prisoners-of-war, however, despite having been certified by the Anglo-Italian Mixed Medical Commissions and despite previous German agreement having been given to the trains crossing southern France, were taken over by the Germans and shipped north to camps in Germany and Austria. The British protested vigorously but the Germans gave as their reason that they did not recognize the findings of the Italian MMCs. However, after many months in German custody, the men were quietly included in the second Anglo-German exchange at Barcelona in May 1944.[1]

A VERY CURIOUS EXCHANGE

When Italy declared war on the British Empire on 11 June 1940 the country's East African Empire, consisting of Eritrea, Ethiopia and Italian Somaliland, immediately found itself cut off from the homeland and from the only other Italian African possession, Libya. The grandiosely named Italian Red Sea Fleet, based at the Eritrean port of Massawa (modern Mitswa), was also ill-suited for its task, comprising seven destroyers, eight submarines, a colonial sloop (the *Eritrea*), and a number of smaller vessels. This fleet was not only much smaller than the British and French naval forces in the area, but was also desperately short of ammunition, torpedoes, fuel and spare parts, for none of which was there any prospect of resupply.

Italian naval operations achieved some minor initial successes but losses quickly mounted and, with the British Army advancing overland and fuel supplies virtually exhausted, it was decided to abandon the naval campaign altogether. Accordingly, four submarines made a remarkable voyage, sailing around Africa to the newly created Italian submarine base at Brest in France, while the *Eritrea* did equally well, sailing eastwards across the British-dominated Indian Ocean to reach Japan. These were undoubted successes but the remaining operations were much less so. *Supermarina*, the Italian naval high command in Rome, ordered that the surviving destroyers form two three-ship squadrons for an attack on the British base at Port Sudan, the major Sudanese harbour on the Red Sea coast (modern Bur Sudan), which was some 300 miles distant from Massawa. The attack was to be carried out on the night of 31 March/1 April 1941, the approach being made at high speed and in darkness, but the prospect of survival for both ships and crew was considered minimal. In effect, it was a suicide mission.

The operation got off to a poor start when one destroyer ran aground just outside Massawa harbour. Then, about two hours later, the British, who were already aware of the operation, sent in RAF bombers to attack the advancing flotilla, but without causing serious damage. However, the engines of one of the older ships, *Battisti*, gave up under the strain and her captain was ordered to proceed across the Red Sea to the coast of Saudi Arabia and then, once inside territorial waters, to scuttle his ship, all of which he duly did. By dawn the remaining four ships were some 30 miles short of Port Sudan and came under heavy British air and sea attack; two of the Italian ships managed to survive for a short period, but the other two, *Pantera* and *Tigre*, were ordered, like *Battisti*, to proceed to the coast of Arabia and scuttle themselves.

At that time Saudi Arabia was a backward desert kingdom, largely cut off from the outside world and neutral in the war, so the arrival of some 600 Italian sailors was a considerable embarrassment. They were not, of course, prisoners-of-war but, like the German survivors from the *Graf Spee* who had arrived in neutral Argentina in December 1939, they had to be interned. Unfortunately for the Saudis, this meant that they had to be accommodated, fed, guarded and provided with medical treatment, all of which imposed a serious and unwanted administrative load. As a result, the Saudi government made several approaches to the British government seeking some way to rid themselves of these unwanted guests, while, on the British side, there was a desire to prevent so many able-bodied sailors from returning to the still-active Italian fleet, although there was also concern at having such a large group of potentially hostile men on the British Imperial lines-of-communication between Egypt and India.

The vital link was provided by the Turkish government which, in June 1942, suggested that the Italian internees be exchanged for an equivalent number of British naval prisoners-of-war then being held in Italy.[2] This was welcomed by the Saudi and Italian governments, and in October Turkey put the proposal to the British, who were quick to agree and even suggested that they would include some other prisoners-of-war, also in their custody.

By the standards of the day, events then moved fairly quickly. The British government accepted the proposal on 11 October 1942, the Italian government confirmed its acceptance on 22 January 1943 and the exchange duly took place at the Turkish port of Mersin on 20 March 1943. The actual exchange was unusual in that all the ships involved were at anchor and the repatriates were taken by boat from one ship to another; at no time did anyone go ashore.

The figures involved in the exchange are difficult to reconcile. The official war complements of *Pantera* and *Tigre* were each 206 and of *Battisti* 155, making a total of 567, but the number actually exchanged was 788. This leaves a balance of 221, which seems somewhat greater than the 'few Italian civilians and some German sailors' mentioned in the British papers, although it is also possible that the three Italian warships had carried some supernumeraries during their final sortie. The British even added 25 German sailors, for good measure.

This exchange was unusual in several major respects. First, only governments participated, the Red Cross not being involved at all. Secondly, it involved fit-and-well prisoners-of-war, and internees not sick or wounded. Thirdly it was outside the terms of the Geneva Convention, which had an effect on a minor sequel when a sailor officially questioned whether, or not, he could serve in a combatant role (see Chapter 11).

9

The French

The drafters of the 1929 Geneva Convention could not possibly have foreseen the status in which France would find itself during World War Two and, as a result, there were major problems concerning prisoners-of-war. France was allied to the UK from August 1939 until it signed armistices with the Germans (22 June 1940) and the Italians (24 June 1940). Among the many terms in the Armistice Agreement with the Germans (which was the only one of the two that mattered), the French government retained full autonomy over southern France, which formed about 40 per cent of the whole, while the northern part of the country, including the entire length of both the Channel and Atlantic coasts, was placed under German occupation – as, indeed, were all airfields, even those in 'Unoccupied France'. A small part of eastern France was occupied by Italy and as a final indignity the costs of both occupation forces was borne by the French government. This arrangement lasted until 11 November 1942, when the Germans occupied the remaining 40 per cent of southern France.

Throughout all this, Marshal Pétain's Vichy government remained the legal civil authority across the whole of the metropolitan territory, including the 'occupied' zones. The implementation of the Armistice and supervision of its continuance lay in the hands of a joint German–French Commission, which was responsible for regulating and supervising the Armistice '… in accordance with the direction of the German High Command'.[1] This was a very powerful body and it became a constant refrain when dealing with French authorities in the colonial empire that any exchanges should be done without the knowledge of the Armistice Commission.

The French government, established at Vichy, was responsible for the civilian administration of the whole of France, but with complete control only of the Unoccupied Territory. The Vichy government also retained responsibility for all French overseas territories and was allowed a small army and navy to achieve this. In international legal terms, the Vichy government was neutral in the war, but in view of the German occupation, it generally had little choice but to comply with German wishes. However, numerous foreign countries regarded the Vichy government as the *de jure* government and maintained diplomatic and consular relations with it, including the United States and Canada, although the British withdrew recognition in 1940.

Meanwhile, Brigadier-General de Gaulle had escaped to England, from where he broadcast on 18 June 1940 calling for the establishment of a Free French government and armed forces. From then until mid 1944 France's considerable overseas territories were faced with the dilemma of whether or not to remain loyal to the de facto French government in Vichy, or to declare for the Free French government in London. Some territories declared for de Gaulle from the very start, a few others followed, more or less peaceably later, but some only did so as a result of direct military force.

The precise status caused many complications. The British recognized de Gaulle and not only did not recognize Vichy but struck militarily at many of its overseas territories – Iraq, Lebanon, Madagascar and Syria successfully, but with complete failure against Dakar. The United States recognized the Vichy government and had an ambassador there (Admiral Leahy), as did Australia. In the Far East the Japanese moved into French Indochina in 1941, leaving the French colonial administration, which was loyal to Vichy, in nominal control, but eventually it took over the country in March 1945.

This brief and by no means comprehensive summary illustrates the complexity of the situation. But somewhere among all this were a variety of prisoners, who, because the status of France itself was unclear, were in an unenviable position and the question of exchange was even more complicated.

The British took over all French warships in British ports on 28 June 1940. Some crews surrendered willingly, some under protest and some resisted, such as that of the giant submarine *Surcouf*, where two British officers and one French seaman were killed. The French sailors who did not choose to transfer to de Gaulle were imprisoned, but the British initially refused to treat them as prisoners-of-war, which meant that they were outside the purview of the Geneva Convention, were not visited by a Protecting Power and did not receive Red Cross parcels. After some protests, however, the British changed their minds.[2] The British also captured some Vichy French in combat, including the crews of the submarines *Ajax*, sunk during the unsuccessful attack on Dakar on 24 September 1940, and *Poncelet*, scuttled after attacking a British sloop off Libreville (Gabon) on 7 November 1940.

By later 1942, there were small groups of Vichy French military and civilians held in the UK and various Dominions, but the most substantial number came with the surrender in Madagascar in November 1942, when some 8,000, of which 6,000 were Malagasies and 1,500 Senegalese, fell into British hands.

The Vichy French had problems, too. One was that they found themselves playing unwilling hosts to a number of merchant seamen in North Africa who were nationals of countries under German occupation. These included 12 Belgians, one Dane, 22 Greeks, and approximately 140 Norwegians.[3] These men refused to go home, but there was no way in which their governments-in-exile could look after them, so they simply languished in a very hot and dry camp known as the *Centre de Sejour Surveille de Sidi El Ayachi*. They were neither prisoners-of-war nor civilian internees and the French stated that they were simply 'under surveillance' although they did allow the camp to be inspected from time to time by the US Vice-Consul at Casablanca, who reported that conditions were 'not too bad' and that the inmates were allowed out for short walks.[4] In late 1942, the Vichy French held some 800 British: 241 in metropolitan France; 528 in North Africa; and 79 in West Africa.

THE ALLENDE AFFAIR

The exchange of the crew of the British merchant ship, SS *Allende*, on the Gambia/Senegal frontier in July 1942, illustrates some of the complexities of exchanges with the Vichy French.[5] *Allende* was a typical British interwar tramp steamer, completed in 1929, with a displacement of 5,081 tons and a crew of 38. On the outbreak of war she continued her task of carrying general cargo, but now usually of a military nature, and the crew was provided with two antiquated light machine guns and several rifles, although quite what these were supposed to achieve was never made clear.

In March 1942 she was sailing along the west coast of Africa towards Freetown in the British colony of Sierra Leone, where her captain intended to refuel before joining a homeward-bound convoy to England. Sailing alone and emitting a dense cloud of smoke, *Allende* was an ideal target for submarine attack and, sure enough, just after nightfall on 17 March 1942, she was hit without warning by a torpedo from a German U-boat, *U-68*. Five men were killed instantly but the remaining 33 survived and abandoned ship, boarding a jollyboat (12 men) and a lifeboat (21 men). Despite the damage, *Allende* did not sink so, 16 minutes after the first, the U-boat launched a second torpedo from point-blank range, which quickly dispatched its victim. The U-boat then surfaced to establish the ship's identity and captain's name, and then, having given the survivors the compass bearing for the nearest land, it disappeared.

The two boats drifted apart, but after two very unpleasant days at sea both crews reached the shore without further loss, although, unfortunately for them, the current had carried them along the coast. As a result, their landfall was not, as they had expected, in Liberia, but in the Ivory Coast, a French colony firmly under the control of Marshal Pétain's collaborationist government in Vichy.

After excellent hospitality in a village, the lifeboat survivors were collected by a French official and taken to the local port of Tabou, where, four days later, they were joined by the remainder of the crew, who had taken to the jollyboat. Armed guards made it clear that the 33 men were not guests but captives, which was reinforced when they were taken aboard a French Navy sloop and roughly handled by the sailors, who, no doubt, remembered the British destruction of the French fleet in Mers-el-Kebir in June 1940 and the naval attack on Dakar three months later.

Once back on shore the survivors commenced a long journey by road, rail and river along the coast to Daloa and then inland to Bouake and onwards until they eventually reached Timbuktu, over 1,000 miles from the coast. By now the crew were wasting away, sick and with very low morale as there seemed no end, nor, indeed, any point, to their wanderings. Some among them thought that the Vichy French simply did not know what to do with a captured merchant navy crew, who were neither military prisoners-of-war nor civilian internees, and they were just being passed from one administrative body to another. They remained in Timbuktu for over two months, where they were treated with great callousness – the food was inadequate and of dreadful quality and requests for visits by a medical officer were met only rarely, and he was rude and unhelpful when he did appear. Somewhat sinisterly, when two men were eventually removed for treatment in hospital both were reported to have died within hours. They were buried in the local cemetery, but the crew were, at least, allowed to conduct the funeral.[6]

On the sixty-third day the French suddenly underwent a complete change of heart and the crew were assembled to be told that there had been a major misunderstanding and that they would be released as soon as possible. They were given food and clothing that had hitherto been unavailable and then, having paid their final respects to two graves of their colleagues, they got into trucks and set off for home. They travelled in the trucks for eight days, eventually crossing the Niger river and being delivered to the railroad station at Bamako. There they were put into the 'European section' of the next available train for a two-day journey to Tambacounda in Senegal, except for one man who was admitted to the local hospital for an operation. Once in Senegal the men were transferred to trucks once again, but this time only for a two-hour journey to Brifu in The Gambia where, on 16 July, they were handed over to the British authorities.[7] They were moved to the capital, Freetown, where one more man died, but the crew then divided and went their various ways. Some made it back to England, but records do not show what happened to the remainder.

The reason for the French change of heart dated back to late March when the Governor-General of French West Africa proposed an exchange of various small groups of seamen interned in the French and British colonies. He wrote to the British on 3 April 1942[8] suggesting such an exchange but with the proviso that this should be kept from the Armistice Commission. This was sent to the British West African Governors' Conference, which body forwarded it to the Colonial Office in London, who approved on 11 April. Once again, the question of head-for-head exchanges arose, as there were 33 white French in British hands, as opposed to 23 British and 7 non-whites in French hands, but after some discussion it was decided to proceed, anyway.

What seemed to be a simple operation eventually involved the State Department in Washington; the Foreign Office, Department of War Transport, Colonial Office and the US Ambassador in London; the French government in Vichy; and various British and French colonial governors, as well as several US consuls in Africa. Nevertheless, the exchange was eventually achieved, with *Allende* crewmen being exchanged for 13 French held by the British, with the man who had been detained in a French hospital following on 7 August.[9]

FRANCO-GERMAN EXCHANGES

The Free French were not party to the Allies–Germany exchange at Barcelona on 17 May 1944, but did agree to allow some wounded German PoWs they held to be included. These men simply counted against the Allied total and no equivalent gesture was asked for from the Germans. Later in the year, and following severe fighting in the Savoy and upper Savoy regions, the Free French became very keen to undertake an exchange of seriously sick and wounded. There was no Protecting Power representing French interests in Germany (nor vice versa) so the French approached the ICRC to act as intermediary. This was done and the Germans responded very positively – possibly due to the earlier French gesture – and suggested that the exchange should take place at Konstancz, and this was duly achieved on 1 November 1944, when 841 French were exchanged for 863 Germans.

Following this success negotiations started for a further exchange, which this time would include not only seriously sick and wounded, but also French senior officers, who had been prevented by the Germans from appearing before an MMC for the previous exchange. The French were also keen to recover colonial troops who were finding the European winters increasingly trying, as well as some medical personnel, and civilian workers. This was still under negotiation in May 1945 when the German collapse rendered it unnecessary.

FLIGHT-LIEUTENANT SIMPSON

In a totally different category was the repatriation of Flight-Lieutenant W. Simpson of the British Royal Air Force, who was very badly wounded when shot down in a Fairey Battle light bomber on 10 May 1940, the very first day of the German attack. The French, at that time allied to and fighting alongside the

British, took him to a military hospital in Roanne, some 55 miles north of Lyon, where he was nursed and operated on for over a year, when, the British having long since been forced to leave by the Germans, he was transferred to another French Army hospital in Marseilles in June 1941. The Germans knew about him, but his injuries were so severe that they chose to overlook him, although they had to become officially aware of him when he persuaded the US Consul in Marseilles to request that he be examined by an MMC. A special board was duly convened, consisting of three doctors, a Swede representing the Germans, an American representing the British, and a Frenchman, which unanimously recommended him for repatriation. After a further move to a hospital in Lyons, in October 1941, he was sent via Grenoble, Barcelona and Madrid to Lisbon, from where he flew aboard a normal commercial flight to England.[10]

It would appear that Simpson was repatriated rather than exchanged, since there is no mention of a corresponding German being released. Everyone involved, particularly the Germans and the Vichy French, seems to have taken a thoroughly pragmatic view and the outcome reflects credit on all those involved.

10

Red Cross Parcels for Camps on Mainland Europe

There is a vast amount of literature and a large number of films and TV programmes on Allied PoW camps during World War Two. Almost all of these give a passing mention to the 'Red Cross parcels' that turned up – at least in camps in Germany and Italy – virtually every week, as if by magic. Few of those sources, however, devote more than passing attention to how those parcels got there. But, in the years 1939–1945, the British Red Cross alone sent just under 20 million parcels at an average weight of 11 lb each, to camps on mainland Europe at a cost (in 2008 figures) of some £300 million. This was, by any standard, a sophisticated and remarkably efficient operation, which required close cooperation with the Allies, neutral and Axis powers.

From its inception, the Red Cross saw its primary wartime mission as aid to the wounded and the sick, so that the provision of parcels for prisoners-of-war and civilian internees was, in many ways, a secondary task. However, the activity quickly proved to be highly necessary for those in the camps, not only in terms of maintaining a balanced diet but also as a highly significant morale factor, in being a constant reminder to those in the camps that they were not forgotten by relatives and friends at home. In addition to this, however, the scheme attained a great hold on the public consciousness, so much so that for many people the parcels were seen as the Red Cross's primary task, with their timely and regular delivery becoming what almost amounted to a sacred duty. As a result, official statements were regularly made in the various parliaments and the Red Cross was constantly being subjected to unwarranted criticism for 'failing in its mission'.

The original plan, devised within weeks of the outbreak of World War Two, was to send five types of parcel.[1] The first would be an initial parcel to a newly captured prisoner-of-war, which would be addressed to him by name and at a specific camp. This would then be followed by regular food parcels, sent to every prisoner three times every fortnight and each weighing approximately 11 lb, as well as separate parcels containing medical comforts and fresh bread. There would also be scope for personal parcels, later known as the 'next-of-kin parcel'.

The Red Cross quickly encountered a number of problems. First, the method of addressing parcels to named individuals at a specific location had, despite its good intentions, some serious shortcomings. The main difficulty was that the national Red Cross had to await notification of a capture from its national authorities (in the case of the British Red Cross, for example, from the War Office London), which had been told by the ICRC in Geneva, who had been notified by the enemy. Since the parcel was treated with respect by both the German and PoW authorities and could only be handed over to the named recipient, this was inevitably a slow process, which meant that the first parcel could take a very long time to catch up with its addressee. The next problem was that prisoners were often moved, again adding to the delivery time as the parcel chased them from one camp to another. When news of these problems reached London and Geneva individual addressing was soon discontinued; thereafter Red Cross food parcels were sent to camps on the basis of one per man using the latest strength return known to the Red Cross. Then, because the supply chain was long, slow and unpredictable it also quickly became apparent that sending perishable items such as bread was impracticable, so it was discontinued in May 1940 and flour and biscuits added to the contents of the normal parcel.

The next major factor was that the number of PoWs increased rapidly, so that the sheer scale of the operation became enormous (see Table 5, opposite). Finally, governments quickly started to lay down stipulations about what could or could not be included.

British and Dominion/Commonwealth PoWs were generally considered as a group, although the parcels were packed within a number of countries. Thus, parcels were sent to camps from the Canadian, New Zealand and South African Red Cross, while parcels intended for Indian PoWs were specially designed to suit their needs (see Table 6, Type 7). The latter amounted to 20,000 per week.

Not surprisingly, it required huge numbers of items to fill some 20 million parcels. Sample figures covering the whole of the war are:

Meats (hot, cold, bacon, sausages)	50.7 million tins
Fish	16.1 million tins
Dairy products (butter, margarine, cheese)	36.6 million tins
Chocolate, sweets, chewing gum	23.3 million packets

Packing this vast quantity of parcels became a sophisticated operation. Initially, manufacturers delivered direct to the few packing centres, but as the volume of supplies and the number of packing centres increased, the Red Cross set up its own supply depots where goods could be sorted and stock maintained to meet unexpected crises, such as increases in demand, damage due to enemy action, or civil catastrophe.

The aim was to provide one parcel per man per week, later three per fortnight, which, in combination with the always inadequate camp rations, was aimed at supplying an optimum combination of calories, nutriments and vitamins. The Red Cross also sought to achieve a variety by having various types of parcel – see

Table 5: Prisoner-of-War Parcels Dispatched by the British Red Cross: 1939–1945

	Nov 1939– Dec 1940	1941	1942	1943	1944	Jan–May 1945	TOTALS
Parcels sent	537,328	2,962,729	5,552,151	4,889,878	4,167,934	1,553,171	**19,663,191**
Approx cost to Red Cross*	10s:0d	10s:0d	9s:5¼d	10s:3¼d	10s:8¼d	11s:0d	
Total cost (£)	268,664	1,481,369	2,619,921	2,511,156	2,227,240	854,244	**9,962,594**
2008 equiv (£) approx	12 million	53 million	78 million	74 million	64 million	25 million	**306 million**

*Contents plus packing materials plus transport from depot in UK to camp in Germany.

Note: £1 = 20 shillings; 1 shilling = 12 pence.

Table 6 below – although there was only one type of parcel for Indian prisoners-of-war.

Table 6: British Red Cross Parcels being Packed in 1944–1945

Commodity		Weight	Parcel Type						
Nature	*Type*	*oz*	*1*	*2*	*3*	*4*	*5*	*6*	*7**
Biscuits	Service	8	X	X	X	X	X		X
	Healthy Life	16						X	
Cheese		3.25	X	X	X	X	X	X	X
Chocolate		4	X	X	X	X	X	X	X
Fish	Pilchards	8			X	X	X		
	Pilchards	16							X
	Salmon	8	X	X				X	X
Fruit/ puddings	Creamed rice	12				X			
	Fruit, dried	8	X	X			X		
	Fruit, tinned	8							X
	Puddings, assorted	12			X				
		6							X
Jam		12	X		X	X	X		
Syrup		8		X				X	
Butter		8	X		X		X		
Margarine		8		X		X		X	X
Meat, hot		16	X	X	X	X	X	X	
Meat, cold	Beef loaf	12		X	X			X	
	Chopped ham, etc.	12	X			X	X		
Sausages		8			X				
Bacon		8	X	X			X	X	
Milk	Condensed	14	X	X	X	X	X	X	
	Condensed (Vit. C)	14							X
Sugar		4	X	X	X	X	X	X	X
Tea		2	X	X	X	X	X	X	X
Vegetables		10	X	X		X	X		
Cocoa		4	X	X	X	X	X		

Commodity		Weight	Parcel Type						
Nature	Type	oz	1	2	3	4	5	6	7*
Mustard or pepper		1		X					
Salt		1.5	X					X	
		2							X
Eggs, dried		1.5		X	X	X	X	X	X
Oatmeal		8						X	
Oats rolled		5	X	X		X	X		
Oatmeal		1.75				X			
Pancake batter		6.5			X				
Sweets		2						X	
Atta		16							X
Curry powder		2							X
Dhal		16							X
Rice		16							X
Soap		2							X
WEIGHT OF CONTENTS (lb)			8.1	7.9	7.9	8.2	8.3	7.6	8.8

* Type 7 parcel was for Indian troops.
Source: Red Cross and St John War History, p. 143.

DOMINIONS

Canada was the first dominion to start sending parcels, starting in January 1941, with its output peaking at 80,000 per week in mid 1943. Australia produced some of its own parcels, but a large quantity were produced on its behalf in Canada. New Zealand and South Africa also produced Red Cross parcels.

UNITED STATES RED CROSS PARCELS

The United States Red Cross also sent parcels – 27 million of them. Like their British counterparts, these parcels were a uniform size – 10 inches x 10 inches x 4½ inches – and weighed 11 lb. These were packed in special parcel depots in Chicago, New York City, Philadelphia, and St Louis by a staff of some 13,500 volunteers. In addition to food parcels – see Table 7 – other parcels contained items such as medical supplies, clothing, toilet articles, and seeds and gardening materials.

Table 7: Contents of Typical US Red Cross Parcels in 1944

Commodity		Weight	Parcel Type	
Nature	Type	oz	A-1	10-1
Milk	Whole, powdered	16	X	X
Spreads	Cheese, processed, American	8	X	X
	Margarine (with added Vitamin A)			X
	'Army' (butter and cheese)	7.5	X	
	Peanut butter	8	X	
	Jam, various	6	X	X
	Liver paste	6		X
Soup	Chicken noodle, dehydrated	2.5	X	
Meat	Corned beef	12	X	X
	Pork luncheon meat	12	X	X
Fish	Salmon	8	X	
	Salmon or tuna	8		X
Eggs	Whole, spray dried	5	X	
Fruit	Prunes or raisins	15	X	X
Biscuits	US Army Type K3	7	X	
	US Army Types 1 or 2	7		X
Chocolate	Bar, Ration D	8	X	X
Sugar	Lump	8	X	X
Coffee	Soluble	2	X	X
Condiments	Salt and pepper	1	X	X
Tablets	Multivitamin	16 tabs	X	X
Cigarettes	Packets, 4		X	X

Source: Prisoner of War Bulletin, US Red Cross, Volume 3, Number 4, Page 4.

OTHER PARCELS

The popular term 'Red Cross parcel' is almost always used generically, although what the users normally mean by that is the standard food parcel, but there were other types as well. The special Christmas parcels, which were in addition to the normal supply, tried to reflect the special occasion with a combination of slightly more luxurious food items. For example, the British Red Cross Christmas parcel for 1942 still weighed 11 lb but contained the following. The main items were one tin each of: chocolate biscuits; plum pudding; Christmas cake; cheese; jam; butter; steak and spaghetti; condensed milk; and sweets. Other contents included soap (one tablet); tea (one packet); sugar (three sticks); and chocolate (one block).

There were also parcels of clothing and other necessities. The 'First Parcel', also weighing about 10 lb, was sent as soon as notification of capture was received by the Red Cross. It contained: vest (T-shirt); short-sleeved pullover; blanket; muffler (scarf); socks (two pairs); pants (trunks); treasure bag; towel; soap; razor and blades; shaving stick; housewife (clothing repair kit containing needles, thread, buttons, etc.); handkerchiefs (two); patch for underwear; chewing gum; chocolate; toothbrush; and tooth powder.[2]

There were eventually 17 packing centres located around the UK, which were staffed by some paid staff but predominantly by volunteers who were packing up to 163,000 parcels per week.

Apart from their contents, the Red Cross parcels had one unintended, but nevertheless very beneficial consequence, which was that every bit of the packaging and materials was treated with great respect and put to a wide variety of uses to make up for shortages in the camps. This applied not just to the more obvious materials such as the wrapping paper and string, but also the empty tins, greaseproof paper and the wood from the crates.

TRANSPORT

Transporting these parcels, plus all the other goods intended for the camps, was a major logistical undertaking. It started with the parcels being completed in the packing centres, where they were then handed over to the General Post Office (GPO), who became responsible for the first leg of the journey. In World War One and for the first few months of World War Two the parcels had been shipped across the English Channel to Ostende and then taken by rail across France to Switzerland, but once the Germans had overrun France in June 1940 that was no longer possible, so a new route had to be devised, but this was done remarkably quickly and the new arrangement started on 24 July 1940.

This new route involved the GPO taking the parcels to ports where they were loaded aboard ships and taken to Lisbon, Portugal. This part of the journey was a straight commercial proposition, as for any other mail, and involved normal merchant ships renting space to the GPO. The ships sailed in normal convoys without any special status such as 'safe passage' but, despite this, not one parcel was lost throughout the war on this leg of the journey.

Once in Lisbon the parcels were transferred to large warehouses that had been rented for this purpose by the Red Cross and St John's Joint War Organization.

Initially, the parcels were then taken by train across Portugal, Spain and France to Switzerland. This was slow and involved three changes of gauge, but it also proved unreliable. As with ships, goods wagons were at a premium and there were disputes over repositioning them after each journey, while parts of the Spanish system were in bad repair after heavy floods. Unaware of the difficulties, the complexity of the system and the strenuous efforts being made to overcome them, numerous PoWs and families complained about the intermittent nature of the supplies.

As a result, the ICRC established a new system in which the parcels were shipped to Lisbon, as before, but were then moved in ships chartered for the purpose by the ICRC, which sailed along a safe-passage route down the Portuguese coast, through the Straits of Gibraltar and then north-east to French Mediterranean ports, either Marseilles or Toulon. From these ports the parcels and other mail were taken by train to Geneva, where they were stockpiled in Red Cross warehouses. From there they were taken by train to the nearest sidings to the camps, where they were unloaded, often by the prisoners themselves, and taken to a central area for breaking bulk and then issuing to individuals.

This route was opened in December 1940 at a time when Marseilles was in Unoccupied France. There was a brief hiatus when the Germans extended their occupation to cover the whole of France in November 1942, but the Red Cross route resumed after a break of no more than 18 days. This continued, despite Allied air attacks on the German-controlled rail network and the ever-increasing demands of the German military on its diminishing resources, until early 1945, when the ICRC began to use trucks as well as trains for distribution within Germany.

The system for parcels and other Red Cross supplies from the United States was generally similar. Starting in December 1942, they were shipped from Philadelphia direct to Marseilles or Toulon, in Swiss-flagged vessels, with the ship following a safe-passage route the whole way. This avoided the unprotected leg and trans-shipment at Lisbon that were necessary for the British parcels.

THE RED CROSS 'FLEET'

The requirements to transport Red Cross and other relief supplies on the Lisbon–Marseilles/Toulon and Philadelphia–Marseilles/Toulon routes were met in two ways. First, there were a number of ships that were bought and operated by a charitable foundation which operated as a subsidiary of Swiss Re, the reinsurance company. The foundation, which was founded in 1942 specifically for this purpose, had its headquarters in Zurich. It owned and operated three ships: *Caritas I* (3,950 tons deadweight, built 1903); *Caritas II* (3,950 tons, 1929) and *Henri Dunant* (8,500 tons, 1910). Of these, *Caritas I,* an elderly vessel that had changed hands many times in the preceding 40 years, completed 12 trans-Atlantic voyages for the Red Cross, in the course of which she successfully delivered no less than 28,636 tons of parcels, mail and other relief supplies.

The ICRC also chartered ships. It needed neutrally owned and manned ships and few such were available during the war years when cargo ships were at a premium. Thus, the ships it obtained in this way tended to be small, elderly and slow, but they did the job. Some were on long-term charters, others on as little as a 'one-voyage-at-a-time' basis.

The ships owned by or under charter to the ICRC are shown in Table 8 below:

Table 8: Voyages Carried Out by Ships Owned by or Under Charter to the ICRC: 1941–1945

National flag	Ship	Voyages	Tons carried	*Totals*
Portugal	*Ambriz*	53	19,395	
	Congo	9	20,924	
	Costeiro T	3	2,350	
	Goncalo V	2	2,786	
	Lobito	6	12,585	
	Malange	5	11,029	
	Padua	18	8,700	
	S. Gouveia	5	2,610	
	Tagus	29	29,927	
	Ze Manuel	34	19,785	**130,091**
Spain	*Abando*	1	1,023	
	Nuria	8	12,491	
	Urola	3	8,405	
	Villafranca	2	2,486	
	Villareal	3	6,059	**30,464**
Sweden	*Cristina*	1	2,191	
	Embla	40	28,082	
	Kanangoora	0	0	
	Mangalore	7	41,088	
	Rosa Smith	2	2,460	
	Saivo	3	19,273	

(continued)

National flag	Ship	Voyages	Tons carried	*Totals*
	Stureborg	1	1,815	
	Sven Salen	1	6,203	
	Travancore	5	30,708	
	Vega	44	35,605	**167,425**
Switzerland	Calanda	2	10,229	
	Caritas I	12	28,636	
	Caritas II	5	14,231	
	Eiger	1	580	
	Finn	9	18,080	
	H Dunant	5	13,983	
	Lugano	1	5,379	
	Nereus	1	6,720	
	Zurich	2	2,288	**100,126**
GRAND TOTALS		**321**		**428,106**

Source: Red Cross

Kanangoora is shown in the table as having made zero voyages, which is correct, but she was chartered by the American Red Cross to take relief supplies to PoWs in the Far East, although this was never permitted by the Japanese – see Chapter 14. *Vega* completed 44 voyages for the Red Cross, of which 38 were on the Lisbon–Marseilles route, but the last six involved taking desperately needed relief to the Channel Islands in 1944–1945.

When on Red Cross missions, all these ships displayed large red crosses on white backgrounds painted on the sides fore and aft, plus the words 'C. International' on both sides amidships. They were brightly illuminated at all times, and followed set 'safe passage' courses. They were liable to be stopped by either side and searched at any time.

Considering that these ships operated almost entirely in hotly contested waters and were liable to attack by surface warships, submarines or aircraft – and, more insidiously, by mines – the casualties were remarkably few. *Padua* was mined off Marseilles in October 1943 and lost with all six hands. In March 1944, *Embla* was bombed twice within a few days by unknown aircraft and sank after the second attack, with the loss of 19 lives. Two months later, *Cristina* was bombed but survived. Finally, *Vega*, although not attacked, suffered twice from the hazards of the sea, colliding with a French ship in December 1942 and being driven ashore in a storm in October 1943; she was repaired on each occasion and survived the war.

11

Re-Employment of Repatriates

The position of military repatriates was laid down very clearly – and unusually succinctly – in the Geneva Convention, 1929:

ARTICLE 74. No repatriated person shall be employed on active military service.

In general, the belligerent nations involved in World War Two interpreted this in much the same way and the British Army Council Instruction (ACI) on the subject, which was promulgated to the entire army, can be taken as typical:

ARMY COUNCIL INSTRUCTION 2205/1942

Employment of Repatriated Prisoners of War

1. In accordance with the provisions of Article 74 of the International Convention Relative to the Treatment of Prisoners of War (Geneva, 1929), which states that 'No repatriated person shall be employed on active military service', sick and seriously wounded prisoners of war who are repatriated after examination by a mixed medical commission will not be employed with an expeditionary force overseas or with a field force unit in the United Kingdom.

2. Such prisoners may, if fit for such employment, be employed with an administrative, training or non-operational unit in the United Kingdom.

3. The above provisions do not apply to prisoners of war repatriated as being personnel protected by the provisions of the International Convention for the Amelioration of the Condition of the Wounded and Sick in Armies in the Field (Geneva, 1929) who under Articles 9 and 12 of that Convention are not to be treated as prisoners of war, *i.e.*, chaplains and personnel of the medical services who will in any event be employed after repatriation on medical, etc., duties only and not in any combatant capacity.[1]

Paragraphs 1 and 2 covered the situation where a man from a combatant service or arm was repatriated from a prisoner-of-war camp having been passed by a Mixed Medical Commission. All such men would usually have been required by the Detaining Power before leaving their custody to sign a certificate that they would not again take up arms.[2] If, however, they subsequently recovered sufficiently to return to duty, they would be told and their documentary records would confirm that they could not be re-employed in a combatant role. Such men could, however, be employed in an administrative or training unit, although, it should be noted, this effectively released another man for a combatant role.

As was made clear in paragraph 3 of the ACI, the rules for 'protected personnel' were different, since they were, by definition, not combatants. This included doctors, nurses, medical orderlies, stretcher-bearers and other medical personnel, as well as chaplains. These were entitled to repatriation as of right and did not have to be sick or wounded, and thus once back in their home country they were fit to be re-employed.[3] However, that re-employment had to be in the same non-combatant duties.

In early 1945 the Soviet Army captured a number of German infantrymen who, it discovered, had formerly been medical orderlies, captured by the British and then exchanged as 'protected personnel'. Once back in Germany the manpower crisis, especially on the Eastern Front, was so serious that these men had been reassigned as combat infantrymen. The Soviets brought this to the attention of the British, who immediately protested to Germany, via the Swiss government. Although they had plenty of other matters to worry about as the Allies squeezed their country towards defeat, the German General Staff tacitly admitted the error by sending a letter to Berne, certifying that personnel of the *Sanitätdienst* (Medical Service) released as protected personnel would only ever be re-employed within that corps.[4]

In another area, there was a curious sequel to the Anglo-Italian exchange that had taken place on 20 March 1943 (Chapter 8), which, it will be recalled, involved fit men only. In early August 1943 one of the repatriated British sailors requested a formal interview with the commodore commanding the Royal Navy barracks at Devonport to seek clarification of his status. The sailor told his commanding officer that he had signed a number of forms prior to leaving his prisoner-of-war camp in Italy, one of which he believed to have stated that he would not take up arms again against any of the Axis powers. The sailor was not seeking to avoid a return to active service, but wished to be absolutely clear about his status.

This was a serious issue since, as explained above, normal exchanges of sick and wounded prisoners-of-war (i.e., under the terms of the 1929 Geneva Convention) certainly did include the undertaking that '... no repatriated person shall be employed on active military service'. Thus, anyone caught breaking such a condition, for example, by being captured for a second time, would almost certainly be guilty of an offence punishable under the captor's military disciplinary code. The commanding officer, clearly well aware of this, did not brush the sailor aside and he and his superiors treated his question with the seriousness and thoroughness it deserved.

The commodore's first reaction was to interview at least 25 other men who had been involved in the same exchange and who happened to be in the local area. From these it was established that before leaving the camps in Italy all had been obliged to sign four documents. It was then established in yet further investigations that three of these were actually three copies of the same form, which reduced the possibilities to two. Both forms had been in Italian and no translation was offered, but the sailors had duly signed, probably because they were eager to get home, whatever the conditions. To add to the confusion, in several instances (although by no means all) the Italian guards nearby had made verbal remarks to the effect that the British sailors would not be able to fight again.

It was eventually established that the form causing concern recorded that the individual had been released from Italian custody, and gave his name, personal details, where he had been captured, and date of release, together with details of pay received from the Italians and any further pay owed. It was, in effect, an administrative document of the type known in many armed forces as a 'clearance certificate'.

After considerable discussion the British authorities concluded that there was no dispute concerning the validity of Article 74 of the Geneva Convention of 1929, but that the Anglo-Italian exchange at Mersin had been outside the Convention. This was because the Italian repatriates had not been prisoners-of-war, but internees in a neutral country, and although the British sailors had undeniably been prisoners-of-war, they were neither sick nor wounded, and thus outside the Geneva Convention. In addition, at no point had the Red Cross or any similar body been involved.

In fact, the British lawyers advised, the exchange was a 'matter of expediency' negotiated between the British and Italian governments, which had been intended to resolve a very particular problem. The negotiations had involved the British and Italian governments, with the Turkish government acting as disinterested intermediaries, and at no time during the negotiations had a 'no further fighting' stipulation been mentioned and, if it had and had been agreed, then it would have been necessary to include a clause to that effect in the written agreement – which was not included. Finally, the British stated that, for their part, they did not consider that the Italian sailors they had returned to Italy were under any obligation not to return to fully active military service.

The British were still investigating the situation when the Italians signed the Armistice with the Allies on 8 September 1943. It might thereafter have been argued that if an agreement for 'no further service' had been signed between the British and Italian governments in January 1943 it would have become null-and-void, anyway, since the German government was neither involved nor mentioned. But, while this possibility was mentioned, it was never tested.

This incident shows that the conditions under which servicemen were exchanged were regarded as a very serious matter and that the possible consequences for an individual if he failed to comply with the Geneva Convention were not to be taken lightly. It is also greatly to the credit of the Royal Navy and the Admiralty that in the middle of a global conflict an issue raised by an individual sailor was examined with such care.[5]

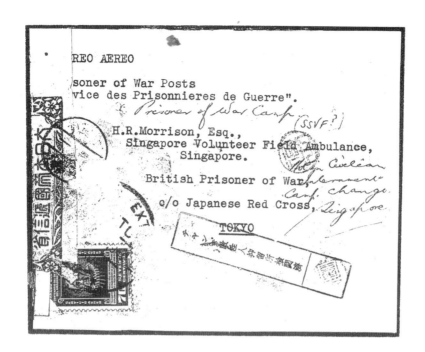

1. Postal Letter Book: This letter, posted in Ecuador, was opened and resealed three times – in the USA, Tokyo, and Singapore, where it was sent to the Civilian Internment Camp before being redirected to the Prisoner-of-War Camp. Despite the state of war and travelling over ten thousand miles many officials cooperated, perhaps without realising it, to ensure that Mr Morrison received his mail. (D. Tett, Esq)

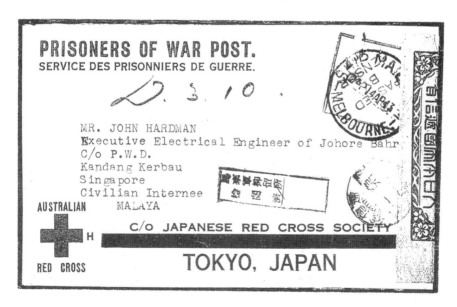

2. Postal Letter Book: Postal covers are excellent records. Posted on April 14, 1943, in Sydney, Australia (circular ship stamp over square Australian censor mark, top right), it passed through Tokyo where it was opened (resealing strip/circular stamp on right) and was delivered to Mr Hardman who was in Block D, Level 3, Cell 10 (manuscript mark above his name) in Changi Jail, Singapore in March-May 1944. (D Tett, Esq)

Left: 3. Levitt Family: Identity document issued by the Swiss Embassy in Berlin to Mrs Kathleen Levitt (28) and her children, Wendy (2) and Peter (6). They were en route to join Kathleen's husband in South Africa when their ship, SS *Zamzam*, was sunk by German raider, *Atlantis*. The Levitts were interned in Germany but later released via Palestine. (P. Levitt, Esq)

Below: 4. *Aramis*: French liner, *Aramis*, was taken over by the Japanese as *Teia Maru* and carried exchangees for the second US/Japanese exchange at Mormugao, India. It is seen here in late 1941 as an armed merchant cruiser, *X-2*, of the French Navy (French Navy)

Right: 5. *Gripsholm*: Swedish-owned liner, *Gripsholm*, was repeatedly used by the US Government to exchange prisoners-of-war and civilian internees. Here she arrives in New York harbor in 1943, bringing many hundreds of happy returnees back to their homeland. The prominent markings ensured that she was never once attacked during her many hazardous voyages. (US Navy Official)

6. Bishop Bury: Despite the ferocity in the trenches during World War One, British Bishop Herbert Bury was invited by the German government to enter their country to visit British civilian internees. He is seen here on November 26, 1916, with some of the internees at Ruhleben camp, a former horse-racing track situated just outside Berlin, Germany.

PARTICULARS OF HOLDER.

NAME (in full)...... *David Nelson*

Rank or
Appointment...... *Captain, S. S. V. F.*

returned to the Issuing Officer

Date of Issue..... 14 JUL 1941

Left: 7. Captain David Nelson: New Zealander Captain David Nelson was captured in Singapore in 1942 and spent the rest of the war as a prisoner of the Japanese. He compiled personal records of virtually every Allied prisoner in Malaya, Thailand, Singapore and Indonesia between December 1941 and August 1945. A courageous and modest man, he never received the awards he richly deserved.
(Mason Nelson Esq)

Below: 8. *Queenfish:* Due to a series of misunderstandings, by no means all of them the fault of her crew, USS *Queenfish* (SS-393), seen here post-war, sank the Japanese liner *Awa Maru,* sailing under "safe conduct" protection. It was learnt later that the Japanese ship was carrying passengers and cargo which breached that agreement.
(US Navy Official)

12

Selection for Repatriation

For PoWs to be repatriated, the first step was examination by a Mixed Medical Commission (MMC), as required by Articles 69 to 73 of the Geneva Convention, 1929 (see Appendix A). These MMCs were required to see and consider prisoners or internees nominated by the hospital commandant or camp doctor, those who requested to appear and any who had been nominated by another agency, for example, their own government or their fellow inmates. It was laid down that each MMC would normally consist of three doctors, two from neutral countries, one of whom was the chairman, and one from the Detaining Power, and decisions were reached by majority vote. The normal routine was to undertake two 'tours' to each area per year; either the MMC visited the camps or it set up in a convenient central location and candidates were brought to them.

Although not specified in the Convention, it was tacitly understood that these were to be very experienced and skilled men.

Attached to the Convention was a document known as 'The Model Agreement' (see Appendix B) that set out the agreed list of medical criteria. In general, all MMCs seem to have used the principle that prisoners should be demonstrably unable to serve again in the current conflict, combined with the inability of the Detaining Power to provide the necessary treatment. In order to progress smoothly through the MMC, all cases required a great deal of preliminary work prior to the commission's arrival, with examinations by the prison doctor, who was usually of the same nationality as the applicant, and then by the doctors of the Detaining Power, combined with the necessary tests and examinations. Some cases were so self-evident, such as blindness or the loss of a limb, that they took up little time. Next came those that were less clear-cut, which required both preliminary investigation by medical staff and detailed inquiry by the MMC itself, but if there was agreement between the national and Detaining Power's medical staff, they stood a good chance of being accepted. Thirdly, came those that were agreed by the national medical staff but not by those of the Detaining Power; for example, what appeared to be an early shadow on a lung, where a certain degree of opinion and judgement was required. Lastly, there were those who put themselves forward, but without recommendation by either the national or Detaining Power's medical staff; the chances of success in such cases were very slim, but not unknown.

At the start of the war, Germany was the first to take steps in accordance with the Convention, submitting a proposal through Switzerland to the UK on 10 June 1940, which included the information that they had already set up their own MMC.[1] However, the British were subsequently indignant when they discovered in November 1940 that the Germans, by applying a very narrow interpretation of the Geneva Convention, were only assessing prisoners who were in a camp within the geographical borders of Germany and not those held in camps that were in German-occupied countries such as Belgium and France.

The UK moved more slowly, with the War Office proposing two respected Swiss doctors resident in the UK – Dr Rast and Dr Schroeter – although MI5 objected to the former on security grounds. This was a problem that took until 4 October to resolve, when MI5 was overruled. With that out of the way, the War Office then named as the British member Colonel H. H. Blake, a recently retired doctor in the army's Royal Army Medical Corps (RAMC). There are always minor administrative complications in such matters and in the case of the British MMC this concerned pay and allowances for the two Swiss doctors. These, it was agreed by Germany and the UK, would be set at the level paid to a lieutenant-colonel in the Swiss Army. This did not worry Dr Rast, who declared that he was delighted to serve in an honorary capacity, but Dr Schroeter objected vociferously and continued to do so throughout the war – but never to the extent of actually withdrawing his services.

The British MMC held its first informal meeting on 28 October 1940, at which Dr Rast was elected chairman. It was also agreed that this MMC would represent all Commonwealth governments in the UK, except for Canada, which had announced its intention to establish its own MMC. The three members also agreed on their method of operation and designed 'case sheets' that had to be completed by hospitals prior to the team's arrival. They also agreed that they would undertake 'tours' in which they would travel around the country according to a predetermined programme, their first starting at the Royal Herbert Military Hospital at Woolwich in east London on 5–6 December 1940, followed by Oldham, outside Manchester, on 11–12 December and Swanwick (20 miles north-west of Nottingham) on 19 December. This first tour was comparatively brief because at this stage in the war the UK held only a small number of German prisoners.

The British MMC used the criteria laid down in the Model Agreement (see Appendix B) and in the early stages placed applicants into one of three categories:

- to be repatriated to his home country
- to be seen again in three months
- rejected.

There was originally to have been a fourth option of a move to a neutral country, but as this was never actually implemented by the governments it was dropped from consideration by the MMC.

The MMCs were supposed to see all those presented to them by the hospital or camp medical officers, but there were instances where this did not happen and it proved possible for the Detaining Power to decide who did, or did not, appear before an MMC. The British Admiralty was against any U-boat crews being repatriated, while the Germans, especially later in the war, were reluctant to repatriate aircrew. The British also criticized the Italians whom they suspected of preventing senior officers from appearing in front of the Italian MMC.

One major difficulty in the UK was that the British government had a policy of dispersing prisoners-of-war to Commonwealth countries, such as Australia, Canada, India, New Zealand, and South Africa. This greatly eased the pressure in the UK but caused some problems over repatriation and there were several instances where prisoners-of-war in the UK appeared before an MMC and were then sent abroad, only to be selected for repatriation, which meant that they had to be brought back again. The authorities must have known that the prisoner had appeared before an MMC and it seems odd that the man should have been sent abroad while the result was still pending and could only have occurred as a result of some administrative oversight or confusion. Rather more common was that protected personnel were sent abroad and had to be brought back to fill the agreed numbers on a forthcoming exchange.

It was the policy of German MMCs to tell the applicant immediately whether or not he met the medical criteria for repatriation. This was by no means a guarantee of a place on either the next, or even subsequent, exchanges, but it tended, not surprisingly, to raise the individual's sense of expectation. The British, on the other hand, did not tell anyone whether or not they had passed until they had been actually selected for a forthcoming exchange.

Some prisoners-of-war were so desperate to escape that they set out deliberately to fool the MMC. One example was witnessed by A. F. Gibbs[2] who was working as a medical orderly in a prisoner-of-war hospital in Hildburghausen, in southern central Germany (Lazaret Nummer 1251). A French prisoner-of-war asked for help in being repatriated to which the camp doctors, using Gibbs as an intermediary, agreed, provided the Frenchman understood that it would be tough. The plan was to feign a gastric ulcer, for which the soldier was required to do arduous physical training from 5 to 7 a.m. every day, unseen by anyone else, to take the absolute minimum of food and drink and to keep to his bed throughout the day. When questioned, he had to point to the spot (as designated by the doctors) where he felt the pain. Over a period of about a year the Frenchman lost a great deal of weight and began to look dreadful. It was known that he would be X-rayed, so the final requirement was for him to swallow a ball of silver paper at a precise interval before being photographed, so that it showed up in the correct place in his intestines. All went well, the MMC was duly misled and he was repatriated to France, where he quickly regained his weight and health.

A stratagem tried by a number of PoWs was to feign insanity, since the Model Agreement's definition was very vague, referring only to: '… All unquestionable cases of mental afflictions'. An American named Tabor at *Stalag Luft III* was the author of a series of increasingly eccentric ideas that, coupled with some very odd behaviour, eventually led to him being declared mentally unstable by an MMC and repatriated in mid 1944. His erstwhile comrades in *Stalag Luft III* learnt of his success when they received a postcard from the United States bearing the briefest of messages: 'Who's crazy now?'[3]

A British officer and inveterate escaper, Flight Lieutenant Eric Foster, RAF, also at *Stalag Luft III*, spent weeks in the camp library thoroughly researching the symptoms of insanity and then implemented them so successfully that he fooled the MMC and was repatriated. Unfortunately for him, each repatriate was accompanied by full medical documentation, and on reading his case notes the British promptly committed him to a lunatic asylum. The result was that having proved himself insane to the Germans, he now found himself in the ironic position of having to prove to the RAF medical authorities that he was actually sane.[4]

Although the Geneva Convention stated that repatriation was to be purely on medical grounds without restriction on numbers, in reality the number taking part in a specific exchange was sometimes fixed by outside factors, such as the number the enemy was offering to return or the accommodation available in a particular ship or train. This meant that if the numbers approved by the MMC exceeded the number of places available there had to be a degree of selection, which appears to have been done within the medical establishment of the Detaining Power. As a result someone faking an illness who was then accepted by the MMC and selected for repatriation might well be taking the place of someone who was genuinely ill or disabled. This presented a moral dilemma to both the individual and to anyone within the PoW community who knew that the malady was only a pretence.

The term 'protected personnel' appeared in the Geneva Convention 1906 and covered specific members of the armed forces responsible for the physical and spiritual welfare of the troops: doctors, nurses, medical orderlies and dentists. According to the conventions, they were not considered to be prisoners-of-war, but should be repatriated as soon as possible. However, the Geneva Convention 1929 included the following:

ARTICLE 14

... It shall be lawful for belligerents reciprocally to authorize each other, by means of special agreements, the retention in the camps of doctors and medical orderlies to care for prisoners of their own country ...

In reality, such personnel could only be detained in PoW camps where, of course, they were very usefully employed caring for the combatant PoWs. Further, although protected personnel were repatriated in a separate category from the sick and wounded, in practice it was the Detaining Power alone that decided which of them was to be retained, and who was to be released and when.

Although it is clear that protected personnel were aware of their right to be repatriated, few if any appear to have tried to insist on this and resigned themselves to staying in the camps 'for the duration'. The news that they were to be repatriated almost invariably came as a bolt from the blue. Typical was Private A. Ross of the RAMC, who was entitled to be repatriated, and who was at Colditz. He recorded that: 'Hauptmann Püpke came into the courtyard and he called me down. "Good news, Ross," he says. "You're going home."'[5]

13

Education and Other Support

The first Allied prisoners-of-war and civilian internees commenced their captivity in 1939–1940. There was no repatriation for the fit and healthy prisoners-of-war and by no means all civilian internees were repatriated, so the vast majority remained there until May 1945, with their numbers ever increasing as more fell into German hands. World War One experience had shown bodies such as the Red Cross, Saint John Ambulance, the Young Men's Christian Association (YMCA) and many others, that apart from providing additional nutrition by way of food parcels, there would also be a need for educational and recreational facilities, all of which had to be collected in the Allied countries and then dispatched by way of a neutral country until they were delivered, with German, and until September 1943, Italian cooperation, to the camps.

The Indoor Recreation Section of the Red Cross Prisoner-of-War Department was set up in mid 1940 and its first priority was to help establish camp libraries. A wide variety of reading matter was supplied, ranging from the escapist, such as Westerns, thrillers, detective and adventure stories, through light and serious novels and classics, to non-fiction items such as dictionaries, reference and educational text books. By 1945 over 250,000 volumes had been supplied, representing many hundreds of tons to be transported and delivered. There was also a well-developed request system in which, as in any library, the staff would search for and, if available, supply a specific book, except that in this case it took many months to achieve. The only limitation was that care had to be taken not to offend the political sensibilities of the Detaining Power, so that books on subjects such as World War One prisoner-of-war escapes were definitely not supplied.

Music provided great solace to both individuals and groups, and their needs were catered for by the supply of instruments and musical scores. All tastes had to be satisfied, ranging from military music, through orchestral works, string quartets, operas and operettas to dance bands and community singing. Some 14,000 instruments were supplied to British PoWs covering a vast range from mouth organs and Irish flutes, through banjos, ukeleles, violins and guitars, to cornets, euphoniums and trumpets – even 14 sets of bagpipes. Although few camps rose to such heights, mention should be made of the Oflag VII/B Music Festival that ran for two weeks in February 1944, with 33 separate events involving 120 musicians with a total audience of over 6,000 people. Performances included a wide variety of serious works – symphony, choral, orchestral, chamber music – as well as dance bands and singalongs.

Many camps featured stage events such as plays, sketches, monologues and pantomimes, as well as operas and operettas. These were supported from the UK by supplies of scripts, together with 'how-to' manuals on set design and construction, lighting, make-up, costume design and manufacture, and stage management.

There was a natural desire among the prisoners for games, both indoor and outdoor. The YMCA took on responsibility for obtaining all this equipment and dispatching it to Lisbon, where, as with mail and parcels, it was handed over to the representatives of the ICRC who arranged for its onward transport to Geneva from where it was distributed to the camps. The range was vast. There were indoor board games, such as chess, draughts and halma, through card games and dominoes, to table tennis and deck quoits. Equipment for outdoor games was also sent, including balls of all types, cricket bats, stumps and pads, boxing gloves, hockey sticks, and a wide variety of boots and team clothing.

There was open space in virtually all camps for gardens. The most practical were kitchen gardens growing vegetables and fruit that could supplement the diet, but decorative gardens were not neglected, with flowers and shrubs being sown and even, in some cases, lawns being laid. In the UK, the Royal Horticultural Society advised what should be sent and when.

The Educational Books Section of the Red Cross was established in London in early 1940, but in December business was so heavy that it moved to the New Bodleian Library in Oxford, where it was run, with splendid efficiency, by Miss Ethel Herdman. She organized the book service but also took on the examinations, putting prisoners-of-war and civilian internees in contact with professional bodies relevant to their intended course of study.

Once the student was ready he was provided with a course of study and a list of books, which were then obtained from institutions, colleges and schools, as well as from new and second-hand booksellers and public appeals. There was even a pool of some 50,000 of the more commonly requested books at Geneva. By February 1945 when the movement of prisoners in Germany made further study almost impossible, some 263,000 books had been dispatched, most of them in small parcels intended for individual addressees.

Nor was this all, because the students also had to be supplied with paper, exercise books, pens and pencils, rulers and mathematical instruments, while the lecturers needed blackboards and chalk. There were some prisoners who did not want to undertake formal study but sought directed reading, for example, in the Classics; the system coped with these, too, their programmes being devised by volunteer experts in the subject and the books dispatched.

In most camps the German authorities were reasonably cooperative, but only as far as making rooms or even, in one or two cases, buildings available; in other camps they simply let the prisoners manage themselves, while in a few they were actively unhelpful. However, there was universal agreement among the prisoners that the Germans never interfered with examinations: the question papers arrived properly sealed, examination periods were respected and the papers returned to the UK with dispatch; there was no censorship in either direction. There was even one case where a parcel of live frogs arrived for a medical examination; five were alive, the sixth was dead, but a note was attached with an apology and an assurance (perhaps tongue-in-cheek) that the death was not the fault of the Third Reich.

Some 120 bodies held examinations in the camps, which covered a vast array of subjects and the success rate was just under 80 per cent. Thus, for many of those in the camps, not only was at least part of their time usefully filled, but, in addition, they gained qualifications that were to stand them in good stead at the end of the war, in some cases in professions that they might well never have considered had this opportunity not been offered.

Officers were not required to do physical work at all, so that, if nothing else, these courses were both useful and time-filling. Senior NCOs could work if they wished and some did so, but stopped when they found that their time could be more productively filled by education. Junior NCOs and private soldiers (and their equivalents in the other services) were required to work, but some still found the time at the end of a long day to carry on studying. Here, too, the Germans made minor concessions in that men on *Arbeitskommandos* (work parties) were allowed to return to their base camp for up to six weeks of concentrated study before an examination.

Educational activities tended to vary between the camps, although foreign languages were popular across the board, including such esoteric ones as Chinese, Japanese, Serbo-Croat, Maori and Swahili. In the Milag (internment camp for Merchant Navy personnel) there was a heavy emphasis on Masters, Mates and Engineers examinations, while in the civilian internment camps teenage children were prepared for their matriculation. Indeed, some adults who had missed the opportunity also studied for matriculation and it was by no means unknown for illiterates to be taught to read and write.

The whole education programme was completed by a well-attended post-war conference for camp education officers, held at the New Bodleian Library on 11–12 August 1945.[1] One of the main features was a deep and heartfelt expression of gratitude to the staff at the New Bodleian Library and, in particular, to Miss Herdman. All were convinced of the value of the scheme and the majority agreed that, in general, the Germans had been very helpful.

One of the most successful schools was that at *Stalag Luft VI*, an NCOs-only camp at Heydekrug in Memelland (present-day Lithuania). It originally accommodated British and Canadian air force NCOs but from June 1944 there were US PoWs as well. In July 1943, the school issued an illuminated prospectus, a copy of which was sent to England where it received the personal endorsement of King George VI and Queen Elizabeth.[2]

This prospectus showed that in mid 1943 there were over 1,000 students attending the school, for which 'the status of prisoner-of-war is the only qualification for entry' and which was organized into five faculties: arts, science, medicine, law and professional studies. There were 54 lecturers and the subjects they covered illustrate the scope of the school's activities: accountancy, agriculture, art, banking, biology, bookkeeping, botany, building, chemistry, commerce, economics, engineering, English, French, Latin, geography, Greek, history, hotel management, Italian, law, local government, mathematics, medicine, metallurgy, meteorology, motor trade, navigation, physics, Portuguese, German, secretarial practice, Spanish and typography. In common with many such schools, two of the limiting factors were properly qualified lecturers and space. In the case of *Stalag VI* there were only five lecture rooms, of which three were used solely for education but the other two were combined with other functions. These rooms were programmed in one-hour blocks from 09.00–12.00, 13.00–17.00 and 18.00–20.00, except for Sundays when they started at 11.00. One of these three rooms was permanently allocated to examinations from 13.00–17.00 Monday to Saturday. The fiction library was used as a library from 13.00–17.00 Monday to Saturday, while the hairdressing shop was only available for classes from 18.00 onwards. It all bespeaks a very busy schedule and an active and rewarding programme.

The spirit of the whole education enterprise was summarized in the story of Sergeant Horsley, the education officer at *Stalag 344* (Lamsdorf), a centre for *Arbeitskommandos* (working parties) in East Prussia. A set of examination papers had just arrived in early 1945 when, due to the Russian advance, the Germans ordered the entire prisoner population to march to *Stalag VIIIA*. Sergeant Horsley took the papers with him and on arrival at their new camp, and despite their tiredness and hunger, the cold and the repeated power cuts, the candidates insisted on sitting the papers that involved 18 hours' work over a period of three days. This had hardly been completed when they were ordered to march again to yet another camp and Sergeant Horsley carried the completed answers wrapped around his body. Due to the state of chaos as Germany collapsed Horsley never found an opportunity to put the precious papers into the postal system, so he carried them back to England and took them straight to Oxford where he handed them over in person.

14

Japan – The First US Exchange

On the day following the attack on Pearl Harbor, the US and Japan appointed Protecting Powers, with Switzerland representing the United States in Japan, while Japan was represented by Spain in the continental United States and by Sweden in Hawaii. There were many nationals of one country in the territory of the other and within a matter of days it was agreed that there would be exchanges, initially of officials in government employment, particularly the diplomats, with the three major questions to be addressed being: Where would it take place? When, in a fast-moving situation? Who would be eligible?

The location was agreed by mid December. The Japanese suggested Tahiti, which was conveniently halfway across the Pacific, but both quickly settled on Lourenço Marques (now Maputo) in the (then) Portuguese colony of Mozambique. Initially, matters moved rapidly and on 1 January 1942 the Swiss Ambassador in Tokyo, Camillo Gorgé, called on the US Ambassador, Joseph C. Grew, in his beleaguered embassy[1] and handed him a copy of a note from the Japanese with their detailed proposals.[2] There was also early agreement that each party would be responsible for assembling people not actually located in their respective home countries, i.e., the Japanese would be responsible for US citizens in occupied China, Thailand and French Indochina, while the US would be responsible for Japanese in Canada, Central and South America. That left the British, as discussed in Chapter 16, who were responsible for people from Europe and the Commonwealth, less Canada.

One of the factors that bedevilled all exchange negotiations, particularly in the cases of Japan and the United States, was the sheer number of agencies involved on each side and the varying agendas they tended to pursue. On the US side the lead was taken by the Special Warfare Problems Division (SWPD) of the State Department, but they had to consult and, in many cases, carry with them, the Department of the Army, the Department of the Navy, the FBI (headed by the notoriously independently minded Edgar Hoover), the Justice Department and the War Relocation Authority, and within each of those were various divisions, many with their own agendas. In addition, the president and his staff frequently became involved, while members of both Houses of Congress also brought influence to bear. Once all these departmental views had been reconciled, there were Canadian and the Latin American governments to be consulted, while most actions had to be coordinated with the United Kingdom, port facilities negotiated with the neutral Portuguese, and ships obtained from neutral Sweden.

On the Japanese side, overall coordination was carried out by the Central Liaison Office of the Ministry of Foreign Affairs, but they, too, had to deal with many vested interests, particularly in the Navy and Army, which enjoyed power and influence in Japan well beyond their counterparts in Western democracies. Although of lesser importance than for the United States, Japan also had to liaise with allies; with the Germans for safe-passage routes and with Italy for the provision of a ship for the first exchange.

But neither side could deal directly with the other and had to use the good offices of the relevant Protecting Power. Switzerland acted on behalf of the United States in Japan and provided representatives aboard Japanese ships involved in the exchanges, while Spain acted for Japan in the United States, inspecting camps and providing representatives aboard exchange ships sailing from US ports.

Who should or could be excluded from an exchange was as important as who to include. The US was keen to prevent the exchange of any Japanese with specialist, especially military technical, knowledge. The US also insisted that on the first voyage all Japanese taking part must express agreement to be repatriated, although this was relaxed somewhat for the second exchange. The British also complicated the issue for the United States, as they sought a degree of coordination that the latter did not want, not least because the US held many more important Japanese than did the British. The Japanese added to this inter-allied confusion by insisting that all four ships involved in the two exchanges should sail together, although they later dropped this requirement.

Despite all these complicating factors, Japan and the United States exchanged their first lists of names in April 1942 and the US authorities chartered a single ship, the Swedish liner *Gripsholm*, although, since she was moored in Swedish waters, she could not reposition to New York until the end of May. On the other side of the Pacific, two vessels were designated for the exchange: the Japanese liner *Asama Maru* and the Italian *Conte Verde*.

Even when the lists of names had been finalized, there were still complications. In early June, the former Japanese Ambassador to the United States, Nomura Kichisaburo, interfered by producing his own list, with significant differences to that already agreed, which was brusquely rejected by the US government on the grounds that he no longer had any official position. Then, J. Edgar Hoover interfered. The Japanese had stipulated and all US departments had agreed that there would be no search of individuals, but despite this Hoover ordered that all be searched by his agents and in typical high-handed manner, did so without any prior warning. Presented with a fait accompli, the Americans held their breath, but to their relief the Japanese did not respond.

From the start of these negotiations, the Japanese insisted on one principle from which, with one exception, they never shifted throughout the war, which was that they would not permit a ship not owned by a Japanese company or manned by a non-Japanese crew to enter what they regarded as Japanese-controlled waters. This meant that a mutually acceptable neutral port had to be found where the ships could meet and exchange passengers.

The one exception to this was in the first exchange, when they themselves chartered the Italian-owned and -manned *Conte Verde*, which happened to be in Far Eastern waters on the declaration of war in December 1941 and was lying, fully manned but unemployed, at Shanghai. Later in the war as the Allies realized how appallingly their prisoners-of-war were being treated they tried to find ways around this 'principle' in order to help the Japanese overcome their increasing shortage of merchant shipping, but the Japanese never moved their position.

Table 9: Ships Involved in the First US–Japanese Exchange

	Gripsholm	*Asama Maru*	*Conte Verde*
Nationality	Swedish	Japanese	Italian
Owner	Swedish-America Line	Nippon Yūsen Kaisha (NYK)	Lloyd-Triestino
Built	UK	Japan	UK
Completed	1925	1929	1923
Displacement	17,944 grt	16,975 grt	18,800 grt
Length	553 ft	560 ft	570 ft
Crew	320	250	n.k.
Passengers: 1st	129		230
2nd	482	840	290
3rd	1,066		1,880
Engines	2 x diesel	4 x diesel	4 x steam turbine
Cruising speed	16 kt	21 kt	20 kt

The Swedish liner, *Gripsholm* (see Table 9, above), was built for the Swedish-America Line (SAL) in 1925 and was the first major transatlantic liner to be powered by diesel engines. It established a fine reputation for efficiency and comfort, but her work was halted when war broke out and she spent many months moored in her home port, Gothenburg. In May 1942 she was chartered by the US government for the first US–Japanese exchange and sailed for New York on 28 May 1942. For this passage she sailed under 'safe conduct' carrying 194 passengers, many of them US citizens who had been trapped in Norway, Sweden, Finland and Denmark. Both sides sought direct assurance that the rules were being followed, the Germans ordering her to call at Kristiansund, Norway, to be inspected, while the British conducted a similar inspection off the Faroes. These delays, plus a North Atlantic fog, meant that she did not arrive in New York until 9 June 1942. The original departure date was 12 June, but in the event *Gripsholm* was delayed and did not sail until 18 June, carrying some 1,100 passengers. She then proceeded along her safe conduct route to Rio de Janeiro, Brazil, arriving on 2 July, and, having embarked a further 380, sailed again on 4 July for a non-stop voyage to Lourenço Marques, which was reached on 28 July. The great majority of the passengers were Japanese, but there were also a small number of Thais.[3]

It was essential that a safe passage ship such as this be instantly recognizable. Thus the entire hull and upper works were white and painted on the sides were the Swedish national flag flanked by the words in huge letters 'GRIPSHOLM' and 'SVERIGE'. The word 'DIPLOMAT' was also painted on the sides above the flag and on the bridge front. There were vertical stripes of blue-yellow-blue (Sweden's national colours): one set each at the stem and stern and two more down each side. The funnels were the SAL's usual beige, with circular shields bearing Sweden's national crest of three golden crowns on a blue circular backing. As normal with safe passage ships, she was fully lit at night, followed an agreed course at a steady speed, and did not zigzag.[4]

The first of the two Japanese ships carrying repatriates to Lourenço Marques was the Japanese liner, *Asama Maru*,[5] which had been completed in 1929 for service on the trans-Pacific route of the Nippon Yūsen Kaisha (NYK). One of its final pre-war duties came in November 1941 when it embarked Japanese families from Singapore, but once war was declared it was controlled by the army for use as a troopship, although still manned by its civilian NYK crew.

Asama Maru started her exchange voyage in Yokohama, embarking 416 passengers on 18 June. The ship then moved only a very short distance before anchoring, dashing the eager anticipation of her passengers, who then spent a full seven days waiting for her to sail. This caused great apprehension, with some of the passengers threatening to commit suicide if the voyage was called off rather than return to a wartime existence in Japan. It came, therefore, as a great relief to them all when she sailed at 1 a.m. on Thursday 25 June.[6]

On Sunday 29 June *Asama Maru* entered Hong Kong harbour, where more US passengers were embarked, and then sailed for Saigon, arriving on 1 July. Having taken on passengers already assembled in Saigon, the *Asama Mary* took on more from SS *Valaya*, a small Thai ferry that had arrived from Bangkok with a number of American repatriates. The ship then sailed to Singapore, where she anchored near the *Conte Verde*, which had arrived first. Their anchorage was a considerable distance from the harbour, presumably to prevent the passengers from observing any naval activity that could then be passed on as soon as they had been released in Lourenço Marques.[7] The Japanese permitted no contact between the passengers on the two ships, although the Swiss Red Cross representative aboard *Asama Maru* was able to visit the Italian liner, where he obtained a passenger list, which he was then able to show to the passengers aboard the *Asama Maru*.

No new passengers were embarked at Singapore, although there was a curious incident shortly before they sailed when a Japanese-crewed launch approached carrying two blond-haired, Caucasian children – a boy aged about 12 and his younger sister. They had become parted from their parents in the Japanese advance and their boat sailed close by the two ships to enable them to see whether either of their parents was aboard. This failed and the boat sailed away – who these unfortunate children were and what happened to them has never been established.[8]

Having replenished with fuel and water, the two ships raised anchor and sailed via the Sunda Strait and then directly across the Indian Ocean, following the route agreed for 'safe passage' and transmitting their exact position at noon every day on the international frequency.[9] They sailed about half a mile apart, giving their anxious passengers a feeling that if something happened to one ship the other would be there to rescue them. They passed to the north of Madagascar and one day out from Lourenço Marques they joined company with *Gripsholm* and the three ships proceeded into the harbour, where they moored alongside the same pier, with *Gripsholm* in the centre, *Asama Maru* ahead and *Conte Verde* astern.

The actual exchange was far less dramatic than the passengers had expected. The high-ranking diplomats, headed by Grew for the United States and Nomura for Japan, were exchanged with the normal courtesies. The remaining passengers then trooped down one gangplank, walked along the jetty, Americans on one side of a line of freight cars, Japanese on the other so that they would not meet, and then up the gangplank of the ship taking them home. There were no roll calls or officials at desks checking names against a master list, but everything seems to have gone remarkably smoothly.[10]

Asama Maru's markings were distinctive, but different from those of *Gripsholm*. According to Max Hill, '… she was freshly painted black and white, with huge white crosses fore and aft on the sides. Above, bolted on the promenade deck rail was another large white cross, this one studded with light bulbs to blaze a night warning of safe conduct …'[11]

Conte Verde was an Italian-owned and operated ship that had been built in the 1920s for the Italy–Far East service. It was operated by the Lloyd-Triestino line and had achieved international fame in 1938 when it was one of several Italian liners that took Jewish refugees from Austria and Germany to Shanghai. On the outbreak of war in Europe in September 1939, *Conte Verde* was in Far Eastern waters and since she obviously risked capture by the British or French if attempting to return home, she made for Shanghai where she lay, with full crew, until chartered by the Japanese government in 1942 for the first US–Japanese exchange.

Conte Verde sailed from Shanghai on 28 June carrying some 640 passengers, the great majority of whom were US citizens who had been working in China. But there were also some other groups, such as a small number of US consular staff from the Philippines who had been taken by ship to Formosa and then flown to Shanghai. She sailed direct to Singapore, where she met *Asama Maru*, anchored, victualled and refuelled and then, as described above, the two sailed in company to Lourenço Marques.

Asama Maru and *Conte Verde* embarked their passengers at Lourenço Marques on 24 July and sailed in company to Singapore for fuel and water and to disembark a few passengers. They then proceeded, still in company and still on safe passage, to Japan. *Asama Maru* then returned to her troop-carrying duties, while *Conte Verde* returned to Shanghai.[12]

Gripsholm sailed on 29 July and arrived at Rio de Janeiro on 10 August. After an overnight stop for replenishment and disembarking several passengers, she then proceeded to New York, arriving on 25 August. Every passenger was then interviewed by immigration officials, some 75 even being taken to Ellis Island for two days before being released.

As usual in most exchanges throughout the war, the numbers exchanged were only approximately equal, with the *Gripsholm* returning to the United States with 1,512 aboard, while *Asama Maru* and *Conte Verde* carried 1,424 (789 and 635, respectively). There were several reasons for this, the first being that there were always changes right up to the time of sailing, with individuals or groups being delayed en route to the embarkation port, taken ill, dying, or simply changing their minds. There were also unavoidable events on the high seas. In the case of this particular exchange, a baby was born aboard *Asama Maru* on 15 July 1942[13] and two people died.

Finally, both governments took advantage of these voyages to reassign some members of staff. Thus, 16 Japanese men, plus wives, children and a servant, having arrived at Lourenço Marques from the United States aboard the *Gripsholm*, were reassigned to other diplomatic posts in Europe and departed for Lisbon aboard a Portuguese ship on 6 August 1942, rather than returned to Japan. Similarly, six United States diplomats returning from Japan were reassigned to posts in Africa and did not embark aboard *Gripsholm*.

The voyages aboard *Gripsholm* and *Conte Verde* seem to have been fairly comfortable, with both the Swedish and Italian crews receiving praise for their helpful and willing attitude. Aboard the *Asama Maru* on its outward voyage, however, the passengers found much to complain about. Women, children and the higher-ranking officials seem to have been reasonably accommodated, but the majority of the men were either accommodated four to a two-person cabin, or, even worse, up to 20 per cabin in 'steerage', below the waterline and in some cases – adding insult to injury – were served steerage-type food, as well. This caused considerable discontent, not least because all non-governmental passengers were being charged a flat-rate fee by the US Government. However, the two officials responsible for cabin allocation had given themselves the worst cabins on the ship and when complainants became too strident offered to swap with them, which invariably ended the discussion.

Almost without exception, the ship's stewards were uncooperative and surly, providing the minimum of service, above which everything had to be paid for in the form of 'tips'. Great attention was paid to security, with the views of some anchorages being blocked off by screens, while at sea the usual map of the world, common to almost every liner, was removed. The unfortunate Red Cross representative, a Japan-based Swiss, aboard the *Asama Maru* served as the official liaison between the passengers and the crew.

PASSENGERS JAPAN–US

The original purpose of these voyages was for Japan and the United States to return the diplomatic staff who had been isolated in the other's country on the declaration of war, a procedure required by international practice. Thus, among those returning to the United States were Ambassador and Mrs Grew and the complete staff of the US Embassy in Tokyo, together with Ambassador and Mrs Peck from the US Embassy in Bangkok, Thailand, and Richard Buttrick, the counsellor at the US Embassy in Peking. There were also US consular staff, including some from the Philippines who had been taken by sea to Takao in Formosa and then flown to Shanghai. Naval and military attachés counted as diplomatic staff, but, despite the US's best efforts, the Japanese refused to give the Marine Corps guards from the Peking Embassy diplomatic status, since this would have made them eligible for exchange; the Japanese maintained that they were prisoners-of-war and held them in a camp until August 1945.

In the negotiations it had been agreed that the exchange would include people from Canada and Latin America, so the passenger list included the ambassadors and their wives from Brazil, Colombia, Canada, Mexico and Peru, together with members of their staff.

There were, however, five US nurses who had been captured when the Japanese overwhelmed the Marine Corps garrison on Guam, who were not classified as military by the Japanese and had, therefore, been taken to Japan where they were held in a civilian prison until boarding the *Asama Maru*. This group of nurses included Virginia Fogarty, who met and became engaged to a US consular official,

Frederick Mann, during the voyage from Japan. He was posted to Brazzaville in (then) French Equatorial Africa, so a Portuguese 30-day residency requirement was bent to enable them to marry in Lourenço Marques, whereupon US Navy regulations were also circumvented to enable the new Mrs Mann to be discharged locally and thus avoid being sent back to the United States aboard *Gripsholm*.[14] Japanese policy with regard to prisoners-of-war and internees was seldom consistent. Thus, although these five US nurses from Guam were exchanged, 17 Australian nurses captured in New Britain in January 1942, who reached Japan in July 1942, were never exchanged.[15]

A total of 76 civilian internees were also embarked at Yokohama, who had all been long-term residents of Japan, and did not include any civilians who had been brought to Japan since the outbreak of war.

The largest single group of passengers were missionaries from China, Japan and Korea, predominantly US or Canadian citizens, comprising 117 Roman Catholics and 593 of various Protestant denominations. There was even a small group of pacifists, who described themselves as 'The Friends of Japan' but who, despite their continuing devotion to Japan and all things Japanese – and assembling on *Asama Maru*'s stern to shout '*Banzai*' as she left port (to the disgust of their fellow Americans) – were firmly expelled by the objects of their misplaced devotion.

There were many US businessmen who had been stationed in either Japan or China, virtually all of them high-level executives, including representatives of Standard Oil, National City Bank, Chase Bank, President Lines, Warner Bros and Otis Elevators.

Another significant group was the press. *Asama Maru* carried some 15, who boarded either at Yokohama or Hong Kong, including representatives from *Associated Press*, *United Press*, *New York Times*, *New York Herald Tribune*, *Wall Street Journal*, and the *Detroit News*, as well as radio correspondents from CBS and NBC. There were also some journalists who had been producing their own Japan-based newspapers, such as the *Japan Times & Advertiser*. Aboard *Conte Verde* from Shanghai were more journalists, most of whom had been held in 'Bridge House' where their treatment had been very rough. Virtually all these journalists spent the entire voyage hunched over their typewriters preparing their reports for transmission home as soon as they could find a radio terminal; the remainder of their waking hours was spent, according to one observer, playing poker or drinking, or both. *Gripsholm* brought some Japanese journalists from New York, who were returning to Japan.

CARGO

Very soon after their defeat in the Philippines, the US government began to hear very disquieting rumours about the Japanese treatment of prisoners-of-war. This problem was exacerbated by the Japanese refusal to sign the Geneva Convention, thus preventing visits by Red Cross representatives and, of almost equal importance, the supply of Red Cross parcels and other supplies such as medicines and clothing. Thus, in the absence of any more regular system, as established with Germany and Italy in Europe, the 1942 exchange was seized upon as a vital opportunity to send supplies as well as exchange people.

Thus, on her voyage from New York, *Gripsholm* carried several hundred tons of humanitarian supplies from the US and Canadian Red Cross societies, which included the following intended specifically for US prisoners-of-war in the Philippines: individual Red Cross food parcels: 22,160; foodstuff in bulk: 219 cases; drugs: 271 cases; cigarettes: 25,000 packs; tobacco: 4,869 tins; as well as clothing, footwear, soap and toiletries. These were cross-loaded from *Gripsholm* to *Asama Maru*, while green tea and reading material for Japanese internees in the United States was sent in the opposite direction. Some of the US/Canadian supplies were offloaded at Singapore and Hong Kong, but most were taken back to Japan, from where they were distributed to Japan's decreasing empire somewhat sporadically over the remainder of the war.

The end result of the first US–Japanese exchange was that virtually all known 'officials' (i.e., government employees) on both sides were exchanged, together with a larger number of non-officials. There was, however, another outcome. It was not surprising that the return of such numbers from enemy territory should generate a great deal of public interest, particularly in the news-hungry United States, and while many of the repatriates disappeared quickly into their usual obscurity, a significant number published accounts of their stay in Japanese hands, in newspapers, magazines, books and in radio talks. These included books by journalists such as Max Hill (*Associated Press*) and Gwen Dew (*Detroit News*), many articles in newspapers and magazines, such as *Life* (7 September 1942), and lectures by some of the returnees. While these were very informative to the US public, most were not only very uncomplimentary about the Japanese, but some were also accompanied by photographs, which added to their impact. These certainly informed the public of the nature of the enemy, but caused some apprehension in government circles about the willingness of the Japanese to undertake further exchanges if they generated such bad publicity.

15

The Second US–Japanese Exchange

The US State Department started serious planning and negotiations for a second, possibly even a third, exchange before the first had been completed. Indeed, a quick turnaround by the *Gripsholm*, *Asama Maru* and *Conte Verde* was so confidently anticipated that the Spanish Ambassador in London approached the British Foreign Secretary on 1 September 1942 for safe passages for *Asama Maru* and *Conte Verde* to arrive at Lourenço Marques on 1 October. The Special Division had submitted a list of some 1,500 Japanese nationals believed to be wanting repatriation on 29 July and the Japanese replied with their own list on 17 August[1] and confirmed their agreement to an exchange, but with a short delay to 1 October.

The argument that ensued between the two sides was not about the principle of exchanging, nor about the total number of ships or people to be involved – a figure of 1,500 was not in dispute – but about who, precisely, would be on the final list. The Japanese sent one list after another and became progressively more frustrated at what they considered to be American dilatoriness, if not outright obstruction. For the US there were three major difficulties: 538 of those on the Japanese list were deemed to be a threat to US national security; some of those on the list refused to be repatriated; and some could simply not be found. There was always the danger, of course, that the Japanese would simply lose interest, thus preventing the return of US citizens to the US – which was a matter close to the hearts of many Congressmen and thus to the Administration.

Both sides, however, suffered from domestic problems, one of the most important on the US side concerning the security clearance of many of those requested by the Japanese government, and, in particular, Hawaii-domiciled Japanese. This problem was compounded by the multiplicity of government agencies involved; someone estimated this to be at least 18. Some of these agencies sincerely wanted to help, but others, including the influential FBI and the navy and army intelligence organizations, had their own agendas. The Japanese appear to have had similar problems. By mid 1943 the internees on both sides had been held for 18 months and the majority of US departments suddenly withdrew their security objections.

The original exchange port was to have been Lourenço Marques, but at a late stage the Japanese suggested that this should be changed to Mormugao in the

Portuguese Indian enclave of Goa, thus saving them (but not the Americans) about a week on the sailing time. This port was on the west coast of India, involving a dog-leg route for the Japanese ships around British Ceylon[2] and when agreeing the safe passage route the British insisted that the Japanese ship should sail much further from the coast than the Japanese had planned.

Table 10: Ships Involved in the Second US–Japanese Exchange

	Gripsholm	*Teia Maru*
Nationality	*Swedish*	*Japanese*
Owner	Swedish-America Line	Nippon Yūsen Kaisha (NYK)
Built	UK	France
Completed	1925	1931
Displacement	17,944 grt	17,537 grt
Length	553 ft	575 ft
Crew	320	350
Passengers:		
1st class	129	196
2nd class	482	110
Steerage	1,066	1,183
Engines	2 x diesel	2 x diesel
Cruising speed	16 kt	16 kt

Having returned to New York on 25 August 1942 *Gripsholm* seemed to be on the verge of departure for a second exchange for many months, with demurrage being paid by the US government at $5,000 per day.[3] She remained there for just over a year and it was not until 2 September 1943 that she sailed, carrying 1,340 passengers, of whom 1,248 were from the US, 61 from Canada and 31 from Mexico. She called in at two ports in South America to pick up further passengers, 89 in Rio de Janeiro and 84 in Montevideo, and then set off across the South Atlantic. She called at Port Elizabeth in South Africa for water and then crossed the Indian Ocean to arrive at Mormugao on 16 October with 1,513 for exchange.

The Japanese troopship *Teia Maru* (see Table 10, above) had been built for the French line, Messageries Maritime, as a passenger liner named *Aramis*, for their Far Eastern route. She was powered by two diesel engines and, in line with a brief fad in the 1920s and 1930s, had two very squat, square stacks, giving her an instantly recognizable appearance. She was in French Indochina on the outbreak of World War Two where she was requisitioned by the colonial government and converted to an armed merchant cruiser with an armament of eight 5.4 in

(138 mm) guns, plus a number of lighter weapons. She was employed in this role on patrols in the China Sea under the designation *X-1*, but in 1942 the Japanese, already short of ships, seized her, removed the armament, and, having renamed her *Teia Maru*, employed her as passenger transport.

Teia Maru's exchange voyage began in Yokohama, sailing on 13 September, followed by an overnight stop at Osaka (15–16 September) and then on to Shanghai arriving on 18 September, loading passengers on 19 September (who included 31 stretcher cases) and sailed in the early hours of 20 September. She called at Stanley Bay, Hong Kong (22–23 September) and then at San Fernando in the Philippines (25–26 September) and Saigon (29–30 September), picking up passengers in all three ports, before anchoring off Singapore for water and supplies (2–4 October). She then went on through the Sunda Strait to Mormugao, arriving on 15 October, the day before *Gripsholm*. She carried 13 passengers from neutral countries plus 1,503 repatriated Americans, of whom 660 were missionaries and their families. One of the missionaries died just as they reached Mormugao and was buried there.

The two ships moored adjacent to each other at the same pier and cross-loading of passengers, mail and cargo took place on 19 October. The Japanese ship then left first on 21 October with some 1,500 passengers and returned home calling at Singapore (1–3 November), and Manila (7–8 November) before reaching Yokohama on 14 November. *Gripsholm* sailed on 22 October with 1,507 passengers, and called at Port Elizabeth (2–4 November), and Rio de Janeiro (14–16 November) before reaching New York on 1 December.

Gripsholm delivered some 140,000 packages to Mormugao that had been sent by various agencies, primarily the Red Cross, in the United States and Canada. Some of this cargo had originally been intended for delivery by *Kanangoora* in 1942, but there were also parcels from PoWs' next-of-kin, as well as welfare goods, such as books, recreational equipment and religious material. These were all cross-loaded to *Teia Maru*, but how much was delivered is an open question.

The State Department had learnt from the first exchange voyage and issued firm instructions on how the passengers were to organize themselves from the time the first of them embarked in Yokohama and the Swiss government representative, Mr Abegg, who sailed aboard the ship, duly passed these on.[4] The first step was for the passengers to form a committee, whose tasks were to assist Mr Abegg, to look after passengers' interests, and to prepare a complete and detailed list to be used as the basis for allocating accommodation aboard the *Gripsholm*. Chairman of the committee was Claude A. Buss, a senior Foreign Service officer with the State Department.[5] There were also a number of Japanese government representatives aboard, headed by Baron Hayashi.

The committee had its work cut out and met daily, finding it necessary to provide a round-the-clock response, as well as setting up 11 sub-committees, with liaison officers for each part of the ship and for national groups.[6] A clear response chain was established, with complaints going first to the liaison officer, then to the general committee and thence to the Swiss delegate and, if necessary, onward from him to the captain, the purser, or one of the Japanese government officers aboard.

The cabin allocation was done partly on the basis of official rank but with some preference being given to those who were known to have been imprisoned by the Japanese. A major consequence was that in many cases able-bodied men and women occupied superior accommodation while others who were sick or in some form of distress were either in the hold or sharing cabins with many other occupants. The accommodations sub-committee struggled to sort this out, their task being hampered by the disinclination of some passengers to move and the insistence of the Japanese purser that any moves could only take place with his authority, all of which was complicated by some stewards selling their own cabins to the highest bidder. The final accommodation task for the sub-committee was to prepare a plan for the *Gripsholm*, of which the State Department required no fewer than 24 copies. They worked very hard to fulfil this request, only to discover when they boarded the Swedish ship at Mormugao that a plan had already been prepared and their work was wasted.

The ship's Japanese doctor would only deal with illnesses or injuries incurred aboard the *Teia Maru*, which meant that doctors among the repatriates had to be pressed into service and a clinic created, but they suffered from a lack of resources, drugs and medicines throughout the voyage.

It is quite clear that the ship was in a bad state of repair and had probably not undergone any proper maintenance since its days as a French-run ocean liner. One of the major problems throughout the voyage was a shortage of water, both for drinking and for washing, which even extended to neither water nor coffee being served at many meals. In many parts of the ship water for passengers was produced in containers, which were only set out at certain hours, and the shortage was particularly acute for those crammed into the hold. This became the subject of numerous official complaints through Mr Abegg to the captain, who apologized, explaining that the problem lay not in the quantity of water, but with shortcomings in the water distribution system.

Another problem was that the electrical wiring was in an appalling state and there were several minor fires. The lifeboats were also in a poor state and there were only 1,000 lifebelts for some 1,800 aboard. Despite several requests from the passengers, led by a number of master mariners among the passengers, there were no emergency drills during the voyage.

The stewards proved to be a major problem, being uncooperative and unhelpful, and demanding tips for almost every service they provided, varying from US$2.00 for a glass of water, through $10.00 for clean bed linen to a massive $100 for a day's use of a deckchair. The medical steward also rented out the hospital ward to 'interested couples'.

Unfortunately, some of the passengers definitely misbehaved, with liquor becoming a serious problem. One small group managed to steal some saki, while others obtained wine or hard liquor that were available by the bottle from the bars – or from the stewards at exorbitant prices. There were several very unpleasant incidents, including fights, assaults and molesting young women, and on several occasions the committee had no option but to take the humiliating course of asking the Japanese captain to exercise his disciplinary powers and place the American culprits in the brig.

Another – and equally humiliating – problem arose because one of the women passengers took to emptying her children's chamber pots out of the cabin window, but unfortunately the contents were carried by the wind into a kitchen further along the hull. Not surprisingly, this upset the kitchen staff on the receiving end, who complained bitterly and the committee had no choice but to offer an apology to the captain and crew.

There were also sub-committees for entertainment, welfare, children under five, children over five, and teenagers, as well as for baggage and finance.

At the request of the State Department, a warning against 'loose talk' was posted which stated that there was: '… reason to believe that wide publicity given on the occasion of the first exchange of nationals to stories of mistreatment of American citizens in the Far East was a factor in delaying the bringing about of the present exchange and in causing subsequent deterioration in the treatment accorded to civilians and prisoners of war held in the Far East.' All passengers were therefore urged that they '… should not lose sight of the consequences which might follow from loose or careless talk on their part lest such talk, whether or not strictly accurate, might cause resentment in quarters which could cause retaliation against those of our fellow citizens who have not yet been afforded an opportunity of repatriation.'

The final triumph of the main committee came on arrival in Mormugao where the public order sub-committee ensured an orderly disembarkation that lasted precisely one hour and 12 minutes, and the baggage sub-committee ensured that the massive quantity of luggage was cross-loaded to *Gripsholm* without fuss.

PERSONAL EXPERIENCES

Among the passengers to board at Hong Kong were the noted American author, Emily Hahn (known to all as 'Mickey') and her infant daughter, Carola.[7] Mickey was an extraordinary character to whom the normal rules did not seem to apply, who tended to be friends with all, and dismissive of officialdom. In this case, when she boarded she found the accommodation committee members 'bossy' as they directed her to a cabin, although they were probably only trying to do their job quickly and efficiently. As the voyage progressed she was soon on speaking terms with most on board, including the group of gamblers and drinkers who caused Mr Buss and his committee such problems. Mickey described the drinkers as the 'Dead-End Kids', and she was duly sent to deliver a message from the committee that they were to behave, although in view of the subsequent arrests this seems to have fallen on deaf ears.

Also among those to board *Teia Maru* at Hong Kong were two Canadian Army nurses: Lieutenants Kay Christie and May Waters. They had been captured with the rest of the Canadian contingent when the colony surrendered on 25 December 1941 and, after initially being allowed to continue nursing, were then put into a civilian internment camp, since the Japanese did not classify them as soldiers. They were included in the 1943 exchange where Kay described conditions aboard the *Teia Maru* as 'worse than the internment camp'.[8]

The British Consul-General at Mormugao watched the exchange operation and was impressed by the efficiency of the US arrangements. He noted the confusion caused as a result of the last-minute refusal by some 200 Japanese to leave the United States, which had come too late for their luggage to be removed from the ship's holds. These people had then been replaced by 200 other Japanese, whose baggage could not be loaded in time. This resulted in considerable confusion on the dockside at the exchange point.

More than this, however, he was greatly amused by the confusion caused by the Portuguese former Consul-General in Shanghai, who, although a neutral, had taken the opportunity to return home. He had fathered an illegitimate child in Shanghai and, being fond of it, had purchased it from its mother for 25,000 Chinese dollars and boarded *Teia Maru* together with the infant and a Chinese nurse. Meanwhile, the mother presented the cheque at a local bank, where it was immediately dishonoured, so she rushed aboard the ship, grabbed her baby and just made it back to the shore before the ship sailed. Unfortunately, the nurse could not be found in time, so that on landing in Mormugao, the Consul-General found himself with a nanny but without a baby – and a lot of explaining to do.[9]

16

The British–Japanese Exchange

Immediately following the Japanese attacks in South-East Asia, the British appointed a Protecting Power, initially selecting Argentina, but when this proved unacceptable to the Japanese, settled on Switzerland instead. As soon as this was resolved, the two countries negotiated to exchange their diplomats and other nationals. The original plan, proposed by the Japanese, was that the US and British exchanges should be conducted concurrently, which seemed to offer economies of effort and coordination. The British government bureaucracy took some time to respond, a major issue being that they wanted to ensure that no Japanese with valuable information on British matters, including any intended for the US–Japanese exchange, should be allowed to take part. The US government, however, quickly scotched both the idea of a coordinated exchange and of British involvement in who the Americans selected for exchange. As a result, the British were forced to proceed on their own and without any say on who was included in the US–Japanese exchange.

There are two misconceptions about this exchange. The first is that it was a single operation on the same lines as the US–Japanese exchange. But, as will be shown, in reality it consisted of two exchanges with only one Japanese ship in Lourenço Marques at any one time and, as a consequence, the Japanese ships did not sail in company with each other in either direction. The second misconception is that, as the name seems to suggest, it was a solely British affair. In fact, those covered by the term 'British' included not only Australians, New Zealanders, Indians, Egyptians and Sinhalese, but also a large number of citizens of European countries such as France, Norway and Poland.

For the United States, their two exchanges involved only one ship, *Gripsholm*, which sailed from New York to Lourenço Marques or Mormugao and back again, calling only at South American or South African ports to take on or disembark small numbers of passengers. The British were, however, faced with different problems because they had to assemble people for exchange from all Dominion countries except Canada. The outcome was a movement plan that involved no fewer than six ships – four British and two Japanese (see Table 11).

The *El Nil* was the most elderly ship involved, having been built in Germany and completed in 1914 as the *Marie Woerman*. She was requisitioned by the Allies in 1918 and purchased by the Dutch, following which she changed

Table 11: Ships Involved in the British–Japanese Exchange

	El Nil	City of Paris	City of Canterbury	Narkunda	Tatuta Maru	Kamakura Maru
Nationality	Egyptian*	British	British	British	Japanese	Japanese
Owner	Misr	Ellerman	Ellerman	P&O	NYK	NYK
Built	Germany	UK	UK	UK	Japan	Japan
Completed	1914	1922	1923	1920	1930	1930
Displacement	7,690 grt	10,902 grt	8,439 grt	16,227 grt	17,000 grt	17,500 grt
Length	426 ft	147.7 ft	136.7 ft	581 ft	583 ft	583 ft
Crew	c.250	196	196	c.300	250	250
Passengers:**						
1st	48	199	130	426		
2nd	52		48	247	840	840
Deck	1067					
Speed	14 kt	14.5 kt	13.5 kt	17 kt	21 kt	21 kt

*Chartered by British as troopship 1940.

**Peacetime figures.

hands several times before being bought by the Egyptian line, Misr, in 1933. During World War Two she was chartered by the British government for use as a troopship, while retaining her crew of British deck and engineer officers, and Egyptian purser and crew. Her departure from Liverpool, England, for Lourenço Marques did not go smoothly and she had to return to port twice. The first time was because confirmation of her safe passage had not been received from Germany and Italy, the second because some Japanese had been inadvertently left behind. However, on 30 July the ship finally set sail for Africa. She carried 73 Japanese and 43 Thais. Among these were over 30 members of the former Japanese Embassy in London, 27 of whom had been held in the internment camp in the Isle of Man, and five Thais who, on the outbreak of war, had been stranded in the Irish Republic.[1] The ship replenished at the Cape Verde Islands (9 August) and Walvis Bay (22 August), arriving at Lourenço Marques on 31 August 1942. *El Nil* was clearly painted for this voyage, with yellow upper works, black hull, and on each side large Union Jacks and the word 'DIPLOMAT' in huge letters. She travelled alone, was brightly lit and did not zigzag.[2]

The *City of Paris* was owned by the British Ellerman Line, a company well known for its smart and efficient ships. She was used to bring some 832 Japanese and Thais from India, where they had been interned, leaving Bombay on 13 August and arriving in Lourenço Marques on 28 August, the first British ship to arrive. She and the other Ellerman ship, *City of Canterbury*, were marked as follows, all the signs being illuminated at all times at night:[3]

- Three horizontal stripes in red, white and blue each 3 metres wide on decks fore and aft for recognition from the air.
- On each side of the hull, fore and aft, three vertical stripes, also red, white and blue.
- On each side amidships a large Union Jack and above it in large lettering the word 'DIPLOMAT'.

The *City of Canterbury*, also an Ellerman Line ship, was in Colombo, Ceylon, when chartered by the British government for this operation. She sailed on 13 July and arrived in Melbourne, Australia, on 4 August, where she was repainted to match *City of Paris*. Having embarked no fewer than 834 passengers and a strong contingent of military police, she sailed on 16 August, arriving in Lourenço Marques on 9 September.

The fourth British ship, the P&O company's *Narkunda*, sailed from the UK on a normal trooping voyage, delivering her passengers to Freetown, Sierra Leone, on 10 August. She then continued to Durban, South Africa, where she picked up 23 Japanese passengers, and, only now part of the exchange and thus on 'safe passage', sailed on to Lourenço Marques, arriving 1 September.

The two Japanese ships were virtually identical, both being built in Japan and joining the NYK fleet in 1930. Like all other Japanese liners, as soon as war broke out they were quickly requisitioned by the government and continued to be crewed by civilian merchant officers and seamen, but with their tasks and movements controlled by the military authorities. They were marked in the same way as *Asama Maru* on the US–Japanese exchange.

Tatuta Maru sailed from Yokohama on 30 July, with 454 passengers, her first port-of-call being Shanghai, China (3–4 August), where a further 324 embarked, most of whom had been working in China, but including 40 who had been brought from Manila and eight from Hong Kong. The ship then sailed to Saigon in French Indochina, remaining there on 9–10 August, where 144 passengers, 104 of them from Thailand, embarked. She then called at Singapore (12–14 August) where, according to British records, one woman and three children, all Dutch, embarked and, having replenished with fuel and water, she proceeded to Lourenço Marques, arriving on 27 August, the first exchange ship to arrive.

These passengers were a rich mixture. The great majority were 729 nationals of the United Kingdom and Dominions, but the remainder included Belgians (31), Czechs (3), Dutch (69), Egyptians (7), Free French (11), Greeks (6), Norwegians (47) and Poles (23), as well as one Russian and one American. The primary purpose of the voyage was to return diplomats and other government officials and their families, who constituted 312 of the total, the remaining 616 being businessmen, bankers, barristers, teachers, missionaries (including one Polish rabbi) and seamen (see Table 12, below).

Table 12: Passengers aboard *Tatuta Maru* on arrival at Lourenço Marques: 22 August 1942

Country of Origin	Officials		Non-Officials		TOTALS		GRAND TOTAL
	Male	*Family**	*Male*	*Family**	*Official*	*Non-Official*	
British, including Australia, New Zealand, UK	100	95	231	175	195	406	**601**
British-India	4	0	78	41	4	119	**123**
British-Ceylon	1	4	0	0	5	0	**5**
Belgium	6	10	7	8	16	15	**31**
Czechoslovakia	1	1	0	1	2	1	**3**
Egypt	4	3	0	0	7	0	**7**
Free French	4	7	0	0	11	0	**11**

| Country of Origin | Officials | | Non-Officials | | TOTALS | | GRAND TOTAL |
	Male	Family*	Male	Family*	Official	Non-Official	
Greece	2	0	4	0	2	4	6
Netherlands	19	15	30	5	34	35	69
Norway	10	8	20	9	18	29	47
Poland	7	9	5	2	16	7	23
Russia	0	1	0	0	1	0	1
United States	0	1	0	0	1	0	1
TOTALS	158	154	375	241	312	616	928

* Family includes wives, children and infants.
Source: Adapted from Passenger Register at TNA (PRO) FO 369/2737.

On arrival in Lourenço Marques, the British Ambassador to Tokyo, who had sailed aboard *Tatuta Maru*, reported that many of those leaving Japanese territory had been allowed to take only hand baggage, thus leaving behind furniture and other valuable property accumulated over years on station.[4] British people leaving Kobe were not allowed to take books, while at Manila cameras, binoculars and guns were confiscated. Those leaving Yokohama even had to hand over papers such as life insurance policies and bank deposit receipts. The haphazard nature of such seizures suggests that they were locally inspired and in most cases seem to have been little more than officially sanctioned looting. Even such high-level complaints to the Japanese government probably had little or no effect, but infuriating as this doubtless was, it was probably a small price to pay for avoiding three more years of incarceration.

Table 13: Senior Diplomats aboard *Tatuta Maru*

Station → Nation ↓	Japan	Philippines	Hong Kong	Indochina	Thailand
United Kingdom	Ambassador	Consul-General		Consul-General	Minister
Australia	Chargé d'Affaires				
Belgium	Ambassador	Consul	Consul-General		
Egypt	Chargé d'Affaires				

(continued)

Station → Nation ↓	Japan	Philippines	Hong Kong	Indochina	Thailand
Free France		Consul			
Greece	Minister				
Czechoslovakia	Minister				
Netherlands	Counsellor of Legation	Consul- General	Acting Consul- General		Chargé d'Affaires
Norway	Chargé d'Affaires	Acting Consul	Consul		Minister
Poland	Consul				

Kamakura Maru did not leave Yokohama until a full ten days after *Tatuta Maru*, but without any exchange passengers, all of whom (some 900) were embarked at Shanghai on 16–17 August.[5] She then proceeded direct to Singapore, arriving on 23 August and departing, having replenished, the next day. She arrived at Lourenço Marques on 8 September, a full five days after *Tatuta Maru* had left the Portuguese port.[6]

As this was the second exchange at Lourenço Marques the mechanics of the exchange went smoothly. As before, the ships moored alongside the same long pier, although not more than one Japanese ship was in harbour at the same time (see Table 14).

Tatuta Maru was alongside from 27 August to 2 September and embarked all of those from India brought by *City of Paris* (832), plus those from the UK brought by *El Nil* (115). Of these, 42 Thais were landed at Singapore, plus some 571 Japanese. Having disembarked these, *Tatuta Maru* took the remaining passengers to Japan.

Kamakura Maru was alongside in Lourenço Marques from 8 to 11 September. She embarked all those who had come from Australia aboard the *City of Canterbury* (834), plus a few others from other ships, sailing with a total of 870, of whom 450 Japanese and 4 Thais disembarked at Singapore. The majority of the Japanese who disembarked were among those removed from the Dutch East Indies in January, so that having travelled from the East Indies to Australia and thence twice across the Indian Ocean they were back at their posts after an absence of no more than six months.

The British ships spent far longer in Lourenço Marques than did the Japanese. *El Nil* lay alongside for 12 days, but then sailed with some 400 passengers, including the former British Ambassador to Tokyo, Sir Robert Craigie, and his staff, who landed safely at Liverpool on 9 October. *Narkunda*, which was outfitted to accommodate some 1,900 passengers, followed on 13 September with

Table 14: British–Japanese Exchange August–September 1942. Time in Lourenço Marques

Ships	August					September															
	27	28	29	30	31	1	2	3	4	5	6	7	8	9	10	11	12	13	14	15	16
El Nil					■	■	■	■	■	■	■	■	■	■	■	■					
City of Paris		■	■	■	■	■	■	■	■	■	■	■	■	■	■	■	■				
City of Canterbury														■	■	■	■	■	■	■	■
Narkunda						■	■	■	■	■	■	■	■	■	■	■	■	■			
Tatuta Maru	■	■	■	■	■	■	■	■													
Kamakura Maru													■	■	■	■					

only 875 passengers, which meant that she returned to England half empty. Of those, only 874 landed at Liverpool on 9 October, one, a Roman Catholic priest, having died and been buried at sea. Both ships called at Cape Town for a 24-hour stopover, where most of their passengers seized the opportunity for a brief 'run ashore' to a city little affected by wartime restrictions.

City of Paris and *City of Canterbury* sailed on 12 September and 16 September, respectively, both heading south to Durban, where they were repainted in normal wartime colours. Both then sailed in company to Suez, arriving on 11 October. They then proceeded independently, *City of Paris* directly to Bombay (27 October) while *City of Canterbury* called at Basra, Iraq (5–6 November), and Bandar Abbas, Iran (8–10 November), before reaching Bombay (16 November).

One of the odd features of this exchange was that on departing Lourenço Marques only *El Nil* and *Narkunda* made their complete return voyages under 'safe passage' rules, while the other two ships were on 'safe passage' only as far as Durban. This meant that passengers heading for India aboard *City of Paris* would be unprotected, as would the Australians and New Zealanders for whom a ship had yet to be found. This caused great discontent at Lourenço Marques, which included a 'sit-down strike' by many of the Indians and verbal protests by the Australians. One proposed solution was that since *Narkunda* was half-empty, she could take the entire party for the UK, releasing *El Nil* to take home the Indians and Australians. The Indians repeated their protests in Durban and eventually forced the government of India to issue them with life insurance for the duration of the voyage. As a result, *City of Paris* returned to Bombay in a series of escorted convoys, rather than sailing alone as she would have done on 'safe passage'.[7] The Australians, on the other hand, both the diplomats returning from Japan and the military police who had escorted the Japanese returnees from Melbourne to Lourenço Marques, were simply placed on the next ship sailing from South Africa to their homeland.

JAPANESE FROM AUSTRALIA

The complexities that often beset these exchanges, particularly for a minor partner, were well illustrated by the Australian involvement in the UK–Japanese exchange. Australia had declared war against Germany on 3 September 1939 and thereafter was a full participant on the Allied side, with its troops active in the Middle East and, from 7 December 1941, in the Far East, as well.

Japanese individuals and families had started spreading across the Far East from the early 1920s, the majority of these early immigrants being legitimate small traders, farmers, teachers, fishermen and the like. In the 1930s, however, the Japanese government instituted an official policy of sending individuals and families to various parts of the Far East, still ostensibly as traders or farmers, but whose real mission was to study local conditions, obtain military and commercial information, make contact with indigenous leaders and, in some cases, make plans for local government once Japan had defeated the military forces. The local colonial security police in territories such as the Dutch East Indies, British Malaya and Straits Settlements and French Indochina were aware of this threat, but were constrained from effective action until the outbreak of war.

In Australia, apart from the Japanese diplomatic staff, there were small numbers of Japanese scattered around the country and these were interned immediately following the outbreak of war, but the Commonwealth also accepted further groups from its neighbours. The Dutch were clear that one of the Japanese intentions was to secure the mineral wealth of the Netherlands East Indies and within days of the outbreak of war their security police had rounded up some 1,700 Japanese suspected subversives. They did not wish to hold them in camps close to any military operations, so, following an inter-government agreement, they were sent to Australia.

There they were interned in a newly constructed complex of prisoner-of-war and civilian internment camps, centred on a hamlet named Loveday in south Australia. Apart from the Japanese from the Dutch East Indies, the civilian internees in Loveday included Germans, Italians and Japanese who had been living in Australia, together with others who had been sent from the United Kingdom, New Zealand, the Pacific Islands, and the Middle East. Designed to hold a maximum of 5,000 internees, the numbers actually peaked at fractionally under 4,000 in March 1942.

A second group of Japanese was in French-ruled New Caledonia, who were mainly interested in the commercial possibilities, especially oil, nickel and chrome. The French colonial government in this territory was one of the first to 'rally' to de Gaulle and in December 1941 they quickly rounded up some 1,000 of these Japanese and, not wanting a camp on their own territory, also sent them to Australia.

As a result, the Japanese military found themselves deprived of their carefully planted 'eyes-and-ears' so, when negotiating the proposed exchange with the British, the names of most of these men, plus their families, were included in their list. For reasons that, with hindsight, appear inexplicable, almost every person asked for by the Japanese was agreed by the British, even those whose potential military roles had been correctly identified by Dutch and French security police. Whether this was due to regarding the return of British internees as being of greater importance, or, perhaps, to placate the Japanese so as not to prejudice future exchanges is not clear, but it could also have been an oversight or simple administrative incompetence.

For their part, the Australians also submitted a list of their nationals to the

British negotiators, which was duly passed on to the Japanese. This list included all the Australian diplomatic and consular staff in Japan and Japanese-conquered territories. The Japanese agreed to include the Australians from the legation in Tokyo, but told the British that they were unable to locate two particular named individuals: V. G. Bowden, who had been the Commonwealth's representative in Singapore, and D. Ross, who had been the consul in Dili in Portuguese Timor.

The Australians were dismayed and protested strongly to the British government and the position was reached where the Australians were on the verge of refusing to proceed, which could have meant either that no Australians at all would be included in the exchange or even that the whole exchange was wrecked. Accordingly, the British Deputy Prime Minister, Clement Atlee, cabled the Australians asking them not to prejudice the overall success of the exchange,[8] and, with understandable reluctance, the Australian prime minister agreed.[9]

This meant that the Japanese gained the return of many hundreds of their people who had been in the Dutch East Indies and New Caledonia. Nor was this the only advantage obtained by the Japanese, since they also retained a previous concession under which the British allowed them the valuable opportunity to send a number of diplomats to Lourenço Marques aboard the exchange ships who would then, with British permission, move to Japanese diplomatic posts in German-occupied Europe.[10]

When the *City of Canterbury* left Australia she carried 872 returnees, of whom 32 were Japanese diplomatic and consular officials, including the former ambassador, Kawai Tatsuo, and 834 (638 males, 90 females and 106 children) were Japanese from the internment camps.[11] The remainder had not been interned but wished to be repatriated: one Japanese woman, plus five Thais (one male, four female).[12] In return, Australia gained seven diplomats and 23 non-officials, not one of whom came from Singapore.[13] A further source of Australian discontent was that while 104 people were repatriated from Thailand, including British, Belgians and Dutch, not one Australian was repatriated from that country.[14] It is scarcely surprising that the Australian government felt that it had been badly treated in the whole affair, a feeling made worse when the Japanese government formally complained that its nationals had been harshly treated and poorly accommodated aboard the *City of Canterbury*.

PERSONAL EXPERIENCES

Peter Petersen,[15] an Englishman accompanied by his wife, Sybil, was the manager of the Hong Kong and Shanghai Bank branch on the island of Kulangsu, an 'international settlement' off the port of Amoy (now Xiamen). Control of the settlement was seized by Japanese troops at 4 a.m., 7 December 1941 and all non-Japanese in the international community were confined to their houses, but were otherwise not badly treated. In April 1942 they were told that they would be repatriated and in early May the entire international community was moved by a small coaster on a five-day voyage to Shanghai. There, together with people from other 'outstations', they were accommodated and fed in a hotel and given a monthly allowance by the Japanese, who also permitted them some freedom of movement.

The Americans in the group were repatriated aboard the *Conte Verde*, following which the Petersens and many others moved into the now empty American Club to await the British exchange. The Petersens then awaited the arrival of the *Tatuta Maru*, which sailed on 4 August. Their impressions were very favourable. The ship had huge white crosses painted on the sides and was brilliantly lit and not only were conditions and food good, but the waiters and stewards seem to have been friendly and cooperative. *Tatuta Maru* was the first to arrive at Lourenço Marques and to alleviate the wait the passengers were issued with a small allowance of Portuguese escudos by the Japanese and allowed ashore. It is clear that from the time they were interned to the time they left *Tatuta Maru* the Petersens had few complaints and considered their treatment to have been both proper and reasonable.

The Streatfields[16] were a British expatriate family living in Thailand when, on Monday 8 December 1941, the Japanese took over responsibility for foreigners. They were confined to their own house for a short period and then moved into a hotel, where food was less than they were used to, but on 23 December they were moved again, this time to a camp in the University of Moral and Political Sciences in Bangkok, where they were held, together with US and Dutch expatriates. The food was again less than usual, but was supplemented by supplies from friendly Thais. The camp was guarded by Thai nationals, under Japanese supervision, and, since it was officially classified as a civilian internment camp, it was visited periodically by a member of the Swiss consular staff.

Information that they were to be repatriated also came from the Swiss Consul, who on 3 April told the Americans that they would be going home, and on 13 April gave similar news to the British and Dutch. The Americans left for Saigon in late June, but the British and Dutch had to wait until 4 August when they boarded a small steamer that took them to Saigon, where they boarded the *Tatuta Maru*. Like the Petersens, Mrs Streatfield found it a 'lovely ship, fearfully overcrowded, of course, but the Japanese provided wonderful food: butter, meat, vegetables and fresh fruit'. During the four-day wait in Lourenço Marques the Streatfields went ashore every day, where they were well looked after by the British community. They then boarded *El Nil* for the voyage to Liverpool.

Farmer[17] was a civilian working in the International Concession at Canton when it was taken over by the Japanese army on 8 December 1941. He and his fellow internees were treated correctly and then taken by ship to Shanghai where they were accommodated in the Cathay Hotel. Again they were treated well, even being allowed out into the city, provided they told the reception desk where they were going and when they would be due back. They boarded *Tatuta Maru* 4 August and sailed for Lourenço Marques. Farmer's only comments on the ship were that she was overcrowded and there were too few toilet and washing facilities.

Among those exchanged were a number of Norwegians, including diplomats from the embassy and consulates, as well as 12 merchant seamen, plus two of their wives and a child. Captain K. W. Nyquist had been the master of the Panamanian-registered SS *Foch* (2,894 grt), an elderly ship (built in 1905) and he was aboard his ship in Yokohama on 8 December 1941. He was immediately interned, while his ship was requisitioned and renamed *Hoshi Maru*. Nyquist was held by the Yokohama police until 29 December when he was sent to Negishi internment camp. But he was selected for exchange and sent to a camp near Tokyo on 24 June 1942, before boarding *Tatuta Maru* on 30 July at Yokohama and there must have been great delight in Shanghai when his wife and son joined him for the voyage to Lourenço Marques.

Another Norwegian to join *Tatuta Maru* in Yokohama was Ordinary Seaman Trygve Lindeberg who had been paid off from his ship in 1938 with TB and had remained in Japanese hospitals ever since. He was told he would be on the first exchange, but as this was confined to citizens of North and South America this did not happen, although he was then included in the second exchange. The British took him from Lourenço Marques to South Africa where he was again admitted to hospital.

A major feature of the Japanese exchanges was a lack of consistency between the various parts of the Japanese Empire and its occupied territories. Thus, the Japanese wife and son of a US businessman, all resident in Japan, were prevented from accompanying him to the United States on the US–Japanese exchange a month previously, because the authorities were not prepared to see one of their own race depart for the hated West. But, on this British–Japanese exchange Mrs Clarke, the wife of a British banker, and Mrs A. J. Smith, the wife of a British official, both ethnic Japanese, and both accompanied by their sons, left China without fuss and reached England safely aboard *El Nil*.

17

Relief Supplies to Prisoners-of-War and Civilian Internees in the Far East

As soon as it was clear that the Japanese had captured large numbers of its citizens, both as prisoners-of-war and as civilian internees, the United States government began to devote considerable effort towards ameliorating their lot. Primarily, this involved negotiating the delivery of relief supplies.

In its first effort, in early/mid 1942, the US government chartered a Swedish vessel, the *Vasaland*, then lying in Gothenburg, Sweden, to carry relief supplies from the United States to the Far East. *Vasaland* was normally used to carry iron ore across the Baltic to Germany and the German government would not allow her to exit the Baltic, although whether this denial of safe passage was in order not to offend its ally, Japan, or for economic reasons as it did not want to lose trans-Baltic shipping capacity, has not been established.

The next attempt came about as a direct result of a talk given by a US army colonel to the San Francisco Press Club on the terrible experiences of US soldiers at Bataan. The club immediately coordinated an appeal fund, which raised enough money to purchase supplies and, in cooperation with the American Red Cross, chartered a ship to carry them across the Pacific.

The ship selected was M/S *Kanangoora*, owned by Rederi AB Transatlantic of Gothenburg, Sweden, a modern vessel, completed in 1938, with a gross registered tonnage of 8,226 and a speed of 13 knots. The ship was immediately taken to a San Francisco shipyard where she was refitted and repainted in preparation for the mission, which included painting her white overall, with several very large red crosses on either side of the hull.[1]

The plan was to load her with food and medical supplies to the value of US$1,000,000 (1942 prices) and send her under 'safe passage' either to deliver her cargo to a Japanese port or to cross-load it into a Japanese freighter at some mutually convenient spot, possibly Lourenço Marques in Mozambique or Mormugao. Yet a third possibility was that the ship would sail to a port designated by the Japanese where not only the supplies, but the ship as well would be handed over to a Japanese crew, which would sail it around the Pacific distributing the supplies and then return the ship to the neutral port and its original crew. *Kanangoora* was diesel-powered and ship's systems of that period were generally very similar and relatively unsophisticated, so such a transfer to a totally new crew would probably not have taken more than about 48 hours.

Refit and painting was completed in August 1942, following which most of the supplies were assembled and loaded, but to no avail, as the Japanese refused to sanction the project and it had to be dropped. *Kanangoora* subsequently sailed to New York where most of the stores were cross-loaded to the liner *Gripsholm* for her second exchange at Mormugao in October 1943.

The prospect of using the ships involved in the Lourenço Marques exchange proved more realistic. All passenger liners had a cargo-carrying capability, if only for passengers' baggage, although most were usually capable of carrying somewhat more. Thus, when she left Lourenço Marques, *Gripsholm* carried several hundred tons of green tea for distribution to Japanese internees in the US, which had been brought to the exchange aboard *Asama Maru*. Returning eastwards, *Asama Maru* carried the stores brought from the US and Canada by *Gripsholm*, plus others from South Africa that had been brought to Lourenço Marques by train. The total carried was 22,160 food parcels (each weighing 11 lb), 271 cases of drugs, 25,000 packs of cigarettes and 4,869 tins of tobacco, as well as large quantities of clothing, shoes and toiletries. As far as is known, the second ship, *Conte Verde*, did not carry any relief supplies on its return to the Far East.

The second US–Japanese exchange at Mormugao in October 1943 built on the success of the first and *Gripsholm* delivered some 140,000 packages with a value of US$1.5 million, which had been sent by various agencies in the United States and Canada. Some of this had originally been intended for delivery by *Kanangoora*, but there were also next-of-kin parcels, together with welfare goods, such as books, recreational equipment and religious material.

The British also sent goods for delivery to their PoWs and civil internees, in this case in Singapore and Hong Kong. These were delivered in the British ships to Lourenço Marques, where they were loaded aboard the *Tatuta Maru* and *Kamakura Maru*.

Many of the American passengers aboard the *Gripsholm* on the first exchange gave their horror stories to the press as soon as they got home and as a result the US government became increasingly concerned about the welfare of those still in Japanese custody. Thus, in early 1943 a new tack was tried, and the US Ambassador in Moscow, Rear-Admiral (retired) William Harrison Standley, approached the Soviet government, which although allied with the US and the UK against Germany was neutral with regard to Japan. Standley made his original proposal in February 1943 and repeated it in March and April, but the Soviet government clearly thought it a very minor matter in comparison with its fight for survival against Nazi Germany and in August 1943 Standley was told that the matter was closed.

Within days of being told of that decision, Standley took advantage of his farewell meeting with Stalin to raise the subject direct with the Soviet dictator and implied that a renewal of the Lend-Lease agreement would be dependent on help in moving relief supplies to Japan. This was reinforced by a detailed proposal submitted by the State Department a few days later and Stalin formally agreed, although it was clear that he still considered it much less important than did the Americans.

The Soviet agreement was given on 26 August 1943, and within days Soviet cargo ships began arriving at Portland, Oregon, where they collected a mixture of Lend-Lease and Red Cross relief supplies. The first ship sailed in late September, followed by three more in October and the fifth in December, and between them these ships carried 2,500 tons of relief supplies, 1,000 tons more than the Soviets had actually agreed to. All these supplies were landed at Vladivostok.

There then followed a further long delay while three-way negotiations took place with the Japanese, via the Swiss, and direct with the Soviets, and it was not until 6 June 1944 that agreement was reached, albeit with some important provisos. On the Soviet side, they refused to allow Japanese ships into Vladivostok harbour for reasons of national security; war against Japan was a distinct possibility and Japanese inspection of the main Soviet Far Eastern military base was clearly not wanted. The Soviets did, however, agree to the one-time use of the smaller, less important port of Nakhodka, which was some 100 miles by rail and 60 miles by air from Vladivostok.

The Japanese were much more demanding, because they realized how desperate the Americans were to get aid to their fellow citizens. In the first place, the Americans wanted the supplies to be moved onwards in one large ship, which the Japanese refused, stipulating that they would employ a number of small ships. This may have been because they wanted to see how the system would work, but the more likely explanation is that their merchant fleet was already badly depleted and they were just not prepared to divert larger ships to what they regarded as much less essential tasks. In addition, the Japanese were able to induce the US government to agree that a ship carrying relief supplies could also carry whatever passengers and other cargo the Japanese saw fit, that no US ship or submarine would approach, nor would the US board and search any such vessel, even if they suspected it was carrying contraband goods. Such an agreement was without precedent and the 'no searching' went beyond the international rules even for hospital ships and gave the Japanese carte blanche to carry virtually whatever they wished.

The first requirement was to move the relief supplies from the Soviet Union to Japan and the ship selected was the *Hakusan Maru*,[2] a 4,300-ton vessel belonging to the Japan Sea Steamship Company (Nippon Yūsen Kaisha = NYK). The Japanese notified this to the US government (via the Swiss) on 21 October 1944, together with the proposed route from Niigata in Japan to Najin in north-eastern Korea and then to Nakhodka, where it would load 1,000 tons of US-supplied

Red Cross relief that had, in the meantime, been moved from Vladivostok to Nakhodka by the Soviet authorities. *Hakusan Maru* would then return to Japan, calling once again at Najin and then at Moji, before completing her voyage in Osaka. The Japanese scheduled dates for each stage of the journey.

The Japanese subsequently altered the schedule, but were careful to inform the US authorities, who, in turn, told the fleet. Even so, *Hakusan Maru* left Nakhodka four days ahead of the revised schedule, although, once again, the US was told, as was the Soviet Ministry of Foreign Affairs in Moscow.

Hakusan Maru delivered 91 passengers and stores to Najin, where she remained for three days. This was permitted in the agreement made with the United States, but it was contrary to the spirit of 'safe passage' as understood by the international community, as it was, in effect, using a ship engaged in carrying humanitarian supplies to move their own nationals, almost certainly for military reasons.

Be that as it may, *Hakusan Maru* then proceeded to Nakhodka where she off-loaded mail and relief supplies (73 cases of books and 32 tons of Japanese tea) for onward dispatch to Japanese internees in Australia, the UK and the US. *Hakusan Maru* then loaded approximately 2,000 tons of US relief supplies (more than in the agreement) and after only 36 hours in the Soviet port sailed again. She spent 24 hours at Najin, where she offloaded 100 tons of supplies for US prisoners in Korea, and arrived at Kobe one day later than scheduled.

According to the American Red Cross *Hakusan Maru*'s cargo comprised relief supplies from four sources. From the American Red Cross came: food parcels: 205,932; drugs: 2,516 cases; tropical clothing: 15,040 sets; heavy clothing: 4,465 sets; overcoats: 7,050; shoes: 4,176 pairs; shoe repair kits: 123; comfort sets: 15,630; and cigarettes: 99 cases. British Red Cross supplies comprised: food parcels: 81,534; miscellaneous foodstuffs: 37 cases; and shoes: 195 pairs. The Canadian Red Cross supplied 42,016 food parcels. Finally, there were 294 cases of recreational and educational supplies from the YMCA.

There were now some 1,900 tons of relief supplies in warehouses in Japan, of which 800 tons were immediately distributed to PoW camps in Japan, leaving 1,100 tons to be transported overseas. On 23 December 1944 the Japanese government informed the United States that the first onward delivery would be to US prisoners-of-war in camps in China. This would be undertaken by *Hoshi Maru* (2,583 tons), formerly the Panamanian-registered *Foch*, which had been seized in Yokohama on 7 December 1941. She was an antiquated vessel, having been completed in 1905, but the Japanese needed every ship they could get their hands on, so she was renamed *Hoshi Maru* and given a Japanese crew.

The plan passed to the US government was for her to sail from Moji on 7 January 1945, going direct to Shanghai, returning to Moji on 28 January. The United States was told that she would carry 275 tons of food and medicines for

PoWs and internees, but what they were not told was that she would also carry 15 tons of gold bullion and 7.5 billion newly minted Chinese Yuan, required to bolster banks in the Japanese-occupied territory's failing economy.

The Japanese master was told before sailing that he must adhere to the schedule communicated to the United States, but, despite that, he left one day late then drove his ancient ship so hard that he arrived at Shanghai one day early. Once there, he was reminded yet again to stick to the plan but still declined to do so, leaving Shanghai a day early and going to Tsingtao empty where he loaded with coal and pig iron (plus some whiskey and opium for senior officers), then returned to Kobe, Japan, rather than Moji, as in the schedule. The US Navy was aware, through intercepts and decrypts, that these transgressions were taking place, but refrained from taking action or even making any comment. Apart from the relief stores, the goods transported were in breach of the spirit, if not the letter, of the agreement.

The failure to stick to the agreed schedule by the masters of both *Hakusan Maru* and *Hoshi Maru* is sometimes given as an example of bad faith, but there could well have been valid reasons for this. When sailing in a wartime convoy, merchant ship masters had no choice but to comply with the rules as to course, speed, arrival times, and so on, but in this case the safe-conduct ship was sailing on its own, thus inevitably increasing the master's apprehension for the safety of his ship and crew. The voyage planners in Tokyo and Washington, who were far removed from the realities of the sea, agreed on a very slow speed for the ships, apparently to make it more obvious to US submarines, but this went against all the beliefs of merchant masters for four reasons.

First, in peacetime it was common working practice among merchant ship masters to arrive at their destination one day early, in order to meet their company's schedule. In peacetime there was no threat, so they would then wait offshore for a pilot to become available, but in wartime this was clearly ill advised so they would enter harbour as soon as practicable. Secondly, it was a widely held view among merchant ship captains that proceeding at maximum speed reduced the chance of a successful attack by a submarine. Thirdly, a ship sailing slowly was much more difficult to steer and control, particularly in heavy seas, making it very uncomfortable, even for experienced mariners. Finally, weather would have been a major consideration. In January the Sea of Japan is subject to the North East Monsoon and a contemporary authority states that: 'The strength of the wind in the open sea averages about Beaufort Force 5 (fresh) in the north, rising to 6 (strong breeze) ... At the height of the season in December and January, winds are likely to reach Beaufort Force 7 (near gale) or above on 6–10 days per month over much of the area between Indo-China, the Northern Philippines, Formosa and Japan; the stormiest area is to the eastward of the Northern Philippines and Formosa, where winds of this strength are likely on over 11 days per month. In the Yellow Sea their frequency is about 3–6 days per month, while south of the tenth parallel it decreases to 1–3 days per month or less.' Also: 'The weather in the vicinity of land is greatly affected by the exposure to the prevailing monsoon; where the latter blows ashore, and especially when the coast is backed by high ground, cloud amounts are larger and rainfall heavier than in the open sea, while to leeward of high ground fairer conditions prevail. In the open ocean visibility is good except when reduced by rain. Off the coast of China and Indo-China however, poor visibility becomes increasingly frequent after December …' Thus, the master of a relatively small merchant vessel, heavily loaded, in waters patrolled by US submarines, and with potentially extreme weather to contend with had plenty to worry about and the schedule laid down by distant bureaucrats must have seemed among the least of his worries.

According to post-war research by the International Committee of the Red Cross (ICRC) a total of 225,000 Red Cross parcels were loaded aboard Japanese ships at Lourenço Marques and Mormugao, and were delivered as follows:

- First US–Japanese exchange (September 1942). *Asama Maru*: 6,993 parcels, all delivered to Japan.
- Second US–Japanese exchange (1943). *Teia Maru*: 48,760 parcels split between Singapore, Manila and Japan.
- British–Japanese exchange. *Tatuta Mar*: 48,818 parcels, all to Singapore. *Kamakura Maru*: 32,940 parcels, all to Hong Kong.

There were also other relief stores, such as those listed for *Hakusan Maru* above.

What really mattered was not what was carried by the ships, or offloaded at the ports, but how much was actually received by the prisoners-of-war and civilian internees in the camps, who needed them so desperately. In a post-war study the New Zealand government concluded that average actual issues to PoWs and civilian internees over the entire period of their incarceration (i.e., from approximately January 1942 to August 1945) were:

- In camps in mainland Japan, an average of four to five food parcels per prisoner, except those in Zentsuji who, for unexplained reasons, received anything up to 20 parcels.
- In China and Hong Kong PoWs and civilians also received about four or five parcels, in addition to a certain amount of bulk food that was used to augment the camp meals.
- In Singapore both PoWs and civilians received a fraction of a food parcel (sometimes as low as one-sixteenth) on three occasions, as well as some bulk food.
- PoWs in the work parties in Thailand received a fraction (as little as one-seventeenth) on one occasion, in 1944.

- In Java and Sumatra PoWs received fractions of a parcel on two occasions; civilians, a tiny fraction on one occasion.
- Men in Macassar received nothing at all.

There were several reports that after the camps were liberated stockpiles of food parcels and other supplies were found, but why these had never been distributed was never properly established. In some cases it may have been a deliberate policy on the part of Japanese higher authority, in some, malevolence on the part of the camp staff, but in others, simple incompetence or inefficiency.

18

The Sinking of the Awa Maru

When analysed, many of the worst military tragedies are usually found not to be the result of one single disastrous pronouncement, miscalculation or act, but rather the consequence of a series of minor, perhaps even trivial, events or decisions. Further, hindsight will often show that if the outcome of any one of those contributory events had been different, the disaster might well have been averted. Few cases prove this more conclusively than the sinking of the Japanese liner, *Awa Maru*, on the night of 1 April 1945 with the loss of approximately 2,000 lives, even though she was sailing under a properly authorized safe conduct, and despite being correctly marked and on the agreed course.[1] This disaster was perpetrated by torpedoes from USS *Queenfish* (SS-393), a well-found and efficiently run submarine, commanded by a competent, experienced and conscientious captain and manned by a well-trained and experienced crew.

There were three types of ship that could travel with (supposed) immunity from attack in wartime. First were hospital ships, usually converted liners, which were permitted to carry only wounded or sick personnel and, under the Hague (1907) and Geneva (1929) Conventions, the doctors, nurses and other medical personnel were 'protected personnel'. In addition, the ship's crew were considered to be equally protected, in the same way as stretcher-bearers or ambulance drivers, since they were essential to the operation. Hospital ships generally sailed between ports on the same side, for example, from the UK to Canada, or Australia to the US and by international agreement were painted white all over, marked with large red crosses, and were well lit at night. In addition, such ships were registered with the ICRC at Geneva, who informed all concerned of their names, appearance and characteristics. Even this did not protect them entirely and an Australian hospital ship, *Centaur*, was sunk on 14 May 1943, with the loss of 238 of its 332-strong crew and medical personnel. It was not carrying any casualties at the time, but nevertheless was fully protected under the Hague and Geneva Conventions.[2]

The second type was a cartel ship that, in time of war and by mutual agreement, moved between two belligerents in performance of a specific mission, usually exchanging wounded prisoners-of-war, protected persons (e.g., doctors, nurses) or civilian internees. In earlier times, such cartel ships had also been used to carry proposals between two hostile powers, although this role had little significance by the time of World War Two when all nations communicated by telegraph or radio. Such a ship was permitted to carry no cargo, ammunition or warlike stores, but was allowed to carry just one gun (and, by inference, the necessary ammunition) for signalling purposes.

The third type was a 'safe conduct' ship (also known as safe passage) that, as a result of a specific agreement, made its way to a particular place in order to undertake a specified mission. This required a documented agreement between the two parties, and at least tacit agreement by any third party through whose waters the ship might pass.

The difference between cartel and safe passage was not entirely clear, even to lawyers, but an example might clarify matters a little. In 1942 the Swedish liner *Gripsholm* was lying in a Swedish port when it was chartered by the US government to take Japanese repatriates from New York to Lourenço Marques and then return with US repatriates to New York. During the voyage New York-Lourenço Marques-New York it was a cartel ship, but it required 'safe passage' from the Germans to pass through the Baltic and those parts of the North Sea controlled by the German Navy as opposed to the British Royal Navy.

The Japanese ship *Awa Maru* was a mixed cargo/passenger liner built for the Nippon Yūsen Kaisha Kisen (Japan Mail Steamship Company = NYK) for use on their profitable Japan-Australia route. The hull was laid down in July 1941 and launched in August 1942, but by that time the war was already six months old and instead of luxurious passenger accommodation the ship was fitted out for military use as a troop/cargo ship, with austere living spaces, maximized cargo capacity and with a light armament of two deck guns and four depth charges mounted aft, although what practical use any of these could have been is open to question.

When completed in March 1943, *Awa Maru* continued to bear her name, even though she had already been requisitioned by the Imperial Japanese Army's Transport Command, to which she was known, more prosaically, as *Ship Number 5032*. The army controlled the ship's movements and loads throughout its working life, although the crew was always civilian and provided by NYK, a practice common among all seafaring nations in wartime. The ship had a full load displacement of 11,249 tons, was 508 feet long and had a beam of 41 feet. Power was provided by a single Mitsubishi 14,000 horsepower diesel engine, giving her a cruising speed of 17 knots. She had a crew of 149 officers and men, the master being Captain Hamada Matsutarō, a capable and efficient officer, who commanded her throughout her working life.

Awa Maru was a valuable asset for the Japanese war effort, being fast, well adapted for her role, and capable of carrying many passengers as well as a considerable amount of cargo and, her final voyage apart, always sailed in fast convoys with ships of similar high performance. As the US Navy's submarine attacks bit deeper these convoys were given as much of an escort as the Imperial Japanese Navy (IJN) could provide, although such protection was always inadequate and most convoys were attacked and suffered losses. Indeed, the IJN anti-submarine capability was so poor that the US submarines frequently attacked on the surface, using radar to aim their torpedoes.

Awa Maru's first convoy left the Japanese port of Moji[3] on 19 July 1943 and called briefly at Takao[4] in Formosa (25–26 July) before reaching Singapore (1 August). Her next known movement was sailing from Singapore (3 November) calling at Takao (10–11 November) and reaching Moji (November 16). There were no losses to the convoy on the outward voyage, but several ships were lost during the return. On her second voyage *Awa Maru* again sailed from Moji to Singapore and back, leaving on 1 February 1944 and returning on 8 April. Her third voyage was again to Singapore, but this time via Manila, returning to Japan on 26 June, during which one ship was lost to a US submarine. So far, *Awa Maru* had been lucky but on her fourth voyage she was hit by two torpedoes but was beached and then recovered by a tug and towed to Manila. Following repairs the ship returned to Japan and undertook yet another voyage to Singapore returning via Saigon with a number of Japanese passengers and some 500 Allied prisoners, who were confined to the holds in atrocious conditions; she arrived in Moji on 13 January 1945. Thus, by this time Captain Hamada and his crew were thoroughly experienced in both wartime conditions and in sailing in the South China Sea.

As soon as she was unloaded in January 1945 *Awa Maru* was sent to the dockyard in Kobe where she was prepared for a 'Safe Passage Mission'. Her entire hull and superstructure were painted green and she was given a number of large white crosses, and additional lights were also fitted so that these crosses could be illuminated at night. While this work was going on she was loaded with her cargo of Red Cross relief supplies for Allied prisoners-of-war, estimates of the amount varying between 800 and 2,000 tons; however, it by no means filled her holds to capacity. There was also a ton of gold for delivery under a government-to-government agreement with Thailand.

Awa Maru was then moved to Ujina, near Hiroshima, where her guns and depth-charges were removed, although special explosive devices for destroying the ship were installed, which were intended to be used if threatened with capture by the enemy. This was, at the very least, a technical breach of the 'safe passage', since such ships were, by custom and practice, liable to be stopped by warships of the opposing navy and searched to make sure that the rules were being obeyed.[5] She was then loaded with military supplies for Japanese forces in Burma, Indochina and Malaya, following which she sailed to Moji, where some of the items just loaded in Ujina were offloaded again. Finally, a small number of passengers came aboard, taking advantage of the opportunity for a safe voyage to Japan's south-eastern conquests.

The humanitarian mission entrusted to Captain Hamada and *Awa Maru* was accomplished as planned, with deliveries of Red Cross supplies being made at Takao in Formosa, Hong Kong (22 February), Saigon (24–28 February), Singapore (2 March) and Batavia in the Dutch East Indies. Following offloading, some of the supplies were undoubtedly pilfered by stevedores and others, but the majority appear to have reached their intended recipients. These were quite proper to be carried in a safe passage ship; but, the military supplies, most of which were landed at Saigon, were not.

The first load for return to Japan had been taken on board during the Saigon stopover, and comprised rice, electrical machinery and some 480 Japanese merchant seamen who had survived the loss of their ships. In Jakarta several thousand tons of baled rubber were loaded and the ship then moved to Muntok, a small port on Banka Island off the north coast of Sumatra where some 2,500 tons of refined and crude oil were loaded, plus tin ingots, tungsten and drilling machinery. Then it was back to Singapore where more tin and rubber was loaded, and, of greater significance in what was to come, some 1,700 passengers, who were a mixture of military and civilian government officials, businessmen and scientists. Even as early as March 1945 there was a clear feeling that Japanese defeat was inevitable and that for many people in what the Japanese government proclaimed to be the 'South-East Asia Co-Prosperity Sphere', *Awa Maru* represented the final opportunity to get home before the total collapse.

On 3 April a large force of USAAF bombers dropped mines in the Shimonoseki Strait astride *Awa Maru*'s homeward route, and so a new route was devised and duly communicated to the American government. *Awa Maru* sailed for Japan on the morning of 28 March 1945 with a heavy load of passengers and cargo; her humanitarian mission had been on the outward leg only, but her safe-passage status covered the homeward leg as well, and, still covered with white crosses, she headed north-eastwards across the South China Sea. The following day two US aircraft overflew the ship, recognized her safe-passage markings and, apart from taking a photograph, allowed her to continue unmolested on her way, and two US submarines, warned of her mission and appearance, also saw her and let her pass in safety. On 1 April the ship, forced, as were all Japan's ships by this time, to hug the shore wherever possible, entered the Straits of Formosa, which run between the island of Formosa (Taiwan) and the mainland province of Fukien.

USS *Queenfish* (SS-393),[6] a Balao-class submarine, had been commissioned on 30 November 1944. She was 311 feet 6 inches long with a submerged displacement of 2,411 tons and was armed with ten 21-inch torpedo-launching tubes, six in the bow and four in the stern, for which she carried a total of 24 torpedoes. Gun armament comprised a single 5 inch gun, one 40 mm and one 20 mm cannon. Her two diesel engines gave her a speed on the surface of

20 knots while her batteries gave her a maximum submerged speed of 9 knots. Maximum depth was 400 feet. Like all US Navy World War Two submarines she was essentially a torpedo boat that fought on the surface, but which could submerge when required to do so, albeit with limited range and endurance. A most important part of her equipment was that she was fitted with an SJ radar that enabled her to detect targets when on the surface and which was sufficiently accurate, when used in conjunction with the torpedo-launching equipment, to aim the torpedoes very precisely.

The commanding officer was Commander Charles Elliott Loughlin, USN, who had five other officers and 60 crew. Commissioned in 1933, Commander Loughlin had served in submarines since 1938 and had commanded the elderly USS *S-14* (SS-119) in 1943 and early 1944, before standing-by *Queenfish* in the final months prior to her commissioning in March 1944, when he took full command. His crew included a large number of men with previous combat experience and were an immediate success in the Pacific war against the Japanese. Once in the Pacific *Queenfish* came under command of Commander Submarines, Pacific (COMSUBPAC), whose headquarters were at Guam.

On his first patrol that lasted 59 days in August–September 1944, Laughlin sank 15,000 tons of Japanese shipping and rescued 18 Allied prisoners-of-war who had survived the sinking of their prison ship en route to Japan. The second patrol lasted 35 days and again resulted in sinking four enemy ships. The third patrol lasted for 32 days and was rather less successful as during a night attack on a convoy on 16/17 January Loughlin launched eight torpedoes, which for reasons unknown failed to hit a single target. On her return to Pearl Harbor *Queenfish* was taken in hand by the dockyard and given much new equipment, including additional radars and sensors, as well as the very latest Mark XVIII-2 torpedoes.

Once the principle of the relief voyage and safe passage had been agreed between the two governments, using Switzerland as an intermediary, the Japanese informed the United States that *Awa Maru* would follow a specified route and be prominently marked with large white crosses. Two of these would be painted on each side of the hull and one on each side of the funnel, with further crosses for aerial identification on the top of the bridge and on the hatch covers of one hold forward and one hold aft. In addition, at night the crosses on the funnels would be floodlit and the ship would display all its usual peacetime navigation lights.

The first message describing the *Awa Maru*, her itinerary and her safe passage was broadcast by Commander-in-Chief Pacific Fleet on 7 February 1945. Because high frequency broadcasts were not always reliable, due to interference, fading and other phenomena, this message was transmitted three times on each of three successive nights, a total of nine times in all. Also, because it contained information already well known to the enemy – and possibly also so that the

Japanese could monitor it and thus be reassured – it was transmitted in plain language.

At this time *Queenfish* was sailing from Hawaii to Saipan from where she would commence her fourth war patrol and it proved to be a period of particularly bad radio reception so that only parts of the message were received. These problems were related to the radio, but for the first time the human factor intervened because experience in all navies throughout the war was that messages of any significance were always encrypted, and it appears that the radio crewmen aboard *Queenfish* may have given a garbled plain language message lower priority than it deserved.

Following the transmission of the first message, the Japanese changed the route and notified the US government accordingly, as a result of which COMSUBPAC transmitted a new message to his submarines. This was again transmitted three times on three successive nights (6–8 March) and was again in plain language.

At this time *Queenfish* was lying alongside a submarine depot ship in Saipan and as was normal practice her radios were closed down and the depot ship's radio room acted as 'communications guard', receiving any messages for the submarines and producing hard copies that were then either delivered by hand or, as happened in this case, collected by one of the submarine's radio crew. Once aboard *Queenfish*, the significance was not appreciated and it was never shown to the commanding officer. This was undoubtedly a major error, but quite why it happened has never been established, except that since, by definition, Commander Loughlin could not know about a message he had not been shown, it was not his fault, although as commanding officer he was responsible for all actions, whether of commission or omission, aboard his ship.

For her forthcoming patrol, *Queenfish* was due to operate in a 'wolf pack' with two other submarines, USS *Spot* (SS-413) and *Sea Fox* (SS-402), and the three commanding officers were given an oral briefing at Saipan before they sailed. This was conducted by a briefing team from COMSUBPAC who flew from Guam for the purpose. Not once during this briefing was the forthcoming voyage of the *Awa Maru* mentioned, which, with hindsight, seems an unusual omission. The three submarines sailed on 24 February (*Spot*), 8 March (*Sea Fox*) and 9 March (*Queenfish*).

Once in her operational area, *Queenfish* formed a 'pack' with *Spot* and *Sea Fox* in the South China Sea-Formosa area, but when *Spot*, having expended all her torpedoes, left to replenish on 17 March, Loughlin, as next senior, took command of the two-boat pack. Despite diligent searches no targets were found but on 28 March, COMSUBPAC, with the sailing of *Awa Maru* from Singapore imminent, sent yet another radio message to all submarines at sea, this time encrypted. The message read, in part:

… Let pass safely the *Awa Maru* carrying prisoner of war supplies. She will be passing through your areas between March 30 and April 4. She is lighted at night and plastered with white crosses …

This message was definitely received by *Queenfish* and for the first time was seen by Loughlin, but in this case the sender failed to stipulate the route to be followed or even the areas through which *Awa Maru* would be passing. Thus, as the message was addressed to all submarines at sea – of which there were dozens covering a huge area from north of Japan to Australia and from the central Pacific to the South China Sea – none of the recipients knew to which of them it was addressed. When Loughlin saw the message he commented on this lack of precision, but since he had not seen either of the two previous messages, he did not appreciate that it might apply to him.

On 29 March *Queenfish* and *Sea Fox* parted company, although still forming part of the same pack with Loughlin in command. *Queenfish* moved northwards to seek targets off the mouth of the Yangtze river, but without success. At 19.40 hours 1 April 1945, *Queenfish* received a message from *Sea Fox* that the latter had attacked a convoy of three merchantmen and four escorts at 13.00 hours but had damaged only one of the freighters before losing contact in dense fog. Loughlin quickly calculated a predicted position for the convoy survivors and set course to intercept.

It was standard operating procedure for US submarines working as members of a wolf pack that as soon as possible after making contact with the enemy they would inform other pack members so that all could converge on the target, thus bringing overwhelming force to bear. It was thus remiss of *Sea Fox* to delay sending the message (although there may have been sound operational reasons for doing so) but the unfortunate – and obviously totally unintended – result was to place *Queenfish* on a converging course not only with the convoy but also with the *Awa Maru*, which, by chance, was in the same area, but not part of the convoy.

Thus, at about 23.00 on the night of 1 April 1945, *Queenfish* was sailing on the surface and heading for the convoy when her radar operator spotted a solitary 'blip' on the screen at a range of 17,000 yards, which was moving at a steady speed of 16 knots and on a straight course (i.e., not zigzagging). Immediately going to battle stations, Loughlin went to the bridge and, with all weapon and sensor crews closed up, *Queenfish* headed straight for the target, which was totally invisible to them due to the dense sea fog. In the experience of the command team aboard *Queenfish* a typical Japanese merchantman sailed at about 8 to 10 knots and followed a zigzag course, whereas this was much faster and from its course appeared to be heading directly for the convoy that *Sea Fox* had attacked earlier. They therefore concluded that this was a Japanese destroyer speeding to bolster the anti-submarine support to the convoy. This conclusion was supported by the relatively small size of the blip on the screen, which matched that of a destroyer, which could well have been because *Awa Maru* was so deeply loaded, although this would, of course, have been totally unknown to them.

The command team took all the evidence available to them and there was no known disagreement at the time that the logical deduction must be that it was a destroyer. Had there been no fog it would have quickly become apparent that the unknown ship was sailing with all lights illuminated which, even had they not related this to the *Awa Maru*, would have been so unusual in wartime as to give them pause for thought. It is at least open to argument that Captain Hamada should have sounded the *Awa Maru*'s foghorn, which would have been normal peacetime practice and would have been a sensible, albeit not mandatory, precaution.

Loughlin had plenty of time – approximately an hour – to plan his attack and decided to use four torpedoes, which, since he had the time available, could be from the stern tubes, so that, should they miss – and because he assumed the target to be a destroyer – he could get away as quickly as possible. Accordingly, he moved in to just under a mile, then turned through 180 degrees and launched the four torpedoes at the position predicted by radar, since they had still not seen the target.

There are numerous variables in a torpedo attack, which include the speed, course, length and draught of the target, and its predicted position at the time the torpedoes reach it – even small errors in any of these can lead to a miss. One way of overcoming this is to fire a spread (i.e., more than one torpedo) in which each is programmed to hit a slightly different point along the target's length. In this case, Loughlin, believing that the target was a destroyer and knowing that the average Japanese destroyer was some 300 feet long, ordered a spread of 290 feet. Similarly, because he did not want the torpedoes to pass under the target he ordered a depth setting of just three feet. Finally, and possibly because of the failure of his attacks in January, he decided to launch four torpedoes.

It is usually taken to be the case that if anything can go wrong it will (Murphy's Law), thus preventing success. In this case, however, everything in the launching and torpedo systems went absolutely right, with the result that the outcome was far more catastrophic than might otherwise have been the case. All four torpedoes ran precisely as intended, all four hit the target and all four exploded – all of which were very unusual, as the US Submarine Service had suffered many problems with unreliable torpedoes earlier in the war. Because they were set for three feet, and because, due to its overloading *Awa Maru* was low in the water, the torpedoes hit the most vulnerable amidships part of the hull. Also, because the spread was 290 feet and the actual length of the target was 600 feet, the hits were concentrated in the centre of the ship. Finally, shrouded in fog and secure in the knowledge that they were protected by a safe conduct, it is very probable (but unverifiable) that the crew and passengers were completely unprepared – watertight doors not closed, damage-control parties not closed up, crew and passengers not wearing lifejackets, and so on. As a result, the four, virtually simultaneous, explosions blew the ship apart. According to *Queenfish's* radar the target disappeared within four minutes, and, as the Japanese authorities never received any distress messages from the ship it must be presumed that the radio crew never had the opportunity to make a transmission.[7]

Loughlin then again followed standard operating procedures and turned towards the target and motored gingerly into the area to try to pick up evidence as to the target's identity and its cargo, and also to rescue at least a few survivors. There were some survivors in the oily water, but only one accepted the offer of rescue, the others preferring, in Japanese fashion, to seek death by drowning rather than the dishonour of capture by the enemy. The survivor, Kantora Shimoda, who did come aboard was taken below to recover, although it was not until some six hours later that he was able to tell his rescuers that the ship they had so successfully sunk was, in fact, the *Awa Maru*, which had been protected by safe passage.

Without a second's hesitation Loughlin radioed this tragic news to COMSUBPAC, where Admiral Lockwood's first reaction was to order both *Queenfish* and *Sea Fox* into the area to search for any further survivors and for any evidence as to what the Japanese ship might have been carrying. No further survivors were found but bales of rubber, various boxes and other debris were found and recovered.

Queenfish returned to Guam on 14 April, where Loughlin was immediately relieved of his command and warned for court martial. So sudden was the sinking of *Awa Maru* that the Japanese authorities only knew that the ship was not answering radio calls and were completely in the dark until 17 April when they were informed by the US government that their ship had been sunk by a US submarine, that there was only one known survivor and that disciplinary action was being taken against the commanding officer.

COMSUBPAC was reluctant to take such a course, but his superiors left him no choice. The court comprised two vice-admirals, two rear-admirals and two captains, with an even spread of experience, two being submariners, two from the surface navy and two naval aviators. Loughlin faced three charges – culpable inefficiency, disobeying a lawful order, and negligence – and having exercised his legal right not to give evidence on his own behalf,[8] he was found 'not guilty' of the first two but 'guilty' of the third, for which he was sentenced to receive a letter of admonition. This enabled the US government to endeavour to draw a line under the incident by making a formal apology, informing the Japanese that the commanding officer had been tried and punished, and offering to replace the *Awa Maru* with an equivalent ship – but which could be used only to transport supplies for prisoners-of-war. This was still under discussion when the war came to an end in August 1945; the repercussions rumbled on for many years, but are outside the scope of this book.

It is clear that Loughlin ought to have known about the *Awa Maru*'s safe-passage status, but everything conspired to ensure that he did not. There were the unread messages, the failure to mention the Japanese ship in the staff officers' briefing, and the classified signal that failed to specify the ship's intended track. Finally, to the fog of war was added the reality of a sea fog that reduced visibility to about 200 yards.

The Japanese undoubtedly and knowingly misused the *Awa Maru* in order to transport military stores and personnel, which, if not against the letter of the agreement was certainly against its spirit. This was compounded when they removed the armament, which seems to indicate that they regarded *Awa Maru* as a cartel ship, in which case there was no question that it should not have carried any military stores or personnel. Finally, if Captain Hamada had sounded his foghorn Loughlin might have hesitated before launching his attack.

Had it been known for certain, in advance of the attack, that *Awa Maru* was carrying contraband goods and thus breaching the rules of cartel/safe passage ships, then the attack might have been justified, but the fact is that Loughlin did not know this, and every decision he took was clearly based on his misappreciation that the target was a destroyer.

19

Postal Services to and from Japanese-Controlled Territories: 1942–1945

According to the Geneva Convention, 1929:

ARTICLE 36

Each of the belligerents shall periodically determine the number of letters and postal cards per month which prisoners of war of the various classes shall be allowed to send, and shall inform the other belligerent of this number.

This article was generally interpreted to mean two letters and four postcards per month and also to include civilian internees. The Japanese were not signatories of this convention but they did announce their intention to abide by this element of it, although this was modified in 1943 when they limited prisoners' letters to 25 words each. Mail was important to all prisoners-of-war and civilian internees wherever they were held, but it was probably of even greater significance to those in the Far East because of the isolation and the excessively bad treatment meted out by the Japanese. A quantity of mail undoubtedly did get through in both directions, but the Japanese distribution system was very poor and after the war some camps were found to have thousands of incoming letters lying in cupboards.

By the time of the Japanese attack on 7 December 1941 the system of mail in Europe between Germany and Italy on the one hand and the UK and British Commonwealth on the other was well established and the United States was included without difficulty. The whole system proved surprisingly robust, even at the end of the war when Germany was in a state of terminal collapse. Unfortunately, matters would run nothing like so smoothly in the Far East. The British government sent a proposal for prisoner-of-war mail to the Japanese government very soon after the fall of Singapore. This was reported in *The Times* newspaper on 6 April 1942 and formally agreed by the Japanese on 22 May 1942, which resulted in a primary overland route by railroad, supplemented by sea routes on an opportunity basis.

For understandable reasons, both sides insisted on censoring outgoing mail and sometimes incoming as well, which was permitted under Articles 39 and 40 of the Convention. This posed a translation problem between European countries, such as Germany and the United Kingdom and United States, but with

Far Eastern mail the different scripts caused even more of a problem. Indeed, the workload on the censor officers was the main reason for the Japanese reducing outgoing letters to 25 words apiece in late 1942.

Before the war there were three routes from Japan, two of which were by sea, either eastwards across the Pacific to North/South America, or westwards via the Suez Canal to Europe. The third route was by rail, the major part lying over the Trans-Siberian Railway, which had been in operation since 1908. Of these three, rail was by far the fastest, official figures for postal services between Japan and Western Europe in 1940 being: ship via US: 23–24 days; ship via Suez: 35–36 days; and rail via Siberia and Moscow: 14–15 days.[1]

Immediately following the Japanese attacks, mail services between Europe and Asia were curtailed as the Japanese advanced, and merchant ships at sea turned away from enemy ports. There was also a problem on the overland (rail) route as, on 19 December 1941, the Swiss authorities notified their public that no further mail for the Far East was being accepted. But, on 29 January 1942, the same authorities declared the route to be open again and stated that the mail would be routed 'via Turkey, the USSR and Siberia',[2] and, since mail could be sent from the UK and North America through Lisbon to Switzerland, there was no reason why PoW mail to prisoners-of-war and civilian internees could not be sent on the same route as well.[3]

Whether, or not, the PoW mail would be sorted and delivered on arrival in Japan was another matter, so, with large numbers of prisoners-of-war and civilian internees now in Japanese hands, both the US and UK governments opened negotiations through the Protecting Powers to restart such services. These bore fruit in April 1942 when the route for the exchange of mail between Japan and Europe, North and South America, and Australasia reopened and remained in use until late July 1945.[4] This main artery consisted of the Trans-Siberian Railway between Moscow and Chita on the Russo-Chinese border and the Trans-Manchurian Railway from Chita to the port of Pusan, Korea, and by May 1945 this route was handling 22,000 items of British mail alone, to the Far East.

Switzerland, which for several years was completely surrounded by Axis-controlled territory, had arrangements with Germany and Italy that enabled them to send and receive mail by train. Thus mail from Switzerland to the Western hemisphere went by railroad through Vichy France and Spain to Portugal, and thence by ship to the UK or North America and onwards – for example, to Australia and New Zealand. Some mail for the UK even went via the United States.

Mail bound for Japan could reach the Trans-Siberian railroad by various routes. One was by sea from North America and the UK to Archangel in northern Russia and then by train to Moscow. Secondly, there was the rail route from Lisbon that handled incoming mail brought by sea from North and South

America and the UK. This route went to Switzerland, whence it went, still by train, via Istanbul, Erzerum and Tiflis, to Moscow. Thirdly, mail from British India, Australasia and South Africa was taken by sea via Colombo, Ceylon, to Basra, Iraq, and thence to Teheran, Persia, and northwards by rail to Moscow. The American Red Cross also established a route, in which mail was carried by ship and rail to Teheran, from where it was sent across the Trans-Siberian Railway. In addition to mail the society also sent drugs by this route and by mid 1945 had sent 604 packages, each containing 2,000 multivitamin capsules, together with 60,000 units of insulin.[5]

There were also air services from England via British Overseas Airways Corporation (BOAC) and from the United States via Pan American Airways (Pan Am) both to Lisbon, Portugal. These were primarily passenger flights but mail was also carried. From Lisbon mail could either be sent by train to Switzerland (as described above) or could continue by air across Africa and then to Teheran, from where it was either flown or transported by rail to Moscow. Prisoner-of-war mail by surface means was free of charge, but airmail had to be paid for, although, at best, the mail was actually transported by aircraft for only part of the way.[6]

In the reverse direction, the prisoners-of-war and civilian internees had no option of selecting and paying for air mail, so any letters they were allowed to send proceeded by sea to Japan and from there to Pusan, where they began their long train journey. However, it would appear that wherever possible Far East mail arriving at Lisbon was sent on to the UK or North America by air in preference to by sea.

In Japan, incoming mail from Europe was taken by railroad to Tokyo, where at least some of it was sorted by the Japanese Red Cross, although the Japanese General Post Office may also have played a part. Mail for Australian, British, Dutch and Indian prisoners-of-war, except those known to be in Japan, was sent by ship to Singapore (known to the Japanese as Syonan) where it was sorted, as described below, by the Bureau of Record and Enquiry (BRE).[7] The BRE distributed the mail for camp inmates and then sorted, bagged and labelled the rest, which was handed over to the Japanese-run GPO in Singapore, who forwarded it by train or merchant ship, as appropriate. Mail for US PoWs was sent separately from Tokyo to the Philippines, although some was occasionally misrouted to the BRE.

Outgoing mail, when permitted by the Japanese, was sorted by the BRE, which also assisted in getting it processed by the Japanese censors before dispatch. It was then sent by ship to Tokyo, from where it went along the Trans-Manchurian and Trans-Siberian railroads to Europe.

It is certainly true that mail was often withheld, both deliberately and accidentally, by the Japanese, but an unquantifiable amount of mail was lost through no fault of theirs. At sea, the loss rate among Japanese-registered merchant shipping was extremely high, some 8.3 million tons being sunk by Allied action and a further 0.27 million tons lost by marine mishaps (collision, grounding, etc.) out of a total of 10.2 million tons. There are no known records indicating which of these carried mail for prisoners-of-war or civilian internees, but many must have done.

There were also occasional losses among aircraft, one known example being that of a BOAC Sunderland flyingboat (G-AGES) that flew into a hillside in the Irish Republic on 28 July 1943. Eighteen of the 28 people aboard survived, but the aircraft was also carrying some 30,000 PoW letters and cards, most of which were destroyed in the ensuing fire. However, approximately 2,500 items were saved by the local inhabitants, carefully sorted from the other debris and then passed to the British GPO who forwarded them, sometimes just scarred remnants, to the original addressees, where these could be identified.[8]

As described earlier (Chapters 14–16), there were three exchanges of diplomatic and civilian internees by ship: two at Lourenço Marques in 1942 and one at Mormugao in 1943. The chartered Swedish liner, *Gripsholm*, carried mail on both outward voyages and the British also placed mail aboard their ships. Such mail was handed over to a Portuguese postal official at the exchange port, who then handed it over to an officer from a Japanese ship, and, of course, in the reverse direction.

On the first US–Japanese exchange in July 1942, *Gripsholm* carried six bags (three from the US; three from Canada)[9] and on her return, 11 lb for Canada and 59 lb for the US. However, it should be noted that the mail sent from and to the United States included items for many other destinations (less Canada), such as Latin America, Western Europe and Australasia. One letter that followed this route left Hong Kong on 30 June 1942, arrived in New York on 25 August 1942, and was delivered to the addressee in Australia on 29 October 1942.

On the Japanese side, the chartered Italian liner, *Conte Verde*, carried no mail in either direction. *Asama Maru*, however, delivered 70 lb of mail to Lourenço Marques where she took on board the mail for US and Canadian PoWs from *Gripsholm*, as well as for South Africans, which had been delivered direct to Lourenço Marques by rail under arrangements made by the South African Red Cross. *Asama Maru* left Lourenço Marques on 26 July, called at Singapore 8–10 August and reached Yokohama on 17 August. The mail was then taken to Tokyo where it was sorted and redistributed, and it is known that several items reached Santo Thomas camp in the Philippines in time for Christmas 1942.

Following the British exchange at Lourenço Marques, *Tatuta Maru* and *Kamakura Maru* called in at Singapore on 16–18 September and 26–28 September, respectively, and it is presumed that one of these ships dropped off the 2,000-odd letters 'from Africa' that, as will be described, arrived in the BRE in October 1942.

As *Narkunda* was the only British ship to stop at a South African port on the way to Lourenço Marques it would appear that she took the mail to the exchange, where she could have passed it over to either of the two Japanese ships.

The US Post Office placed 304 sacks of US mail plus 550 sacks of Canadian parcels aboard *Kanangoora* in San Francisco in July 1942, but when it became clear that she would definitely not be sailing, her mail was transferred in September 1942 to New York to sail aboard *Gripsholm* for the second exchange. Further mail was placed aboard *Gripsholm* prior to her departure in September 1943 and, even then, a further 6,500 lb was flown to Rio de Janeiro to be put on board when she called to refuel. All of this was transferred to *Teia Maru* at Mormugao. *Teia Maru* brought mail to Mormugao, where she transferred some 150,000 items in eight sacks for US and Canadian addresses, plus a further four sacks for UK and India.

Despite the very best efforts of the ICRC and the American and British governments, the supply of Red Cross parcels to prisoners-of-war and civilian internees under Japanese control was very patchy. Based on New Zealand figures, for unknown reasons those in one fortunate camp in Japan received as many as 20, but the average there, as well as in China and Hong Kong, was between four and five, although, in addition, some bulk food was also received that was issued to the cooks to enhance the camp meals. In Singapore, apart from a very small number of Americans, no prisoners or internees received a full food parcel throughout the war, although on three occasions one parcel was issued between 17, and there was one issue of bulk food. Those in Thailand received a fraction (also, as little as one-seventeenth) on one occasion, in 1944, while those in Java and Sumatra received fractions of a parcel on two occasions; civilians received a tiny fraction on one occasion.[10] Some food parcels also went to the Philippines. But, many of those incarcerated by the Japanese received nothing at all.

The Japanese were by no means consistent in their treatment of their captives and in some camps the prisoners were allowed to purchase food from local sources – provided, of course, they had the money to pay for it. The prisoners-of-war were paid by the Japanese and in Singapore, the monthly rate of pay for officers ranged from $220[3] for a colonel to $70 for a second lieutenant, although the Imperial Japanese Army (IJA) immediately deducted a standard $60 per head for the prisoners' 'keep', and, after further stoppages, paid out only $30 to colonels, majors and captains, $25 for lieutenants and $10 for second lieutenants.[4] The prisoners' own camp administration then deducted $15 per month to purchase rations and medicines. A major problem towards the end of the war was that the pay did not rise, but inflation in the local markets certainly did.

Another alternative, employed by the British, but not, so far as is known, by the Americans, was to supply money to the local representatives of the Red Cross or the Protecting Power, who were then empowered to spend it on the purchase of necessities or to pass it to the PoWs themselves to spend on the local market. Such arrangements were made in Singapore, Hong Kong and Thailand, although how much actually got through to the prisoners is unclear. The sums supplied by the British government and Red Cross were, however, quite substantial, sufficiently so to cause the government problems over finding Swiss francs.

In Singapore, for example, the first parcels were received in late September 1942, followed by a bulk supply of Red Cross stores on 8 October, all of which had almost certainly been brought by either *Tatuta Maru* or *Kamakura Maru*, which refuelled in Singapore on their return from the British exchange at Lourenço Marques in early August.[11] The stores were in bulk form and sufficient to issue every man with sweet biscuits (12 oz), corned beef (one tin), condensed milk (one tin), cocoa (8 oz), and sugar (24 oz).[12] Also in Singapore, a further small quantity of 17 parcels was received in November 1943, which were addressed to US prisoners-of-war by name. [13]

No further Red Cross parcels seem to have been received until 1 April 1945 when, without warning, the IJA issued them on a scale of one parcel between 20 PoWs, followed by a similar issue on 8 April. These parcels were almost certainly brought to Singapore by the *Awa Maru* which, as described in Chapter 18, was used to deliver Red Cross parcels and medicines that had been sent by the United States to Japan via the Soviet Union. However, after their surrender the Japanese suddenly found plenty of Red Cross food for issue to the now ex-PoWs, although where they had been hiding them and for what reason was never established.

THE BUREAU OF RECORD AND ENQUIRY (BRE) AND CAPTAIN DAVID NELSON, SSVC

There was one element of the Far East wartime postal system that was unique – the Bureau of Record and Enquiry (BRE), which was set up in the Changi prisoner-of-war camp. Its operation deserves description here because it illustrates how one man could make a very considerable difference to the plight of his fellow prisoners-of-war and how a basic modicum of cooperation with the enemy, without once compromising his personal integrity, could reap enormous dividends for the benefit of all.

Vast numbers of British, Commonwealth, Dutch, Indian and United States prisoners were taken in the Allied collapse in February 1942 and while it was well known that Japan had not signed the Geneva Convention of 1929, it quickly became apparent that, in addition, their administrative services, never particularly efficient, were totally unprepared to deal with prisoners in such huge numbers.

Once a semblance of order had been established in Singapore, the European prisoners were concentrated in the former British military cantonments in and around the Changi peninsula at the eastern end of the island, with interned civilians held in Changi civil gaol itself, and the Indian prisoners at a separate camp.[14] Much of the internal organization of these camps and their prisoners was left to the prisoners themselves, with a prisoner-manned camp headquarters and commandant working to an Imperial Japanese Army (IJA) Liaison Office.

Most of the prisoners were soon put to work in helping to clean up Singapore city and in locating and burying the dead, but on 4 April 1942 the first major working party of 1,125 all ranks was sent overseas, their destination later discovered to be Saigon in French Indochina. Thereafter, there was constant movement of work parties, which varied in size from several hundred to as many as 8,000, who were dispatched, usually at very short notice, to carry out physical labour all over South-East Asia and even in Japan itself. As in Germany, planning such moves must have taken the captors weeks, if not months, of preparation, but for the prisoners everything had to be done at the last minute. Some such parties never returned to Changi, while others passed through Singapore in transit to another destination.

From the start, senior prisoners-of-war realized there was a problem over personnel records. Much had been lost in the chaos of defeat, but the IJA went further and ordered the destruction of virtually all documentation, including unit records and files, diaries (both official and personal) and passports. This was quickly followed by an order banning any new written records covering captives' names, fate and movements. There was also a strong suspicion that the Japanese would not establish a Prisoner-of-War Record Bureau as laid down in the Geneva Convention. This led a small group in Changi to set up the Bureau of Record and Enquiry (BRE), whose aim was to record the names and fate of all prisoners taken by the Japanese, and which was entirely independent of the prisoner-run camp administration. The BRE was originally established to deal with British personnel, and had its own army, navy and air force sections, but later included a Dutch section, while working closely with a similar, but autonomous, Australian section.

This remarkable enterprise started work in mid July 1942, its initial aim being to establish the Allied order of battle as at 8 December 1941 and the subsequent reinforcements that had arrived in a vain effort to stave off defeat. This task was followed by the preparation of nominal rolls listing all the men in all those units. The BRE then went on to try to record the fate of every man involved and of those who had attempted to escape and what had happened to them. The BRE functioned like a vacuum cleaner, garnering information from all possible sources. Every new arrival or transitee was interviewed and milked of information about names, units and ships he had encountered. Every offhand remark by a Japanese officer was recorded; copies of the local Japanese-produced newspaper,

Syonan Shimbun, were obtained whenever possible – and all were analysed for possible information.[15]

Despite the great hardships and the high rates of sickness and death, life was not devoid of all humour or irony. One example was the request from the BRE to the British-run Camp Administration Office for the 0.22 calibre rifle target cards which were known to be held in the Royal Engineer stores and would be ideal for use as record cards. Despite the fact that there was absolutely no other use for these cards, the British staff flatly refused to release them. The problem was unexpectedly solved when, a few weeks later, the IJA suddenly took over the stores, wired them off and placed armed guards on the entrance. At this, the normal PoW processes of cajolery, flattery and bribery quickly resulted in the transfer of the cards to the BRE.

The BRE was set up by a British officer, Major F. H. Francom of the Royal Army Education Corps, but when he was sent to Japan in November 1942 Captain David Nelson took over and remained in charge for the rest of the war. The office was forced to move on numerous occasions and there were frequent changes in staff as the IJA moved their captives around South-Eastern Asia, but the work was never seriously disrupted and Nelson remained in charge throughout.

Although they had not ratified the Geneva Convention, the Japanese periodically allowed PoWs to send letter cards. The text was strictly limited to 25 words, which had to be in capitals, either handwritten or typed. According to Captain Nelson, these cards were issued in Changi on five occasions: June 1942; February 1943; December 1943; August 1944; and March 1945, and cards are known to have been completed at many other prisoner-of-war camps at approximately similar times. All cards were passed through IJA censors, some of whom applied the instructions rigidly, while others were more flexible. The system was not fast: as an example, Captain David Nelson's first card to his wife in New Zealand was posted in June 1942 and reached her in November 1943, and he received news of its safe arrival in September 1944.

Civilian internees in Singapore were also allowed to send cards, but for unknown reasons most were at different times from the PoW cards: June 1942; November 1942; May 1943; August 1944; and October 1944. For the first card, unlike those completed by prisoners-of-war, the civilian internees were not limited to 25 words, but to 15 lines lengthwise or 10 lines breadthwise and although block letters were preferred, those in normal manuscript were allowed through, provided they were readable. Even these limits were lifted for the second, third and fourth cards, although the fifth card appears to have been limited to three or four lines of typescript. The internees took every advantage of these opportunities, Nelson commenting drily that on one occasion a ten-month-old baby managed to write no fewer than 157 words! [16]

These were the only known outgoing mails. The first cards, in both cases, appear to have been carried in Japanese custody aboard either *Tatsuta Maru* or *Kamakura Maru* to the British–Japanese exchange and handed over at Lourenço Marques. They were then sent to the UK, India or Australia, according to their addresses. However, this appears to have been the only occasion when such a route was used, at least for British mail, and the second through fifth cards were sent overland via the Trans-Siberian Railway.

On receiving mail in bulk, the BRE used its increasingly extensive records to sort it. Individual items were then censored in the IJA Liaison Office at a rate of about 400 letters per censor per day. They were then returned to the BRE to be rebagged. Bags were then dispatched to camps all over the Far East, including the Andaman Islands, Burma, Christmas Island, Guam, Hong Kong, Japan, Java, North Borneo, Philippines, Sarawak, Shanghai, Sumatra, Taiwan, and Thailand. There was even some mail for civilians in Singapore that was handed over to a Japanese corporal working in the Japanese-supervised city post office and Nelson later had firm evidence that it was delivered.[17] On one occasion, on 5 December 1944, a Japanese officer visiting Singapore from a camp in Thailand called in to the BRE specifically in order to collect mail for PoWs in his camp to take with him.

There was a separate section within the BRE for Dutch PoWs, while the Australians maintained their own organization, but which cooperated very closely with the BRE. Nelson and his staff looked after all others, even including some hapless Italians, 24 of whom arrived in the camp on 2 May 1944, followed by three more on 23 May.[18] Italy had surrendered to the Allies on 8 September 1943 at which time four Italian submarines in Malayan/Indonesian harbours were seized by the Japanese or Germans and their crews imprisoned. Where these 27 had been in the intervening seven months (and what happened to the approximately 200 others in the crews) is not clear, although Nelson remarks that the uniforms of those arriving at Changi were immaculate, so that their imprisonment cannot have been too arduous. In accordance with by now well-worn procedures, they were simply added to the prisoner-of-war rolls and documented by the BRE.

Although relations with the IJA were reasonable and they clearly knew of the BRE's existence, Nelson maintained duplicate sets of all records, which were always being updated and were hidden and moved regularly. Indeed, so efficient was Captain Nelson's operation that eventually the IJA came to rely on the BRE for accurate nominal rolls and statistics, which were more efficient than their own. Over two million items of mail were handled by the BRE, as shown in Table 15 below:

Table 15: Summary of Incoming Mails Handled by the BRE 1942–1945

| Date arrived at BRE | Quantities[19] | | Remarks |
	Bags	Letters (approx)	
October 1942		2,000	From South Africa, probably aboard *Teia Maru*.
December 1942		4,000	From UK.
March 1943	33	250,000	Mixed from Australia, India, UK, US, etc. UK to Singapore took 9 months.
April 1943	20		Mostly ex-UK. Most recent posted Jul/Aug 1942.
August 1943	26		Mail for Australians (2 bags); British (22); Indians (2). Most recent posted October 1942.
August 1943	40		Most recent posted February 1943.
October 1943	1	5,000	Only known mail from within Far East, including Hong Kong, Shanghai, Korea.
Late 1943	10		From New York for US PoWs in China, Japan, Philippines. Redirected by BRE.
April 1944	23		
May 1944	37	250,000	
June 1944	2		
July 1944	92		89 for PoWs; 3 for civil internees and redirected by BRE.
July 1944	30		26 British, 2 Indian, 2 civilian.
August 1944	15		
October 1944		7,000	
October 1944	71	400,000	
November 1944	19		
March 1945		8,000	May have come aboard *Awa Maru*, which arrived Singapore 2 Mar 1945.
April 1945	9		
June 1945	3		From Australia (½); India (1); UK (1½).
June 1945	12		
July 1945	Few		Most routed through Java and Sumatra.

Source: Nelson, *The Story of Changi*

Captain David Nelson found himself in a very delicately poised position. Unlike committees sitting in London, Washington, Berlin or Tokyo, Nelson did not have to deal with the enemy at a distance through the offices of the Protecting Power; he met them face-to-face and every day – indeed, almost every hour of every day. Further, if he was to have access to whatever limited information the Japanese were prepared to pass on and also try to ensure that they did not interfere with the BRE's work, he and his staff had to maintain a reasonable degree of cooperation, while also showing that their activities were in no way anti-Japanese. This ranged from keeping well clear of clandestine wireless sets, through saluting and reporting in IJA-style whenever a Japanese officer entered the room, to meeting Japanese demands for information and documentation as rapidly as possible.

Nelson adopted a very pragmatic approach. He clearly saw that the purpose of the BRE was so important for two reasons. The first was to record what had happened or was happening to every man in the Far East. The second, which was only possible as a result of the first, was the rapid and efficient sorting and distribution of mail, every item of which was of exceptional importance to the PoWs in the Far East. In order to achieve these, some minor compromises on a day-to-day level had to be accepted.[20] Thus, he maintained a correct relationship with the censor officers and the NCOs in the IJA Supervising Office, even assisting them, on occasion, but always with the aim of getting the mail to the anxious recipients as quickly as possible.

His diary records various personal medical problems, ranging from dysentery to skin complaints:

We are passing through a period when every scratch or break in the skin turns septic. 14th May [1944]: I have some chips of skin off both shins and one arm and they have all turned septic. What a nuisance. It takes half an hour to dress them before breakfast, and again in the evening … We all got over it in time.[21]

This makes it clear that he neither sought nor received any rewards or special treatment for his cooperation, while 'what a nuisance' is the nearest he ever got to complaining. Even the very occasional small gifts, such as a tin of condensed milk from an IJA corporal at Christmas 1943, were immediately shared with others.

Nelson worked hard – seven days a week was routine – and his contribution towards the morale of the prisoners-of-war and their families at home was immense. Immediately following the Japanese surrender his records were eagerly gathered by the British and Commonwealth military authorities and became a vital aid in establishing what had happened to the men and units. But this brave, dedicated and exceptionally modest officer received little formal thanks, his sole award being a 'Mention in Despatches'.[22]

20

Failed Attempts

The two US–Japanese and single UK–Japanese exchange voyages, coupled with the delivery of supplies via Vladivostok and mail via the Trans-Siberian railroad, represent the only positive outcomes of the Allied attempts to provide relief for the prisoners-of-war and civilian internees in Japanese hands. However, there were many other attempts between February 1941 and August 1945 in which the belligerent governments dealt with each other through a third party, but which, for a variety of reasons, failed to achieve success.

Until late 1944 the two major Allies, the US and the UK, persisted in dealing with the Japanese independently, and there is no doubt that the Japanese were only too pleased to take advantage of this. A second major difficulty was the shortage of shipping, which affected both sides, but with the constant sinking of their merchant ships, the Japanese worst of all. Third was the Japanese insistence that no foreign crew, not even from a neutral country such as Sweden, would be permitted to sail in Japanese-controlled waters.

One of the objections that was repeatedly raised by the Japanese was that ethnic Japanese internees in the United States were being unfairly treated by the US authorities. As a result, representatives of the Spanish Embassy in Washington, as the Japanese Protecting Power in the United States, carried out numerous inspections, and sent reassuringly favourable reports to Tokyo, although the Japanese remained suspicious to the end of the war.

Another issue raised by the Japanese was their demand that 331 named pearl fishermen and nautical pilots, who were interned in Australia, had to be included in any exchange. Whether deliberately or by chance on the part of the Japanese, this issue raised a number of inter-Allied problems, which involved not only Washington and London, but also Canberra, and took many months to resolve.

The Australian pearl fishing industry was concentrated around Broome in Western Australia and the depths were such that specially trained divers were essential. Originally, aborigines were employed, but the numbers required and the restrictions imposed by the Australian government resulted in the industry seeking labour overseas. The great majority of these came from the well-established pearl fisheries in Japan, and by 1941 there were some 500 employed there. On the outbreak of war, these were all immediately interned and their luggers destroyed for fear that they might be used to support a possible invasion.

When the possibility was raised that they might be included in an exchange, General Douglas MacArthur, Supreme Allied Commander South-West Pacific, immediately opposed it on the grounds that they could return to Japan with vital information about Australian maritime conditions and defences. The Australian government had little option but to support him, which was not surprising as he was in Australia and was a very forceful character. The authorities in Washington saw it differently, as it seemed far more important to them to recover the US civilians interned by the Japanese, whose health was known to be deteriorating rapidly. In any case, it appeared that the divers' knowledge of Australian defences must be increasingly out of date.

The Joint Chiefs-of-Staff signalled MacArthur in late January 1944 asking him either to relent totally, or, failing that, to agree to a small, carefully selected group being repatriated in order to keep the negotiations going, but he remained intransigent. Having failed to get them included in a potential US exchange, the Japanese then tried to include them in a British exchange, whereupon London, in turn, sought Canberra's agreement, but to no avail. The Australians still felt that, even though the divers were in their hands rather than those of the United States – and despite the fact that at this stage in their history Australia's primary loyalty lay with London rather than Washington – they could not overrule MacArthur. Thus, by mid June and after eight months of negotiation no real progress had been achieved.

At this point a totally separate group of people was brought into play. These were the Japanese diplomatic staff in Argentina, a country then not one of the belligerent powers.[1] The Japanese wanted these back home and asked for them to be included in the next US exchange, but the British, hearing of this, insisted that they would have to be searched. By early July officials in both the United States and the UK had reached a complete impasse – each had the means of resolving the other's problem, but refused to do so. So serious did the situation become that on 14 July 1944 President Roosevelt wrote a personal letter to Prime Minister Churchill which, for sheer reasonableness and even-handedness is worth quoting in full:

> Both you and we are negotiating to exchange Japanese civilian prisoners held by each of us for British and American civilians held by Japan. The likelihood is that such an exchange may be the only way of saving the lives of hundreds of your and our nationals.
>
> There is a snag on both sides. The Japanese want us to release three hundred odd divers and pilots held in Australia; my military people do not agree to their release and as a result your exchange negotiations have bogged down.
>
> In our exchange the snag is that the Japanese Government insists that Japanese

officials coming out shall not be searched, while your people insist on search. The immediate case concerns officials coming out of Argentina. In result our negotiations will bog down when we inform the Japanese of this requirement.

It seems to me that the military considerations in either case are now very small. Japanese officials cannot carry any effective quantities even of valuable contraband. On the other hand, our naval affairs in the Pacific are proceeding well, and the Japanese divers and pilots held in Australia cannot be of great help to the Japanese, even in respect to far eastern installations, in view of our present sea and air superiority.

My suggestion is that you give directions to your people to waive the search of Japanese officials; I will be prepared to recommend to our people that the divers and pilots be exchanged. This at least will give a reasonable chance that both exchanges might go through, saving many hundreds of both American and British from slow death. Please cable me your views. I think the technical people are over-emphasising the importance of considerations quite proper in themselves, but which should be overridden by the higher humanitarian interest.[2]

The president's letter appears to have worked and in early August both the pearl divers and inspection issues were resolved, but it was too late, matters had moved on and even though the war had another year to run there were now other problems to be addressed.

There were two further extraordinary proposals for Japanese–Allied exchanges. By mid 1944 United States' advances had resulted in numerous Japanese garrisons being isolated on various islands in the central Pacific with no hope of relief or resupply. Such garrisons had to be screened to ensure that they did not interfere with ongoing US operations and it was realized that US troops would eventually be required to tackle each in turn, and it was known from previous experience that virtually every Japanese soldier would sell his life dearly. There were also large numbers of Japanese civilians – some 10,000 on Saipan alone. Thus, with the prospect of large numbers of US casualties and in order to relieve US prisoners in Japanese hands, in late June 1944 Admiral Chester Nimitz, Commander-in-Chief Pacific, submitted the following proposal to President Roosevelt:

The Japanese garrisons on Wake, Wotje, Maloelap, Mille, Jaluit, Ocean and Nauru comprise between 23–25,000 Japanese (and Korean laborers), which are isolated, without hope of successful evacuation or supply. They are a military liability to Japan, and it is debatable whether they can be induced to surrender even when it becomes apparent to them that all hope is lost. Should a neutral be induced to arrange an exchange whereby these garrison personnel would be exchanged, rank for rank, for our prisoners of war from Bataan, Corregidor, Guam, Wake and Tientsin, it would retrieve these unfortunate prisoners of war who are suffering from malnutrition and disease, and thereby boost the morale of the American people.

Should the Japanese refuse to consider such a proposal (through a neutral), the morale effect of that refusal should be exploited in order to attack the military and civilian morale of the Japanese. I envision such an exchange as a 'safe-conduct evacuation' to permit 'face-saving,' in view of their doctrine of 'non-surrender.' The removal of those garrisons to be after receipt of, or simultaneous with, a 'safe-conduct evacuation' of American prisoners of war. It is realised that the Japanese will probably raise many obstacles to such a proposal, but it is felt that if there is one chance in a hundred for the success of such a proposal it should be undertaken.[3]

In essence, this proposal was to exchange these cut-off Japanese for a like number of sick and wounded prisoners-of-war and civilians interned by the Japanese. But in this case the US government planned to include Canadian servicemen and civilians as well as nationals of other 'American republics' but not those from other British Commonwealth or European countries, such as Australia, New Zealand and the Netherlands.[4]

This proposal was communicated to the British government in July 1944, not to seek their agreement or comments, but rather just to tell them what the US intended to do. The British were dismayed, but the Australians were incensed, as both they (and the Dutch) had many prisoners-of-war and civilians in Japanese hands and had not been consulted in any way. The Australian government protested particularly strongly, pointing out that there were more Japanese garrisons cut off in the south-west Pacific area than in the central Pacific, including an estimated 60,000 Japanese in New Guinea, 20,000 in Bougainville and 10,000 in New Ireland. This was estimated to be virtually equal to the number of British Commonwealth troops known to be in Japanese hands.

The UK government sent a formal protest to Washington, which resulted in the Americans amending the proposal to cover military prisoners-of-war only, and to include British and Dutch, but they would not agree to the proposal being widened to include the south-west Pacific. Quite why the US government was so dismissive of Australian sensitivities is not clear, especially as the latter were making such a large contribution in the south-west Pacific. Thus, it is not surprising that the authorities in Canberra were so angry.

Once the shock of the initial Japanese attacks had worn off, the Allies realized that one of the enemy's greatest weaknesses was the enormous geographical spread of its conquests, with which the only means of communication was by sea. Thus, the Japanese depended on merchant shipping to move their own troops, supplies, military equipment and wounded, which meant that the transport of relief supplies for prisoners-of-war and civilian internees featured well down their list of priorities.

US attempts to resolve this problem using the Swedish-registered *Vasaland* and *Kanangoora* have already been covered, but the problem did not go away, and there were several more attempts to resolve Japanese reservations in order to get supplies to Allied people in Japanese hands who were known to be in increasingly bad shape.

In early 1944 the American Red Cross came up with a new proposal, this time for two neutral ships that would be crewed under arrangements agreed by the Japanese and implemented under the supervision of the ICRC. These ships would be loaded in the United States, and sailed to a mutually agreed port where they would be handed over to Japanese crews. The ships would then take the relief supplies to the various ports in the Japanese-occupied area and then return to the original port to be handed back to the neutral crews, who would sail back to the United States and start the cycle over again.

In parallel, the British proposed a slightly different scheme, but which was again carefully crafted in an effort to overcome Japanese sensibilities and to prevent them feeling that they had 'lost face'. In this, the supplies would have been taken by Ship A, manned by a neutral crew and under the auspices of the ICRC, to a port designated by the Japanese and on the edge of the area they claimed to control. This ship would have been accompanied by a second freighter, Ship B, also manned by a neutral crew, which, on arrival at the designated port, would have been handed over permanently to the Japanese on the understanding that it was only to be used for distributing relief supplies. The supplies would then have been cross-loaded from Ship A to Ship B, which would then have sailed around various parts of the Japanese territories distributing the supplies, while Ship A would have gone back for more, following which the two ships would have met for a second transfer, and so on. The British also made it clear that supplies from Japan intended for Japanese prisoners and internees in Allied hands would have been carried on the return voyages.[5]

The two schemes were essentially similar except that the British would have handed over one ship permanently and set up a shuttle service, with cross-loading each time they met at the designated port. The Americans, on the other hand, required the ships to be handed over each time at the designated port, which removed the need for cross-loading but increased the complexity of changing crews.

Both these schemes required that two ships be found. In the US scheme two ships would be handed over temporarily, while in the British scheme one ship would be handed over permanently. However, the British scheme involved a second ship permanently committed to shuttling the supplies to the designated port. Both countries looked to Sweden for the use of *Gripsholm* and *Drottningholm*, a somewhat surprising choice since they were liners rather than freighters, but both schemes were emphatically rejected by the Swedish government and that was the end of that.

Similar schemes resurfaced in the last year of the war, but were fated never to reach fruition, usually because of difficulties raised by the Japanese, one of the main issues raised from February 1945 onwards being the sinking of *Awa Maru*, as described in Chapter 18. They were, however, very careful never to end the discussions completely, which continued virtually up to their surrender.

21

Conclusions

The basis of most of this activity was the Convention Relative To The Treatment Of Prisoners Of War dated 27 May 1929 (the Geneva Convention, 1929). This was ratified by virtually all military and naval powers, but unfortunately, two major powers, the Soviet Union and Japan, did not ratify it, although the latter did announce that it would follow the spirit of the Convention in certain respects. It is a matter for speculation whether, if the Soviet Union had been a signatory, that would have improved its position and, in particular, the position of its PoWs in German hands. Nothing can excuse the gross maltreatment and mass murder of Soviet PoWs carried out in Nazi camps – the figures will never be known but probably amount to between three and four million – but it is difficult to avoid the conclusion that if the USSR had signed the Convention then the ICRC might have been able to insist on inspecting at least some of the camps.

Perhaps the greatest single benefit conferred by the Convention lay, quite simply, in the fact that it existed, setting certain civilizing standards by which belligerents could measure their own and their opponents' conduct. In some respects it worked quite well. The MMCs, for example, were set up very early in the war, as was required by the Convention, their composition followed the predetermined pattern, and the Model Agreement gave clear guidance to the doctors. Even the final clause that '... all cases not fitting exactly into the examples cited shall be decided by invoking the spirit of the above governing principles' seems to have worked well and allowed MMCs a degree of flexibility that they were pleased to use. But, even with the MMCs at work, there were still some shortcomings. For example, Detaining Powers sometimes prevented people from attending, and there were occasions when fit PoWs hoodwinked the doctors. The one area where nothing was achieved was the question of PoWs who had spent an excessive time in captivity. The Swiss regularly returned to this subject in an effort to get the longest-serving men out to a neutral country but, despite many negotiations, it was never achieved.

Neutral countries were able to play a crucial role in either the negotiations for these exchanges or in their implementation. Like Switzerland, Sweden had to strike a delicate balance, being placed close to Germany but with the Allies firmly in control of its overseas trade routes. But in its humanitarian role Sweden was of great help to all concerned. It regularly provided the venue for exchanges, which were conducted with great efficiency, usually at Gothenburg. The merchant marine also provided the two liners, *Gripsholm* and *Drottningholm*, which sailed all around the world under charter with an absolutely unblemished record for safety, timekeeping and care of their passengers. The role of Portugal has largely been overlooked by historians, but it helped in a variety of important ways. First, Lisbon was the port through which many exchanges were achieved and through which Red Cross parcels and mail were funnelled, with the Portuguese Post Office playing a vital role. Secondly, the airport provided facilities for both the British Overseas Airway Corporation and Lufthansa, requiring a difficult balancing act by the host nation, but which seems to have been achieved successfully. Thirdly, the harbours of Lourenço Marques and Mormugao in Portuguese overseas territories provided the location and facilities for the three exchanges with Japan to take place.

Spain served as Japan's Protecting Power in the United States, which proved to be a somewhat thankless task. It also enabled several exchanges to take place at Barcelona. Switzerland was Protecting Power for the UK and the US in Germany and played a major role in many negotiations. It also played involuntary host to a large number of foreign internees and was the setting for several exchanges later in the war.

Although not a nation per se, the ICRC was a major player in most of these activities. It organized the onward travel of parcels and welfare and education supplies, inspected camps, set up negotiations and provided liaison officers during the actual exchanges. Its role in relation to the Jews and concentration camps has been the subject of some post-war controversy, but in these PoW and civilian internee exchanges it was undoubtedly very beneficial.

A few of the exchanges involved some or all travel to be by rail, but most were done by sea. The first problem was simply in finding the ships. On the Allied side the transportation of troops, weapons, ammunition and supplies across the Pacific and Atlantic required huge numbers of vessels of all types, with very few left over. For Germany the most shipping that was usually required were trans-Baltic ferries, but when later in the war they needed to transport people over a long distance on the Turkish exchange they chartered the Swedish *Drottningholm*. The Japanese, on the other hand, were always desperately short of shipping, both because of the need to supply their empire and because of the ever-increasing ship losses, particularly to US submarines. At the time of World War Two, the British operated by far the largest mercantile marine in the world and normally used their own flagged ships for these exchanges. The US, on the other hand, never used its own vessels, preferring instead to charter Swedish ships such as *Gripsholm*, *Drottningholm* and *Kanangoora*.

As this book has shown, dozens of ships covered several hundred thousand miles on 'safe passage'. They normally sailed alone, all lights blazing and without zigzagging, thus offering an ideal target and sailed for much of every voyage through hotly-contested waters. Despite this, only three were lost: *Awa Maru*, *Padua* and *Embla*. Many of these ships were neutral, but some belonged to one belligerent and penetrated deep into waters controlled by their enemy. For example, the Japanese ships on the Japanese–US and Japanese–UK exchanges sailed deep into British-controlled areas of the Indian Ocean. Similarly, British liners sailed to and from Sweden through German-controlled waters.

It is also important to bear in mind that these voyages were not undertaken in isolation from other events such as the invasions of Italy, North Africa, France and the Pacific islands. In addition some of the exchanges were exceptionally complicated in their own right, involving the assembly of participants from numerous locations and their safe transport to the point of exchange.

One surprising element is the inconsistencies in treatment and behaviour. The Japanese, for example, allowed some cooperation with the Red Cross and the departure of civilian repatriates from metropolitan Japan, Hong Kong and Thailand, but virtually none from Malaya or the Philippines. The Japanese also allowed no male servicemen to be exchanged, but did exchange uniformed nurses from Guam and Hong Kong, but in the latter case only Canadians not Australians. The Germans, too, were inconsistent. Their treatment of the Jews was generally appalling, but they were prepared to honour Latin American passports, when they, as much as the holders, knew them to have been obtained by dubious means. There was also the very curious episode where a dozen women were simply dumped in Berlin and left to their own devices for many months, something that would have been unimaginable in the United States or United Kingdom.

It is astonishing what a volume of supplies crossed the interface between the Allies and Axis powers. Food parcels, medical supplies, clothing, seeds and bulbs for gardens, and musical instruments all managed to get through. Time and again PoW and civilian internees' reports describe how essential were these parcels and the post. Some letters and parcels, although regrettably few, even got through to the PoWs being held by the Japanese.

In complex matters such as these a few individuals will always shine out to show what could be achieved. There are many dozens, if not hundreds, in the area covered here, but just two can be given as examples. Mary Berg was one – a gentle but thoroughly determined adolescent who endured life in the Warsaw Ghetto and saw sights and underwent experiences no human, let alone a young woman, should have to endure. The other is David Nelson, running the Bureau of Record and Enquiry from early 1942 through to the last days of the Japanese occupation of Singapore. He was able to track and account for men in a way impossible to anyone else and to route mail and parcels that meant so much to the recipients.

It would be wrong to exaggerate the scale of the exchanges and repatriations that took place during World War Two. The war was a highly destructive, global conflict, and even if it was more mobile than World War One, the belligerents fought each other on land, sea and air with unparalleled intensity. It has been estimated that some 105 million men and women were conscripted, of whom about 15 million died and well over two million became prisoners-of-war. The number of civilians involved is incalculable, but it is estimated that somewhere between 26 and 34 million died.[1] Set against those figures, the numbers of PoWs and civilian internees involved in the exchanges and repatriations were very small. However, every single repatriate represented a life saved and an individual returning to his or her homeland, and the very fact that this happened at all was only achieved because the belligerents – however tenuously and even though it was usually through a third party – were communicating with each other.

Appendix A
The Convention of 27 May 1929 Relative to the Treatment of Prisoners-of-War

[Explanatory Note: The Convention is a very lengthy document, so those articles not relevant to this book have been omitted. Those Articles that are quoted are verbatim.]

ARTICLE 1

[Application]

ARTICLES 2–4

[General]

ARTICLES 5–6

[Capture]

ARTICLE 7

[Circumstances of capture]

ARTICLE 8

Belligerents are bound mutually to notify each other of their capture of prisoners within the shortest period possible, through the intermediary of the information bureaus, such as are organized according to Article 77. They are likewise bound to inform each other of the official addresses to which the correspondence of their families may be sent to prisoners-of-war. As soon as possible, every prisoner must be enabled to correspond with his family himself, under the conditions provided in Articles 36 *et seq.* As regards prisoners captured at sea, the provisions of the present article shall be observed as soon as possible after arrival at port.

ARTICLES 9–13

[Camps: siting, food, clothing, sanitary and medical facilities]

ARTICLE 14

… It shall be lawful for belligerents reciprocally to authorize, by means of private arrangements the retention in the camps of physicians and attendants to care for prisoners of their own country …

ARTICLES 15–16

[Medical and religious matters]

ARTICLE 17

So far as possible belligerents shall encourage intellectual diversions and sports organized by prisoners-of-war.

ARTICLES 18–22

[Internal Discipline of Camps]

ARTICLES 23–24

[Financial Resources of Prisoners-of-war]

ARTICLES 25–26

[Moves]

ARTICLES 27–34

[Labour]

ARTICLE 35

[General]

ARTICLE 36

Each of the belligerents shall periodically determine the number of letters and postal cards per month which prisoners-of-war of the various classes shall be allowed to send, and shall inform the other belligerent of this number. These letters and cards shall be transmitted by post by the shortest route. They may not be delayed or retained for disciplinary reasons.

Within a period of not more than one week after his arrival at the camp, and likewise in case of sickness, every prisoner shall be enabled to write his family a postal card informing it of his capture and of the state of his health. The said postal cards shall be forwarded as rapidly as possible and may not be delayed in any manner.

As a general rule, correspondence of prisoners shall be written in their native language. Belligerents may allow correspondence in other languages.

ARTICLE 37

Prisoners-of-war shall be allowed individually to receive parcels by mail, containing foods and other articles intended to supply them with food or clothing. Packages shall be delivered to the addressees and a receipt given.

ARTICLE 38

Letters and consignments of money or valuables, as well as parcels by post intended for prisoners-of-war or dispatched by them, either directly, or by the mediation of the information bureaus provided for in Article 77, shall be exempt from all postal duties in the countries of origin and destination, as well as in the countries they pass through.

Presents and relief in kind for prisoners shall be likewise exempt from all import and other duties, as well as of payments for carriage by the State railways.

Prisoners may, in cases of acknowledged urgency, be allowed to send telegrams, paying the usual charges.

ARTICLE 39

Prisoners-of-war shall be allowed to receive shipments of books individually, which may be subject to censorship.

Representatives of the protecting Powers and duly recognized and authorized aid societies may send books and collections of books to the libraries of prisoners' camps. The transmission of these shipments to libraries may not be delayed under the pretext of censorship difficulties.

ARTICLE 40

Censorship of correspondence must be effected within the shortest possible time. Furthermore, inspection of parcels post must be effected under proper conditions to guarantee the preservation of the products which they may contain and, if possible, in the presence of the addressee or an agent duly recognized by him.

Prohibitions of correspondence promulgated by the belligerents for military or political reasons, must be transient in character and as short as possible.

ARTICLE 41

Belligerents shall assure all facilities for the transmission of instruments, papers or documents intended for prisoners-of-war or signed by them, particularly of powers of attorney and wills.

They shall take the necessary measures to assure, in case of necessity, the authentication of signatures made by prisoners.

ARTICLES 42–44

[Relations between PoWs and Camp Authorities]

ARTICLES 45–67

[Discipline, legal matters, punishments]

ARTICLE 68

Belligerents are bound to send back to their own country, regardless of rank or number, seriously sick and seriously injured prisoners-of-war, after having brought them to a condition where they can be transported.

Agreements between belligerents shall accordingly settle as soon as possible the cases of invalidity or of sickness, entailing direct repatriation, as well as the cases entailing possible hospitalization in a neutral country. While awaiting the conclusion of these agreements, belligerents may have reference to the model agreement annexed, for documentary purposes, to the present Convention.

ARTICLE 69

Upon the outbreak of hostilities, belligerents shall come to an agreement to name Mixed Medical Commissions. These commissions shall be composed of three members, two of them belonging to a neutral country and one appointed by the detaining Power; one of the physicians of the neutral country shall preside. These Mixed Medical Commissions shall proceed to the examination of sick or wounded prisoners and shall make all due decisions regarding them.

Decisions of these commissions shall be by majority and carried out with the least possible delay.

ARTICLE 70

Besides those who are designated by the camp physician, the following prisoners-of-war shall be inspected by the Mixed Medical Commission mentioned in Article 69, with a view to their direct repatriation or their hospitalization in a neutral country:
a) Prisoners who make such a request directly of the camp physician;
b) Prisoners who are presented by the agents provided for in Article 43, acting on their own initiative or at the request of the prisoners themselves;
c) Prisoners who have been proposed by the Power in whose armies they have served or by an aid society duly recognized and authorized by that Power.

ARTICLE 71

Prisoners-of-war who are victims of accidents in connection with work, except those voluntarily injured, shall enjoy the benefit of the same provisions, as far as repatriation or possible hospitalization in a neutral country are concerned.

ARTICLE 72

Throughout the duration of hostilities and for humane considerations, belligerents may conclude agreements with a view to the direct repatriation or hospitalization in a neutral country of able-bodied prisoners-of-war who have undergone a long period of captivity.

ARTICLE 73

The expenses of repatriation or of transportation to a neutral country of prisoners-of-war shall be borne, from the frontiers of the detaining Power, by the Power in whose armies the prisoners have served.

ARTICLE 74

No repatriated person shall be employed on active military service.

ARTICLE 75

[Release and repatriation upon cessation of hostilities]

ARTICLE 76

[Death of prisoners-of-war]

ARTICLE 77

Upon the outbreak of hostilities, each of the belligerent Powers, as well as the neutral Powers which have received belligerents, shall institute an official information bureau for prisoners-of-war who are within their territory.

Within the shortest possible period, each of the belligerent Powers shall inform its information bureau of every capture of prisoners effected by its armies, giving it all the information regarding identity which it has, allowing it quickly to advise the families concerned, and informing it of the official addresses to which families may write to prisoners.

The information bureau shall immediately forward all this information to the interested Powers, through the intervention, on one hand, of the protecting Powers and, on the other, of the central agency provided for in Article 79.

The information bureau, being charged with replying to all inquiries about the war, shall receive from the various services concerned full information respecting internments, and transfers, releases on parole, repatriations, escapes, stays in hospitals, deaths, as well as other information necessary to enable it to make out and keep up to date an individual return for each prisoner-of-war.

The bureau shall state in this return, in so far as is possible and subject to the provisions of Article 5: the regimental number, given names and surname, date and place of birth, rank and unit of the interested party, the given name of the father and the name of the mother, the address of the person to be advised in case of accident, wounds, date and place of capture, internment, wounding, and death, as well as any other important information.

Weekly lists containing all new information likely to facilitate the identification of each prisoner shall be transmitted to the interested Powers.

At the conclusion of peace the individual return of the prisoner-of-war shall be delivered to the Power which he served.

The information bureau shall further be bound to receive all objects of personal use, valuables, letters, pay vouchers, identification marks, etc., which are left by prisoners-of-war who have been repatriated, released on parole, escaped or died, and to transmit them to the countries interested.

ARTICLE 78

Relief societies for prisoners-of-war, which are properly constituted in accordance with the laws of their country and with the object of serving as the channel for charitable effort, shall receive from the belligerents, for themselves and their duly accredited agents, every facility for the efficient performance of their humane task within the bounds imposed by military necessities. Agents of these societies may be admitted to the camps for the purpose of distributing relief, as also to the halting places of repatriated prisoners, if furnished with a personal permit by the military authorities, and on giving an undertaking in writing to comply with all measures of order and police which the latter may issue.

ARTICLE 79

A central information agency for prisoners-of-war shall be created in a neutral country. The International Committee of the Red Cross shall propose the organization of such an agency to the interested Powers, if it considers it necessary.

The function of that agency shall be to centralize all information respecting prisoners, which it may obtain through official or private channels; it shall transmit it as quickly as possible to the country of origin of the prisoners or to the Power which they have served.

These provisions must not be interpreted as restricting the humanitarian activity of the International Committee of the Red Cross.

ARTICLE 80

Information bureaus shall enjoy the privilege of free postage on postal matter, as well as all exemptions provided in Article 38.

ARTICLE 81

[Application to certain classes of civilians]

ARTICLES 82–85

[Execution of the Convention]

ARTICLE 86

The High Contracting Parties recognize that the regular application of the present Convention will find a guaranty in the possibility of collaboration of the protecting Powers charged with safeguarding the interests of belligerents; in this respect, the protecting Powers may, besides their diplomatic personnel, appoint delegates from among their own nationals or from among the nationals of other neutral Powers. These delegates must be subject to the approval of the belligerent near which they exercise their mission.

Representatives of the protecting Power or its accepted delegates shall be permitted to go to any place, without exception, where prisoners-of-war are interned. They shall have access to all places occupied by prisoners and may interview them, as a general rule without witnesses, personally or through interpreters.

Belligerents shall so far as possible facilitate the task of representatives or accepted delegates of the protecting Power. The military authorities shall be informed of their visit.

Belligerents may come to an agreement to allow persons of the same nationality as the prisoners to be permitted to take part in inspection trips.

ARTICLE 87

In case of disagreement between the belligerents as to the application of the provisions of the present Convention, the protecting Powers must, in so far as possible, lend their good offices for the purpose of settling the difference. For this purpose, each of the protecting Powers may, in particular, suggest to the interested belligerents a meeting of representatives thereof, possibly upon a neutral territory suitably chosen. Belligerents shall be bound to accede to proposals in this sense which are made to them. The protecting Power may, if occasion arises, submit for the approval of the Powers concerned a person belonging to a neutral Power or a person delegated by the International Committee of the Red Cross, who shall be summoned to take part in this meeting.

ARTICLES 88–97

[Final provisions]

Appendix B
Geneva Convention 1929: Annex to Article 68.
Model Agreement Concerning Direct Repatriation of
Prisoners-of-War for Reasons of Health

[Explanatory Note: In the original Convention this annex covers hospitalization in a neutral country, as well as direct repatriation. Hospitalization in a neutral country was practised in World War One, but in the very early days of World War Two it was mutually agreed that it served little purpose and was never implemented. For clarity, therefore, those provisions relating only to hospitalization in a neutral country have been omitted. All remaining text is verbatim.]

I. GOVERNING PRINCIPLES FOR DIRECT REPATRIATION AND HOSPITALIZATION IN A NEUTRAL COUNTRY

A. DIRECT REPATRIATION

There shall be repatriated directly:
1. Sick and wounded who, according to medical opinion, are not likely to recover in one year, their condition requiring treatment and their mental or physical fitness appearing to have suffered considerable diminution;
2. Incurable sick and wounded whose mental or physical fitness appears to have suffered considerable diminution;
3. Cured sick and wounded whose mental or physical fitness appears to have suffered considerable diminution.

B, C. HOSPITALIZATION IN AND SUBSEQUENT REPATRIATION FROM A NEUTRAL COUNTRY

[Omitted as never implemented]

II. SPECIAL PRINCIPLES FOR DIRECT REPATRIATION OR HOSPITALIZATION IN A NEUTRAL COUNTRY

A. REPATRIATION

There shall be repatriated:

1. All prisoners-of-war who, as the result of organic injuries, have the following impairments, actual or functional: loss of a member, paralysis, articular or other defects, provided that the loss is at least a foot or a hand, or is equivalent to the loss of a foot or a hand;

2. All wounded or injured prisoners-of-war whose condition is such that it renders them invalids whose cure, within a period of one year, can not be anticipated from a medical standpoint;

3. All the sick whose condition is such that it renders them invalids whose cure, within a period of one year, can not be anticipated from a medical standpoint;

The following, in particular, belong to this category:

a) Progressive tuberculosis of any organs which, according to medical opinion, can no longer be cured or at least considerably improved by a course of treatment in a neutral country;

b) Nontubercular affections of the respiratory organs presumed incurable (such as, above all, strongly developed pulmonary emphysema, with or without bronchitis, bronchiectasis, serious asthma, gas poisoning, etc.);

c) Serious chronic affections of the organs of circulation (for example: valvular affections with tendencies to disorders of compensation, relatively serious affections of the myocardium, pericardium of the vessels, especially inoperable aneurisms of the large vessels, etc.);

d) Serious chronic affections of the digestive organs;

e) Serious chronic affections of the urinary and sexual organs (particularly, for example: all cases of confirmed chronic nephritis with complete semeiology, and most especially when cardiac and vascular impairments already exist; likewise, pyelites and chronic cystitis, etc.);

f) Serious chronic diseases of the central and peripheral nervous system (such as, particularly, serious neurasthenia and hysteria, all unquestionable cases of epilepsy, serious cases of Basedow's disease, etc.);

g) Blindness in both eyes, or in one eye when the vision of the other remains below in spite of the use of corrective glasses; reduction in acuteness of vision in case it is impossible to restore it by correction to the acuteness of 1/2 for one eye at least; other ocular affections coming in the present class (glaucoma, iritis, choroiditis, etc.);

h) Total deafness in both ears, as well as total deafness in one ear in case the partially deaf ear does not discern the ordinary spoken voice at a distance of one meter;

i) All unquestionable cases of mental affections;

j) All serious cases of chronic poisoning by metals or other causes (lead poisoning, mercury poisoning, morphinism, cocainism, alcoholism, gas poisoning, etc.);

k) Chronic affections of the organs of locomotion (arthritis deformans, gout, rheumatism with impairments clinically discoverable), provided they are serious;

l) All malignant growths, if they are not amenable to relatively minor operations without endangering the life of the patient;

m) All cases of malaria with noticeable organic changes (important chronic increase in size of the liver, of the spleen, cachexia, etc.);

n) Serious chronic cutaneous affections, in so far as their nature does not constitute a medical indication for hospitalization in a neutral country;

o) Serious avitaminoses (beriberi, pellagra, chronic scurvy).

B. HOSPITALIZATION IN A NEUTRAL COUNTRY

[Omitted as never implemented]

III. GENERAL OBSERVATIONS

The conditions given above should, generally speaking, be interpreted and applied in as broad a spirit as possible.

This breadth of interpretation should be especially applied to the neuropathic or psychopathic conditions caused or brought to a head by the events of the war or even of the captivity itself (psychasthenia of prisoners-of-war), and also to cases of tuberculosis in all degrees.

It is needless to state that camp physicians and the Mixed Medical Commissions may find themselves confronted with a great number of cases not mentioned among the examples given under Section II, or cases not fitting in with these examples. The examples mentioned above are given only as typical examples; an analogous list of examples of surgical alterations has not been drawn up because, with the exception of cases incontestable by their very nature (amputations), it is difficult to make a list of particular type; experience has shown that a recital of these particular cases was not without disadvantages in practice.

All cases not fitting exactly into the examples cited shall be decided by invoking the spirit of the above governing principles.

Notes

Notes to Chapter 1: The Historical Background

1. Noble = 120 grains of gold. Source: Froissart, J. (1978), *Chronicles*. London: Penguin.
2. This meant that an officer could be exchanged one-for-one for an officer of equal rank, or for a combination of those of lower rank. Thus, for example, a major could be exchanged for one major, or two lieutenants, or a captain and two privates, or eight privates, and so on.
3. Cartel for the Exchange of Prisoners of War Between Great Britain and the United States of America May 12, 1813. See: http://www.yale.edu/lawweb/avalon/diplomacy/britain/cart1812.htm.
4. TNA (PRO) FO 383/283 and FO 283.
5. One sight that made a great impression on Bury was a *nagelfigur* (nail statue), a 12-metre-high wooden carving of Hindenburg, into which civilians hammered nails bought at a special price, with profit going to the German Red Cross. At the time of his visit, the one in Berlin contained an estimated 30 tons of nails! There were many other such statues throughout Germany.
6. *New York Times*, 30 September 1917.

Notes to Chapter 2: British–German Exchanges

1. Vance, J. F. (ed.) (2000), *Encyclopedia of Prisoners-of-War and Internment*. Santa Barbara, CA: ABC-CLIO, pp. 270–71.
2. *Gradisca* had been employed by the Italians as a hospital ship from 1940 to September 1943, when she was taken over by the Germans and employed in a similar role.
3. *Tairea* was a British-India liner, requisitioned for war service as Hospital Ship *Number 35*. *Cuba* was a former French CGT liner taken over by the British in 1940 and then used as a troopship under management by the Cunard company.
4. The total of New Zealanders exchanged at Barcelona and Gothenburg was 395, comprising 169 sick and wounded, and 226 protected personnel.
5. Letter CRA 10 January 1944 in TNA (PRO) CAB 118/27.
6. He was apprehended (for a second time) by the British in May 1945 and held for ten months when he was released without charge.
7. COS383/5 dated 5 March 1945 in TNA (PRO) CAB 121.

Notes to Chapter 3: US–German Exchanges

1. Source: http://home.scarlet.be/ed.ragas/awswissus.html.
2. This was virtually the entire number of Germans held by the Swiss.
3. TNA (PRO) COS(45)27(O) dated 11 January 1945.

Notes to Chapter 4: German Exchanges

1. TNA (PRO) ADM 1/15885.
2. Foreign Office telegram to Stockholm, No 363 dated 10 March 1945.

Notes to Chapter 5: Jewish–German Exchanges

1. The text is at http://www.yale.edu/lawweb/avalon/mideast/balfour.htm.
2. Palestine Mandate, London, 24 July 1922. http://www.yale.edu/lawweb/avalon/mideast/palmanda.htm.
3. Command 6019 of 17 May 1939.
4. Other sections in the Bergen-Belsen complex housed Polish Jews with Latin American passports, Tripolitanian Jews with British passports, Soviet prisoners-of-war, and German political prisoners. It became an official 'concentration camp' in December 1944.
5. It seems very probable that these were the 106 crewmen of the Egyptian passenger ship *Zamzam* (see Chapter 6).
6. Wenck, A.-E. (1997), *Zwischen Menschenhandel und 'Endlösung': Das Konzentrationslager Bergen-Belsen*. Paderborn, Germany: Ferdinand Schöningh, p. 230.
7. *ibid.*, p. 230.
8. This is an extract, showing the first 20 names of some 300, from a document in the Postal Museum, London [Post 33/6057]. It is taken from a Foreign Office telegram dated 25 July 1944.
9. Kasztner emigrated to Israel after the war. His actions were very strongly criticized in certain sections of the Jewish community and he was murdered in 1955.
10. Schulze, R. (2005), 'Keeping Very Clear of Any Kuh-Handel', *Holocaust Genocide Studies*, 19, p. 250 fn. 96, quoting Ladislaus Löb.
11. She shortened her surname to Berg once she had arrived in the United States in 1944.

Notes to Chapter 6: The Zamzam *Affair*

1. These traders were known in American parlance as 'tobacconists'.
2. *Zamzam* was sailing under a complete blackout and zigzagging, allegedly on the advice of the resident Royal Navy officer at Recife, whereas it was normal practice for a neutral ship to have all lights blazing and steer a straight course. *Atlantis'* captain, Rogge, was not prosecuted at the war's end, indicating that the Allies recognized that he correctly and decently observed the rules of war in his operations, which included sinking 16 ships and capturing six.

3. *Bismarck* started her Atlantic foray on 18 May, sank HMS *Hood* 24 May and was herself sunk 27 May 1941.

4. Ironically, these pictures later enabled a British warplane crew to positively identify the *Atlantis*, leading to her sinking on 21 November.

5. In a somewhat surreal scene, the *Zamzam* women danced and sang the Palais Glide to a bemused audience of German women prisoners in the Stuttgart jail. Source: de Graaff-Hunter, p. 24.

6. Those inmates incapable of hard work had been given lethal injections on Hitler's orders, to create space for the *Ilag*.

7. Their expenses were met by their own countries, the money being forwarded to them via the United States Embassy in Berlin, as the Protecting Power.

8. This group included Isabel Guernsey and Mrs Guilding.

9. This section is based on a letter written by Mrs Hankin on 22 March 1943, which was copied to Mrs Levitt and then by her son, Peter, to this author.

10. This Liebenau group included the Levitts, Mrs Nora McWhannell and children Sarah and James, Gwen de Graaff-Hunter and daughter (10). In addition, there were two New Zealand women from Liebenau who were not *Zamzam* survivors.

11. De Graaff-Hunter's release is described in his obituary notice by G. Bonfield in the *Proceedings of the Royal Society*, dated 1967. This mentions the role of Dr Nørlund, but nothing can be discovered about this man apart from the fact that he was a geographer.

12. Captain Smith was certainly there in 1943 when he signed a tribute to the Panama Canal pilots: http://www.usmm.net/panama.html.

13. This could well be the group of '100 Egyptians' who were seen in Vienna by Jews taking part in the third Palestinian exchange. Oppenheim, A. N. (1996), *The Chosen People*. London: Vallentine Mitchell, pp. 148, 176.

14. Letter from Kathleen to Lionel Levitt, Liebenau, 13 May 1942. Courtesy of Peter Levitt.

Notes to Chapter 7: The Channel Islanders

1. Personal interview 23 June 2006.

2. Its full designation was *Ilag VB*.

3. After departure of the second group some 500 Channel Islanders were left at Bad Wurzach, and were subsequently liberated by the advancing French Army.

Notes to Chapter 8: The British–Italian Exchanges

1. Satow, H. and M. See (1948), *History of the Prisoner-of-War Department*. Draft in TNA FO 370/1649.

2. TNA (PRO) ADM 1/13976.

Notes to Chapter 9: The French

1. Article XXII of the 'Armistice Agreement between the German High Command of The Armed Forces and French Plenipotentiaries, Compiègne, June 22, 1940'.
2. Letter WO 0144/7843 in TNA (PRO) ADM 116/4614.
3. There was also one Newfoundlander, but why he was held is not known.
4. M 07380/42 of May 1942 in TNA (PRO) ADM 116/4614.
5. TNA (PRO) ADM 116/4614.
6. Their graves are now considered to be the most remote of any administered by the Commonwealth War Graves Commission.
7. They were joined by a man holding an Irish Republic passport, who had not been interned by the French, but for whom this exchange presumably offered an unexpected means of getting home.
8. PRO (TNA) FO 371/32035.
9. PRO (TNA) FO 371/32036.
10. Clutton-Brock, O. (2003), *Footprints on the Sands of Time, RAF Bomber Command Prisoners of War in Germany 1939–45*. London: Grub Street, p. 172.

Notes to Chapter 10: Red Cross Parcels for Camps on Mainland Europe

1. *The Times*, 12 December 1939.
2. Pamphlet, 'Prisoner of War', Red Cross, 1944, p. 12.

Notes to Chapter 11: Re-Employment of Repatriates

1. ACI 2205/1942 (0103/3690 (P.W. 2 (b) communicated to author by MoD (Army) April 2007.
2. One British colonel, passed by the MMC, travelled from his camp to a port in northern Germany where he was asked to sign such a certificate before sailing to Sweden for exchange. He refused and was taken straight back to the PoW camp he had left only a day earlier.
3. The detaining power was, however, entitled to retain sufficient captured medical staff to provide first aid and hospital service within the PoW camps.
4. Letter from US Embassy London to Foreign Office, 2 January 1945 in TNA (PRO) ADM 16146.
5. Although outside the time frame of this book, it should be mentioned that the 70-strong Royal Marine garrison on the Falkland Islands in 1981 was overwhelmed by the Argentine invaders and immediately deported to Montevideo in Uruguay, whence they returned to the UK. They were then included in the Task Force and fought against the Argentines in the subsequent land campaign. This was totally legal because they were not exchanged under the terms of the Geneva Convention, nor were any conditions placed on their release by the Argentines, who simply dumped them on the tarmac in Uruguay and presumably thought that they would never see them again.

Notes to Chapter 12: Selection for Repatriation

1. TNA (PRO) WO 32/9374.
2. IWM 93/4/1.
3. Durand, A. A. (1989), *Stalag Luft III: The Secret Story*. London: Patrick Stevens, p. 179.
4. *Daily Express*, 29 March 2006, pp. 22–3.
5. Mackenzie, S. P. (2004), *The Colditz Myth: British and Commonwealth Prisoners of War in Nazi Germany*. Oxford: Oxford University Press, p. 146. It should be added that Ross had the misfortune to be batman to Squadron Leader Douglas Bader, who refused point-blank to allow him to go, resulting in Ross spending a further two years as a PoW.

Notes to Chapter 13: Education and Other Support

1. British Library YD.2005b.335.
2. TNA (PRO) AIR 20/6530.

Notes to Chapter 14: Japan – The First US Exchange

1. Grew was now legally the *former* ambassador and his embassy building was under the control of the Japanese authorities, but certain diplomatic niceties continued.
2. Grew, J. C. (1944), *Ten Years in Japan*. London: Hammond & Hammond, p. 439.
3. Previously known as Siam, the country was redesignated Thailand on 24 June 1939.
4. The only ship not to have displayed lights was *Asama Maru* when anchored overnight in Hong Kong harbour, as the local commanding general ordered them switched off. The entire city was routinely blacked out and the general said (not unreasonably) that he had no wish for her to act as a beacon for American bombers, whether or not there was an international agreement on the lighting. Source: Hill, M. (1942), *Exchange Ship*. New York: Farrer & Rinehart, p. 175.
5. The word 'Maru' was suffixed to the names of all Japanese merchant ships. The origin of this custom is obscure but one theory is that it may be based on the meaning of the word as a castle and thus was used as a form of good luck charm to defend the ship and bring it back safely to port.
6. Grew, *op. cit.*, p. 460.
7. Passengers' estimates of the distance from the harbour to where they anchored vary from 60 miles to 18 miles.
8. This incident was reported by several aboard *Asama Maru*, including Max Hill, *op. cit.*, p. 213. It seems just possible, but can be put no stronger than that, that these may have been the two children referred to in Nelson, D. (1974), *The Story of Changi, Singapore*. West Perth, Australia: Changi Publication Ltd, pp. 50–1, whose father was in Changi civil prison. This man's wife and three children were aboard an evacuation ship that was bombed and sunk. All four reached the shore, but then became separated. The mother and elder sister were captured and detained in Palembang Camp in Java, but the other two children, a boy and

a girl, were captured by a different group of IJA soldiers and given to a Dutch woman in a civilian internment camp to look after.

9. This was at 500 kc/s, a frequency monitored by all ships at sea and many coastal stations.

10. One surprising lapse in US efficiency was that a cabin allocation had not been made for *Gripsholm*. A hasty plan had to be made, which resulted in many anomalies, not least being three nuns and one sailor placed in one cabin and three sailors and one nun in another. (For the record, the sailors slept in the saloon.)

11. Hill, *op. cit.*, p. 18.

12. It is certain that *Conte Verde* returned to Shanghai, as she was scuttled there by her crew 8 September 1943, following Italy's surrender.

13. Dew, G. (1943), *Prisoner of the Japs*. New York: Alfred A. Knopf, p. 303; Hill, *op. cit.*, p. 229.

14. Hill, *op. cit.*, p. 257.

15. 'WWII Australian Nurses who were Interned in Yokohama', paper by Mrs Mayumi Komiya, at Seminar of PoW Research Network Japan, Canberra, 2006.

Notes to Chapter 15: The Second US–Japanese Exchange

1. Corbett, P. S. (1987), *Quiet Passages, The Exchange of Civilians between the United States and Japan during the Second World War*. Kent, Ohio: Kent State University Press, p. 73.

2. Now Sri Lanka.

3. Demurrage is the fee paid by a charterer when a ship is detained for reasons other than weather or tide. It is usually calculated on a daily basis.

4. For some obscure reason, never explained, these were written in German and had to be translated before the American passengers knew what was expected of them.

5. Claude A. Buss (1903–1998) served in the US legation in Peiping (1927–1928), then was vice-consul in Nanjing (1931–1934). He then taught at the University of Southern California from 1934 until early 1941 when he returned to government service as executive assistant to the US High Commissioner in the Philippines. He was ordered to stay behind and surrender Manila to the Japanese and was interned until repatriated aboard the *Teia Maru*.

6. On the voyage from Mormugao to New York Mr Buss wrote a detailed report on the work of his committee, from which this summary is taken. A copy is in the British archives at TNA (PRO) DO 35/1203.

7. Carola's father was a British Army officer and former head of intelligence in Hong Kong, Major Charles Boxer. He remained a prisoner-of-war in the camp at Stanley, but survived the war and he and Mickey married in 1946.

8. http://www.hkvca.ca/historical/accounts/christie.htm.

9. TNA (PRO) ADM 1/15869.

Notes to Chapter 16: The British–Japanese Exchange

1. *The Times*, 20 July 1943; p. 3e.

2. *The Times*, 30 July 1942.

3. Navy Office, Canberra, signals dated 23.30 hours, 10 July 1942.

4. British Foreign Office to Berne, 5 September 1942. TNA FO 371/31748.

5. She would probably have carried Japanese passengers and/or cargo for delivery to Shanghai but there is no evidence one way or the other.

6. Unfortunately, despite repeated searches, the passenger list for the *Kamakura Maru* has not been found.

7. TNA FO 371/31748.

8. Attlee to Commonwealth Government, Cablegram 497 dated London, 6 July 1942.

9. Commonwealth Government to Attlee, Cablegram 360 Canberra, 8 July 1942.

10. The alternative route was by submarine to France, which was feasible but lengthy, uncomfortable and dangerous.

11. The breakdown of internees by former residence was: Australia: 28; New Caledonia: 103; and Netherlands East Indies: 703.

12. Source: NAA 962541.

13. At the end of the war it was discovered that Bowden had escaped from Singapore as it fell, but was then found by a Japanese patrol on Banka Island and murdered. Ross had been captured in Dili but then sent with a message demanding the surrender of Australian troops; the latter refused and sent Ross to Australia.

14. Prime Minister of Australia to Secretary of State for Dominion Affairs; 23 November 1942.

15. Mrs S. (Sybil) Petersen, IWM 04/17/1.

16. Mrs U. M. Streatfield, IWM 87/1/1.

17. IWM Misc 153/2355.

Notes to Chapter 17: Relief Supplies to Prisoners-of-War and Civilian Internees in the Far East

1. *Time* magazine, 17 August 1942.

2. This small vessel should not be confused with another ship of the same name, *Hakusan Maru*, which was built in Japan in 1923 as an all-first class passenger liner carrying 175 passengers and 200 crew. That ship measured 10,380 gross tons and was 520 feet long and was torpedoed and sunk by submarine USS *Flier* southwest of Iwo Jima on 4 June 1944.

3. These figures are in Straits (i.e., Singapore and Malaya) dollars, not US dollars.

4. The balance, at least in theory, was paid into a Japanese bank.

Notes to Chapter 18: The Sinking of the *Awa Maru*

1. As a comparison, the loss of life in the *Titanic* disaster was 1,517 (US figures) or 1,490 (British figures).

2. It was not until the 1970s that the Japanese eventually accepted that this had been done by a Japanese submarine, *I-177*, commanded by Lieutenant-Commander Nakagawa Hajime.

3. At the northernmost tip of the island of Kyūshū, this port is now known as Kitakyūshū.

4. Known to the Japanese as Takao, its modern Chinese name is Kaohsiung.

5. *Gripsholm*, for example, was stopped and inspected by the Germans when on her way to the United States in 1942 and nobody disputed their right to do so. On completion of their inspection, the Germans allowed the ship, crew and passengers to proceed unmolested.

6. The US Navy designates its submarines by names, which are frequently repeated to honour an earlier boat, together with a unique number running sequentially from #1. Thus, SS stands for 'submarine, diesel-electric powered' and this *Queenfish* was the 393rd such boat to have served in the US Navy, since SS-1 in 1902.

7. The actual position of sinking was 24° 41'N, 119° 12'E.

8. Loughlin remained silent on the advice of his legal counsel; he was reluctant to do so at the time and regretted it afterwards.

Notes to Chapter 19: Postal Services to and from Japanese-Controlled Territories: 1942–45

1. *Japanese Philately*, 40 (4), August 1985, p. 171.

2. ibid. p. 167.

3. There was an agreement between Switzerland and Germany/Italy that allowed German and Italian trains to transit the country, in return for which Switzerland had rail access to Istanbul and Lisbon. Use of such routes by all parties was very strictly limited to non-military goods, including mail, and no passengers were allowed.

4. The surface route for neutral countries appears to have reopened on 29 January 1942. Source: *Japanese Philately, op. cit.*, p. 167.

5. *Far Eastern Prisoner of War Bulletin*, 1 (1), August 1945, p. 2.

6. TNA (PRO) FO 916/751.

7. Mail received in Singapore by the BRE frequently included items for British work parties in China, Taiwan and even Japan itself. However, it was also known that there was a small sorting facility, similar to the BRE, at Omori, a PoW camp located on an artificial island in Tokyo Bay. This may have handled some mail for prisoners-of-war in Japan alone.

8. Tett, D. (2002), *A Postal History of the Prisoners-of-War and Civilian Internees during the Second World War, Volume 1. Singapore & Malaya 1942–1945*. Bristol: Stuart Rossiter Trust Fund, p. 204.

9. Ruggiero, M. E. (2003), *United States and British Exchanges with Japan, 1942–43*. Schaumburg, IL: International Society for Japanese Philately Inc., p. 8.

10. Kippenberger, H. K. (1954), *The Official History of New Zealand in the Second World War 1939–1945; Prisoners of War*. Wellington, New Zealand: Historical Publications Branch, p. 356.

11. According to Nelson, some Allied PoWs working in the docks pilfered some of the Red Cross stores, as a result of which the Allied camp commander tried and sentenced them to 28 days' detention, a fine of £5 and a loss of amenities. Nelson, D. (1974), *The Story of Changi, Singapore*. West Perth, Australia: Changi Publication Ltd, p. 39.

12. *ibid.*, p. 63.

13. *ibid.*, p. 123.

14. Much of what follows is based on Captain Nelson's book, *ibid.*, published in 1972, hereinafter Nelson. In peacetime Nelson worked for the Singapore government but also served in the Straits Settlements Volunteer Corps (SSVC). His unit was embodied in late 1941 and Nelson became the oldest military PoW in Changi. His excellent book is a remarkably well-balanced and non-judgemental record of his experiences in captivity.

15. Syonan = city of light (Japanese name for Singapore); shimbun = newspaper. This paper was owned and run by the Japanese, but published in the lingua franca of the island – English!

16. Nelson, *op. cit.*, p. 238.

17. Nelson, *op. cit.*, p. 82.

18. Nelson, *op. cit.*, p. 136.

19. Sometimes Nelson quantifies mail by the number of bags, sometimes by the estimated number of letters, and occasionally both.

20. One such was the Selerang Incident in September 1942 when the PoWs refused en masse to sign a form that they would not escape. Some 16,000 were confined in Selerang Barracks, designed to house 800, and surrounded by heavily armed Japanese guards. After three days the British commander ordered everyone to sign. Nelson took his part with the rest, without complaint, but described it in retrospect as 'a fuss about nothing'.

21. Nelson, *op. cit.*, p. 137.

22. This is the most basic formal award in the British Armed Forces, and means that the individual's name has appeared in the relevant commander-in-chief's formal despatch. Visually, it is marked by an oak leaf, which is worn on the medal ribbon for the campaign concerned. This author cannot avoid commenting that David Nelson's selfless service to so many others, in the most trying conditions, at considerable personal danger and over such a protracted period, deserved much more.

Notes to Chapter 20: Failed Attempts

1. It declared war on both Germany and Japan on 27 March 1945.

2. President Roosevelt to Prime Minister Churchill, No 584, dated 14 July 1944, TNA CAB 121/298.

3. Original text quoted in British War Cabinet paper WP (44) 404, dated 23 July 1944, TNA CAB 121/298.

4. Australian Department of External Affairs cablegram B.35169, dated 30 September 1944.

5. British War Cabinet WP (44)183, dated 4 April 1944, TNA CAB 121/298.

Notes to Chapter 21: Conclusions

1. Dupuy, R. and T. Dupuy (1993), *The Collins Encyclopedia of Military History*. London: Harper Collins.

Bibliography

Berg, M. (2006), *The Diary of Mary Berg, Growing Up in the Warsaw Ghetto*. Oxford: One World.

Bury, H. (1917), *Here and There in the War Area*. London: AR Mowbray & Co.

——(1917), *My Visit to Ruhleben*. London: AR Mowbray & Co.

Clutton-Brock, O. (2003), *Footprints on the Sands of Time, RAF Bomber Command Prisoners of War in Germany 1939–45*. London: Grub Street.

Corbett, P. S. (1987), *Quiet Passages, The Exchange of Civilians between the United States and Japan during the Second World War*. Kent, Ohio: Kent State University Press.

Cuthbertson, K. (1998), *Nobody Said Not to Go: The Life, Loves and Adventures of Emily Hahn*. Boston and London: Faber & Faber.

Dew, G. (1943), *Prisoner of the Japs*. New York: Alfred A. Knopf.

Durand, A. A. (1989), *Stalag Luft III: The Secret Story*. London: Patrick Stevens.

Froissart, J. (1978), *Chronicles*. London: Penguin.

Grew, J. C. (1944), *Ten Years in Japan*. London: Hammond & Hammond.

Hahn, E. (1946), *China To Me: A Partial Autobiography*. Philadelphia: The Blakiston Company.

Hill, M. (1942), *Exchange Ship*. New York: Farrer & Rinehart.

Holland, R. W. (1949), *Adversis major: a short history of the Educational Books Scheme of the Prisoners of War Department of the British Red Cross Society and Order of St. John of Jerusalem*. London: Staples Press.

Kippenberger, H. K. (1954), *The Official History of New Zealand in the Second World War 1939–1945; Prisoners of War*. Wellington, New Zealand: Historical Publications Branch.

Mackenzie, S. P. (2004), *The Colditz Myth: British and Commonwealth Prisoners of War in Nazi Germany*. Oxford: Oxford University Press.

Moore, B. and K. Fedorowich (2002), *British Empire and Its Italian Prisoners of War, 1940–1947*. London: Palgrave Macmillan.

Nelson, D. (1974), *The Story of Changi, Singapore*. West Perth, Australia: Changi Publication Ltd.

Oliver, B. (1966), *The British Red Cross in Action*. London: Faber & Faber.

Oppenheim, A. N. (1996), *The Chosen People*. London: Vallentine Mitchell.

Plumridge, J. H. (1975), *Hospital Ships and Ambulance Trains*. London: Seeley Service.

Poulgrain, G. (1993), 'The Loveday Exchange, Australia, 1942: The Japanese Naval Spies Return to Java', *Indonesia*, 55, 140–9.

Red Cross (1948), *Report of the International Committee of the Red Cross on its activities during the Second World War: (September 1, 1939–June 30, 1947) Vol. 1. General Activities; Volume II. The Central Agency for Prisoners of War.* Geneva: International Committee of the Red Cross.

Rohwer, J. and G. Hümmelchen (1992), *Chronology of the War at Sea 1939–1945.* London: Greenhill Books.

Ruggiero, M. E. (2003), *United States and British Exchanges with Japan, 1942–43.* Schaumburg, IL: International Society for Japanese Philately Inc.

Satow, H. and M. See (1948), *History of the Prisoner-of-War Department.* Draft in TNA FO 370/1649.

Schmidt, R. and A. Kludas (1978), *Lazarettschiffe im Zweiten Weltkrieg.* Stuttgart: Motorbuch Verlag.

Schulze, R. (2005), 'Keeping Very Clear of Any Kuh-Handel', *Holocaust Genocide Studies*, 19, 226–51.

Streatfield, U. M., *A Long Way from the Ships – Recollections.* Privately printed and published, IWM 87/1/1.

Talbot-Booth, R. C. (ed.) (1942), *Merchant Ships.* London: Sampson and Low.

Tett, D. (2002), *A Postal History of the Prisoners-of-War and Civilian Internees in East Asia during the Second World War, Volume 1. Singapore & Malaya 1942–1945.* Bristol: Stuart Rossiter Trust Fund.

Vance, J. F. (ed.) (2000), *Encyclopedia of Prisoners-of-War and Internment.* Santa Barbara, CA: ABC-CLIO.

Wenck, A.-E. (1997), *Zwischen Menschenhandel und 'Endlösung': Das Konzentrationslager Bergen-Belsen.* Paderborn, Germany: Ferdinand Schöningh.

Woodley, C. (2004), *BOAC, An Illustrated History.* Stroud: Tempus Publishing.

Index